D1523196

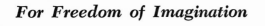

For Freedom of Imagination

For Freedom of Imagination

❧

BY ANDREI SINYAVSKY

translated and with an introduction by

LASZLO TIKOS AND MURRAY PEPPARD

HOLT, RINEHART AND WINSTON

NEW YORK   CHICAGO   SAN FRANCISCO

Published simultaneously in Canada by Holt, Rinehart and Winston of Canada, Limited.

Library of Congress Catalog Card Number:
79–122252

First Edition

SBN: 03–085268–4

Designer: RONALD FARBER

Printed in the United States of America

Acknowledgment is made for permission to reprint
random selections from "The Wood-pile"; "The
Death of the Hired Man"; "The Tuft of Flowers";
"The Star-splitter"; "The Pasture"; and "Birches"
from Complete Poems of Robert Frost. Copyright
1916, 1923, 1930, 1934, 1939 by Holt, Rinehart and
Winston, Inc. Copyright 1944, 1951, © 1958, 1962
by Robert Frost. Copyright © 1967 by Lesley Frost
Ballantine. Reprinted by permission of Holt, Rinehart
and Winston, Inc.

Contents

Introduction	vii
On a Collection of Verses by Anatoly Sofronov	1
No Discount (ON SCIENCE FICTION)	17
The Poetry and Prose of Olga Berggolts	37
"Come Walk with Us" (ON ROBERT FROST'S POEMS)	63
The Unfettered Voice (ON ANNA AKHMATOVA)	72
Pamphlet or Lampoon? (ON A NOVEL BY IVAN SHEVTSOV)	78
There Are Such Verses (ON YEVGENY DOLMATOVSKY'S POETRY)	92
The Poetry of Pasternak	103
In Defense of the Pyramid (ON YEVTUSHENKO'S POETRY)	167
Notes	197

Introduction

From Faith to Disillusionment

Abram Tertz,[1] or to use his real name, Andrei Sinyavsky, followed a well-established literary tradition in Russia: he was active not only as a writer of fiction but also as a literary critic. From Pushkin to Marina Tsvetayeva, from Dostoyevsky to Andrei Sinyavsky, creative artists in Russia often combined creative work with theoretical studies on the problems of their craft. For the most part it was not personal motives only (envy, admiration of other artists' works, etc.) that led them to literary criticism, but rather a feeling of responsibility for the state of literature and for what in Russia has always been closely related to it: politics. They felt that it was their duty to draw a line between "good" and "bad" art and by so doing help to solve not only aesthetic problems but questions of a political nature, too. Because of this feature of literature and literary criticism, writers as well as their critics have often ended their lives in Siberia or other places of exile. Andrei Donatovich Sinyavsky's fate fits this pattern almost to perfection. Both as a literary critic and as a creative writer he aroused the anger of the authorities, and as a result he had to follow the path to exile that so many others before him had taken.

Sinyavsky's life story is typical for his country and generation: born on October 8, 1925, he belongs to the generation that went through the most zealous Communist indoctrination. As a child and young man he experienced the darkest periods of Soviet history: the purges of the thirties, the horrors of the subsequent war, and finally the so-called de-Stalinization with its illusion-destroying revelations. At the age of eighteen he was drafted into the army, but was discharged after brief service. In 1945 he entered Moscow University, where he majored in Russian literature. He was an eager student, and according to a former professor of his, V. D. Duvakin, a "person of great quality" whose "academic and professional qualities were outstanding." [2] While studying at Moscow State University, Sinyavsky wrote a dissertation on Gorky's unfinished novel, Klim Samgin. It was accepted in 1952. Some fourteen years later, at the trial, this dissertation suddenly acquired a topical interest: the prosecution quoted it to demonstrate that Sinyavsky was indeed hypocritical, since in 1952 Sinyavsky had thought about Gorky "quite differently" than he did in his writings published abroad.[3] The dissertation, which has never been published, is not known in the West. However, a long essay of Sinyavsky's, most likely based on this dissertation, was published in 1958 in the first volume of the prestigious Istoriya Russkoy Sovyetskoy Literatury (History of Russian Soviet Literature), sponsored by the Academy of Sciences of the Soviet Union. This certainly indicates that Sinyavsky's ideas on Gorky were, even if not orthodox, definitely conventional by Soviet standards.

After completing his studies with a "state examination" Sinyavsky received an appointment at Moscow State University where, again according to Professor Duvakin, he was a "very popular lecturer." Sometime later—exact dates are not available—he became a member of the Gorky Institute for World Literature, and here he devoted himself entirely to research. His field of special interest was Soviet literature, primarily that written in the early 1920's and during the years of the

Second World War.[4] While still a student at the Moscow University he had come to know the wife of the French Ambassador, Madame Hélène Peltier Zamoyska. As one of the few foreigners of embassy rank who was a native Russian, Madame Zamoyska had the privilege of studying Russian literature at Moscow University. It was she who took Sinyavsky's (and later also Daniel's) manuscripts abroad. According to her testimony Sinyavsky was a "convinced Komsomolets" (member of the Communist Youth League) during his student years, who "saw the Soviet system in the light of the official Soviet propaganda." However, the hard facts of Russian reality soon disillusioned him, as they did so many others who once had harbored idealistic notions. As early as the late 1940's Sinyavsky must have become involved with the moral problems arising from the discrepancy between reality and propaganda. According to Madame Zamoyska his first discussion with her also revolved around this problem: "Was he shocked by the cruelty employed to establish the better order of life about which his father had dreamed? Certainly less than I, a foreigner was. . . . He explained to me that the law of historical progress unfortunately demands some human sacrifices. Nevertheless his conscience could not be content with this easy justification. It is significant that one of our first longer discussions had as its theme the dilemma of Ivan Karamazov: 'Can one build a Crystal Palace on the corpse of a child?' "[5]

Although details about Sinyavsky's career are meager, it is quite probable that his conversion from a "convinced Komsomolets" to a "non-Marxist," as he called himself during the trial,[6] must have begun in 1951. In that year his father was arrested,[7] and this event made a profound impression on the sensitive young man. If formerly his questions were only on the abstract-philosophical level, now for the first time he came into direct contact with the impersonal machinery of state-controlled injustice. Doubts about the justice of the Soviet system aroused by this incident were strengthened by the 1952 anti-Semitic "doctor trials."[8] Stalin's death in 1953 and Khrushchev's revelations of Stalin's "crimes" in 1956 completed the process of disillusionment; and it can be documented that around this time Sinyavsky had already broken completely with his earlier ideals. The disillusionment was of course not confined only to Sinyavsky—it engulfed particularly the intellectual and student circles. "My former comrades at the university," Madame Zamoyska recalls the effect of Khrushchev's speech on the students in Moscow, "suddenly became aware of the tragedy lived through by millions of innocent people in the concentration camps, and they felt themselves personally responsible for these crimes, since in the name of patriotism identified by conformism they had let these things happen. A feeling of shame gave rise to the will not to remain passive, that is, indifferent in the face of the slightest injustice. . . . This was also the reaction of Sinyavsky and Daniel, and it is this which drove them to write." [9]

From an urge to write to publishing abroad under a pseudonym, however, is probably a long way to go for someone who has been reared in a quasi-religious society and who, from the cradle on, has learned to hate all that is connected with the West. We know that both his *On Socialist Realism* and *The Trial Begins* were ready in manuscript in 1956 and also that in December of the same year they were taken abroad by Madame Zamoyska.[10] They were not published until 1959. Even if we allow for some delays of a technical nature (translation, finding a publisher, etc.)[11] the gap between 1956 and 1959 is not explained. It is very likely that the historical circumstances also influenced Sinyavsky—if it was he who caused the delay—in putting off the publication of his manuscripts for a while. One reason may have been the reaction after 1956 in the Soviet Union, which had both literary and political implications: the literary freeze following the aftermath of the bloody suppression of the Hungarian Revolution, and the storm of the "Pasternak affair" (the publication of *Doctor Zhivago* abroad in 1957 and the award of the Nobel Prize in 1958). None of these events could have encouraged Sinyavsky to publish abroad under his real name.

On the other hand, the rapidly spreading aversion to Khrushchev among the Soviet intellectuals, the continuing denial of freedom in the Soviet Union, and Sinyavsky's own personal feeling of frustration at not being able to publish at home must have given him a sense of urgency to give his permission—if that was what was needed—to appear in print as Abram Tertz.

Ironically, the year 1959 not only saw Abram Tertz in print, but also launched Sinyavsky at home on a writing career as a critic and scholar of Soviet literature. Between 1959 and 1965 Sinyavsky-Tertz published a total of twenty-nine pieces of writing; thirty if one includes his essay on Yevtushenko, published two years after Tertz's arrest.

In chronological order they are the following: *On Socialist Realism,* a long essay of literary criticism tearing apart the dogmas of Socialist realism and establishing his artistic credo, was the first work ever published by Sinyavsky under the pseudonym Tertz. *The Trial Begins,* a short novel, applying Sinyavsky's aesthetic credo to his fiction, followed soon after in 1960. Both works were originally written in 1956, although the final pages of *On Socialist Realism,* which define Sinyavsky's artistic principles as "fantastic realism," were added only in 1958.

In the Soviet Union Sinyavsky's name as a literary scholar and critic appears in print for the first time toward the end of 1958, when two of his long essays are published in the above-mentioned *History of Russian Soviet Literature.*[12] The first essay is on Gorky and the other one is on the forgotten Jewish poet from Odessa, Eduard Bagritsky (Dzybin) (1895–1934). Both essays stand out in the collection as the work of a well-informed young scholar who has a respectable command of his material and style and knows the rules of his trade.

From 1959 on Sinyavsky presents his views regularly as a literary critic in the Soviet periodical press. It was particularly the liberal *Novy Mir* that attracted him. Most of the criticism included in this volume was originally written for and published by *Novy Mir.* At the beginning Sinyavsky seems to have preferred to work in a team with a fellow scholar from the Gorky Literary Institute, where Sinyavsky was doing research. In 1959 A. Menshutin and Sinyavsky published together a long essay on a collection of poems, *The Day of Russian Poetry*, in which they analyzed the production of the younger generation, pointed out the artistic merits of good poetry, and derided the would-be poets of the Socialist-realist trend. The same trend can be observed also in another review article, written by Sinyavsky alone, dealing with the lack of any artistic value in the poetry of one of the most powerful party hacks of Soviet poetry: Anatoly Sofronov.[13]

Thus, the first articles which introduced A. Sinyavsky to the Soviet reader did not leave any doubts about his stand in the topical debates of Soviet literary life. True, his essays published by the Academy of Sciences were more conventional, but of course it is hard to say how much of the original text was deleted, edited, or rewritten by the editors and the censors.

His studies, printed in the Soviet Union in 1960, provide us with further evidence that Sinyavsky was in the forefront of the liberal literary forces fighting for higher artistic standards and against the dogmas and representatives of official Socialist-realism. Sinyavsky, for example, realized that establishing new norms and new principles for Soviet literature required not only the discrediting of the official party hacks, but also the restoring of the lost and suppressed values of contemporary Russian literature. The "rehabilitation" of the suppressed works became the fighting slogan of the day. This is how one should understand Sinyavsky's long essay on Olga Berggolts' poetry.[14] He also appeared in print in the Soviet Union with two articles on science fiction, a topic dear to his heart, which interested him greatly because it offered excellent opportunities for exploring a field closely related to his fiction—the correlation between fantasy and reality.[15] The same interest also drove him to study the art of a "fantastic" painter: Pablo Picasso. This interest yielded in 1960 a little-known book on Picasso written together with the art historian Igor Naumovich Golomshtok.[16]

In 1961 a collection of short stories appeared abroad with the title *Fantastic Stories*.[17] It contained five short stories, written between 1955 and 1961. The short story "At the Circus," dating from 1955, is the earliest known fiction of Sinyavsky; "The Tenants" dates from 1959, the "Graphomaniacs" from 1960, and two stories, the "Icicle" and "You and I," date from 1961.

At home in 1961, Sinyavsky participated with two more articles in the struggle for liberalization: "In Favor of Poetic Activity" (*Notes on Young Poets,* 1960)[18] and "Let's Talk Professionally." [19] These essays are part of a "debate" which the reactionary literary periodical *Oktyabr* started about the third volume of the *Istoriya Russko-Sovyetskoi Literatury* to which Sinyavsky had contributed a long essay on the history of Soviet literature during the war period.[20] Thus, only two years after his appearance in print in the Soviet Union, Sinyavsky's position was already clear enough to be singled out by the party and literary Establishment for a severe attack.

In 1962 he published in the Soviet Union an article on a volume of Pasternak's poetry[21] and he was also working on his most mature novel so far available, *The Makepeace Experiment* (*Lyubimov*), which he finished in 1962. (It was not published abroad until much later, in 1965).[22] In 1964 he appeared in the Soviet press with a review article, a very subtle and sensitive appraisal of Robert Frost's poems in Russian translation,[23] and he was also working, together with A. Menshutin, on an ambitious *History of Soviet Poetry of the First Years after the Revolution,* which was published in 1964 by the prestigious publishing house of the Academy of Sciences of the Soviet Union.[24] In 1964 he also wrote a short article on Anna Akhmatova,[25] recommending her warmly for a public rehabilitation. An annihilating criticism of one of the untalented writers of the Socialist-realist Establishment, V. Shevtsov, followed in the same year.[26]

In 1965 he continued his attack upon another member of the Establishment, V. Dolmatovsky,[27] and completed, just before his arrest, editing the publication of a volume of Pasternak's poetry, to which he wrote a long and perceptive introduction.[28] In the summer of 1965 and after his arrest, in 1966, two more (three including the article on Yevtushenko) works appeared abroad: a short story, "Pkhentz" (which some publishers now include in the *Fantastic Stories*),[29] and a collection of aphorisms, *Thoughts Unaware*.[30]

The article on Yevtushenko[31] was also written by Sinyavsky before his arrest and presented for publication to *Novy Mir*. However, *Novy Mir* apparently rejected the article, most probably for political reasons.

Besides the published materials, there must have been unpublished manuscripts in Sinyavsky's possession. An "Essay in Self-Analysis" was mentioned at the trial,[32] as well as some "other manuscripts" which were burned by a friend of his, Miss Dokukina.[33]

Abram Tertz as a Creative Artist

Abram Tertz as a creative artist has a clearly formulated aesthetic credo, expressed in his *On Socialist Realism*: "Right now," he writes in 1958, "I put my hope in a phantasmagoric art, with hypotheses instead of purposes, an art in which the grotesque will replace the realistic description of ordinary life. Such an art would correspond best to the spirit of our time. May the fantastic imagery of Hoffman, Dostoyevsky, or Goya, Chagall, and Mayakovsky (the most Socialist realist of all) and many other realists and nonrealists teach us how to be truthful with the aid of the absurd and the fantastic." [34] With the aid of the fantastic and the grotesque, Sinyavsky-Tertz analyzes the basic situation of life as he sees it: the individual's feeling that he is trapped, that his life is determined, and his urge to attempt an escape from his captivity. The limitations of reality, however, prove to be stronger than the possibilities of escape, and thus a tragic vicious circle is created from which there is no breaking out. The illogical desire of Sinyavsky's heroes to try the impossible anyway leaves them with only one loophole—to resort to the age-old means of phantasts and prophets, that is, to change their subjective reality, or their subjective view of reality.

With the aid of the fantastic and grotesque, Sinyavsky proves that even fantasies are of no avail: he lets his heroes succeed in their desires, but their failure after they have achieved their first goals strikes them with an even greater force, underlining the basic paradox of the human condition.

In the story "At the Circus," for example, Konstantin, the hero of the tale, escapes confining reality by learning the art of creating a new reality for himself from a circus magician. His "wonderful" life, however, comes to an early end, because with the attainment of his goal boredom sets in, and in seeking new excitement Konstantin participates in a criminal raid. During the criminal act he "accidentally" kills his magician teacher, and in so doing he also loses his magic power. (Sinyavsky usually gives a "realistic" explanation for surrealistic phenomena.) After his magic power is gone reality takes over; Konstantin is arrested, sent to a labor camp, and the reader's last view of him is his death (there is no escape from the steadily narrowing circle of determinism) while attempting to flee from the forced labor camp.

The classic situation described in this story is developed in Sinyavsky's fiction in several variations, and at various levels. Thus, for example, the short story "You and I" narrows the determining external circumstances to a minimum and reduces the components of determinism to the Dostoyevskian double nature of man. Here the split personality of the hero—supported by the schizophrenic atmosphere of the post-war Stalinist period in the Soviet Union—erects walls around the freedom of the ego and leaves the hero with only one alternative—the suicide of the critical You (who, by the way, has a red beard, and is a small dwarf-like fellow—a description fitting Sinyavsky himself).

The communal apartment described in "The Tenants" is the classic trap itself, which for the would-be writer-observer and narrator of the story cannot appear as anything but a bewitched, fantastic world populated with witches, water nymphs who are prostitutes, and other ruined characters.

The Makepeace Experiment enriches the structure of the escape mechanism to political and historical forces. The hero of the novel, Lenya Tikhomirov—a peaceful man by nature—is suddenly possessed by a magic power and almost against his will becomes a political leader performing miracles, but this time not for his own sake but for the supposed benefit of the entire community. He has the power to create a new reality based on make-believe for a city whose population, driven also by a hidden desire to escape from everyday reality, happily follows the self-appointed leader toward greater and greater miracles. Reality, however, has a greater force than the soap-bubble miracles of Tikhomirov, and after he has committed a "crime," his magic power dwindles and the radio-directed unmanned tanks of actual historical and political reality destroy his kingdom.

The political implications of this novel in a society with Utopian strivings, like the Soviet Union, and the similarity between certain character traits of Khrushchev and Tikhomirov must have hit the Soviet Establishment very hard. Indeed, this story, along with *The Trial Begins* and *On Socialist Realism*, furnished the material evidence of the prosecutor. However, as Sinyavsky himself said at the trial, he is not a political writer (the complex symbolism of *The Makepeace Experiment* would have precluded political propaganda, Sinyavsky said).[35] Politics appears in his philosophical approach to reality only as part of life, subject to the eternal rules of human behavior.

The Makepeace Experiment and the last story published abroad, "Pkhentz," develop further the device of the escape mechanism in another respect, too, namely in the way Sinyavsky treats his hero after the Makepeace experiment collapses. Tikhomirov, after the destruction of his empire, catches a freight train to Siberia, where he hopes to sink into anonymity and possibly start a new life (whatever this new life may be); and the hunchback hero of "Pkhentz" longs to go back to Siberia and find the secret landing spot where he entered this planet. The unintelligible word "Pkhentz" is the only remaining material proof for the hero that he did belong to another world, where the word "Pkhentz" meant something. (The lost meaning of the word, and the impossibility of finding out its meaning, symbolize the hero's longing for "paradise lost" and his total alienation on this earth.) Thus, the collapse of the make-believe reality does not necessarily lead to the destruction of the hero—he is given a chance to find another beginning—but this new beginning may bring nothing but the cyclical repetition of the former experience with different variables. This is a new departure in Sinyavsky's fiction—a sadness, the feeling of loneliness to a cosmic extent from which only the most logical appearance of religious ideas can mean a positive outcome. This tragic feeling transformed into transcendental optimism permeates the collection of aphorisms (*Thoughts Unaware*) and seems to be, at least for the time being, the final stage of Sinyavsky's philosophical development.

Andrei Sinyavsky as a Literary Critic

"Literary criticism for me was not a mask, it was my life's work," and there was "always a close relationship between my work as a critic and my work as a writer." [36] The closeness of this relationship may be observed in even a casual comparison of his critical writings with his fiction. The necessity of freedom for the flowering of the creative imagination is the central theme of Sinyavsky's essays and reflects the sense of freedom gained by writing under a pseudonym. As Hélène Zamoyska states: "The possibility of writing without constraint taught him that freedom of the conscience and of the word was not a luxury of an anarchist individualist, dangerous for the common good: . . . but a fundamental necessity of man and the condition of all individual and social progress. . . ." [37] The interaction between his secret fiction and his work as a critic may be noted both in his choice of topics to discuss and in his preference for certain authors. His favorite fields are the first exuberant years after the October Revolution and the period of the Second World War. These were times when bureaucratic control and censorship rigidity either had not yet set in or were temporarily lifted. These were times when there was relative freedom in Soviet literature, freedom to experiment and to express what one thought and felt. There was a common goal, inspiring new departures, a spirit of adventure and idealistic sacrifice for a great cause, and as yet no rigid rules nor constricting dogma confined creativity to the narrow and sterile path of Socialist realism.

Sinyavsky's favorite authors are, with the exception of Mayakovsky, writers who were suppressed, ignored, or even imprisoned and persecuted by the Soviet government: Pasternak, Yesenin, Babel, Akhmatova. . . . These authors became his favorites not only from a clear spirit of opposition, but also and more significantly from a critic's sense of quality and a literary historian's appreciation of continuity. Sinyavsky's tastes and judgment were trained by reading the Russian classics of the nineteenth century, and it is to them that he owes his appreciation of form and aesthetics. In addition he learned from the experimental poetry of the 1920's, a period now sometimes referred to as the "Silver Age" of Soviet poetry. The Formalists, the Futurists, and the Acmeists, to mention but a few of the diverse literary groups which were formed during the era before the Stalinist freeze-up, are now no longer in the mainstream of Soviet literature. But the break in continuity which resulted from their suppression is one that Sinyavsky obviously seeks to overcome in his critical writing. Under the circumstances it is not surprising that Sinyavsky has to write carefully and at times in Aesopian language. In his caution he refers almost exclusively to Mayakovsky, an approved and canonized writer. But it soon becomes clear that the name Mayakovsky has become a symbol representing the courage to experiment. Yesenin, who is now slowly being rehabilitated, is another name mentioned more than casually by Sinyavsky, who is discreet in his references, although a reader trained in the kind of language used in dictatorship can easily discern where his sympathies lie.

It is equally easy to discover what authors Sinyavsky dislikes. Here he has been quite bold and has taken some risks, for the authors at whom he has aimed his most devastating criticism are mostly Party favorites. Stalinist poetasters such as Dolmatovsky and Surkov,[38] and A. Sofronov (the editor of *Ogonyok*;[39] said to be an informer), are among his targets.

Sinyavsky has had the courage to write articles exposing their pompous and bombastic doggerel, and in doing so has made no secret of the source of his own high standards. The inferior literature produced in accordance with the doctrines of Socialist realism is, however, not always openly contrasted with models taken from earlier literature. Sometimes Sinyavsky prefers merely to quote a few lines from a poem and let these lines speak for themselves. Usually such quotations are enough to illustrate the falsity and pretentiousness of the poet in question. In other cases he may collect from various poems by the same author certain recurrent mannerisms, a method of criticism that may render the poet quite ridiculous, as in the case of the fixation on shaking hands noted in the review of Sofronov's poems.

It should be pointed out that Sinyavsky never attacks and rarely mentions the pious and patriotic intentions an author professes; it is rather the poetic achievement of the poet that concerns him. Socialist realism favors poets with proletarian backgrounds, and skill in versification is of little importance; it also prefers glorification of the state and the achievements of the Party to stylistic excellence. Patriotic intent, *ideinost* (commitment to Communist ideas) and civic-mindedness are placed above prosodic perfection by all critics who adhere to the Party line. In order to expose the triviality of much of the literature produced by Socialist realism, a quotation from a poem is usually followed by the comment that mere intent is not enough and that the enumeration of the great achievements of the Party and praise of patriotic fervor do not suffice to make a poem. This may seem obvious to Westerners, who are easily dismayed by the fatuous form and sickly sycophancy of many Soviet poems, but what is obviously second-rate to us is printed in large editions in the Soviet Union. To deal with this mass of poor poetry, professional criticism of an incisive kind is urgently needed.

Sinyavsky, often working with his collaborator Menshutin, has done his best against great obstacles and has supplied professional criticism of a high order. He has not only dwelt on negative aspects of the poetry under discussion, but has set up minimum standards and offered advice to the young poets. Some of this advice seems obvious and primitive, composed of truisms and the platitudes of poetics, but it is needed desperately by the new generation of poets and many of the older, Stalinist group. Often Sinyavsky has to suggest that mere enumeration of details is not enough and that these details must be converted into images and living pictures. Discrepancies between a subject and its treatment or between premise and conclusion are never noted without the comment that unity of conception and feeling will help to provide illumination through a special, uniquely personal view. Usually a negative criticism is followed by the citing of a positive example that will illustrate the point, and it is here that Sinyavsky draws on his favorite writers. He is eager to help the poets discover the difference between a "concrete" image and a mere statement. Again and again he calls for an original poetic view, one that is expressed by "concrete delineation" and not by "commonplace judgments."

This advice which he offers so freely comes, however, from a view of man and of art which is at variance with Socialist realism. A special, personal view of the world is demanded, not a collectivized, stereotyped, and widely shared commonplace. Sinyavsky believes that the stature of the individual behind the poem is decisive for the quality of the poem and that this quality will be reflected in the language. Although he appeals to the classics and recommends a study of them—a bold recommendation—he insists on a subjective but self-apparent sense of what great poetry is and on an inward view of what is meant by the artistic authenticity of an image or of a use of language. Originality in language and imagery are called for again and again, as they must be in a society where the norms are set by and for a collective. Realism, falsely understood, may lead to a rejection of imagination and to the death of a poem. If one must have realism, then it should be consistent and appropriate; Sinyavsky's most cutting irony is reserved for those who try to mix and blend the fantastic and pedestrian realism—"On Science Fiction" is evidence for this.

Underneath all the specific comments one can hear, now

distinctly, now more by suggestion, the call for freedom—freedom for the imagination and for liberation from the bonds of Socialist realism. Fetters of any kind lead to falseness. This is, in summary, the great single message of his essays. Man must be free to create. And man must be spiritually free to be creative in language. The freedom Sinyavsky gained by publishing abroad under a pseudonym has suffused all his thinking, and it has led him to hard labor in Siberia.

Arrest and Trial

Sinyavsky was arrested on September 8, 1965. Four days later Daniel was also arrested by the security police.[40] Official notice of the arrests was not given until three and one-half months later, and then in an unusual form, namely by the President of the Union of Writers, A. Surkov, in Paris.[41] The Soviet public did not learn of the affair until the thirteenth of January, 1966.[42] Attacks in the press began toward the end of January, opening with the infamous article of Zoya Kedrina, "Smerdyakov's Successors," [43] and followed by other articles which were reminiscent of the worst days of Stalinism in their savagery. The actual trial did not begin until February 10, 1966. On the fourteenth of the month the sentences were pronounced: seven years of forced labor for Sinyavsky (the maximum penalty) and five years for Daniel.[44] During the spring of the year the condemned men were sent to labor camps.

The preparation for the trial and its actual course were a strange mixture of old Stalinist methods and attempts to preserve a minimum appearance of legality. The fact that the writers were arrested because of the alleged anti-Soviet quality of their works was typically Stalinist, as were the attacks in the press before the trial had even begun. The misuse of paragraph 70 of the Civil Law[45] and the use of quotations out of context remind one of the dark ages of Stalin. The attempt to identify the author's views with random statements made by the fictional characters they had created continued a vicious tradition of the 1930's. But it must be assessed as a sign of a new era that there was a trial at all and that attempts were even made to make it seem like an open, public trial. The defendants were allowed counsel, and the procedure in the courtroom maintained the legal formalities. And not least of all, the defendants were allowed to survive. Nevertheless, the trial represents a throwback to the Stalinist period and a weakening of the "liberal" position in the field of literature. The accused were quickly cut off as soon as political statements were about to be made. The audience was carefully chosen from Stalinist stalwarts.

No material concerning the trial has been published in Russia. The author of the excerpts that reached the West has wisely remained anonymous.[46] Both writers pleaded not guilty, and both continually and firmly rejected the charges against them. Daniel did concede that he regretted the "abuse" of his publications abroad for anti-Soviet purposes, but Sinyavsky did not admit that his works could be used that way. Neither recanted nor confessed his errors, and thus they spoiled the trial as a show or spectacle for the government.

Epilogue

The reaction of the West to the trial was one of indignation from all quarters: writers, politicians, professors sent protests and appeals to the Soviet government, the officials of the party, and to the Writers' Union.[47] Communists in the Western countries joined in this wave of protest as eagerly as the non-Communists. The Communist parties of France and Italy responded to the trial not only by condemning it, but by making freedom of religion and literature a part of their party programs.[48]

The attempts of the government to mobilize criticism of the two authors failed miserably. Not a single writer of stature, except Sholokhov,[49] condemned Sinyavsky and Daniel. Only a few obscure Party hacks lent their names to the cause of the prosecution. The so-called literary "experts" present at the trial consisted of totally unknown members of the Writers'

Union. The controlled press tried by every means to confuse and obfuscate the issues of the trial, even hinting darkly that it was illegal to publish abroad at all. The witnesses at the trial were put in a difficult position by being asked about works which were unobtainable, at least officially, in the Soviet Union; to admit knowing about them would have been dangerous for the witnesses. The moral character of the two writers was attacked, both openly and by innuendo, a tactic well known from Stalinist times.

As subsequent events in the Soviet Union have proved, the Sinyavsky-Daniel trial was not an isolated incident, but an organic part of the struggle which has been going on ever since Stalin's death between the "liberal" (democratic) and the "conservative" (neo-Stalinist) forces of Soviet society. The Sinyavsky-Daniel trial became the focal point of this struggle, both the symbol of dissent and the showpiece of the regime's determination to stifle dissident opinions. It is not necessary to recall all the individual phases of this struggle. Suffice it to say that the growing literary and political underground movement in the Soviet Union, the snowballing effect of dissent and repression since 1965, and finally, even the Soviet-led invasion of dissenting Czechoslovakia clearly indicate that the problems which the Sinyavsky-Daniel trial raised, the principles which have been evoked and violated, are not at an end. The trial—with all the issues it raises—continues.

The selected essays chosen for translation provide evidence for the basic unity of the works of Sinyavsky-Tertz. We feel that a study of the essays[50] contributes to a more profound understanding of A. Tertz's fiction. Also, since Sinyavsky has for some time been recognized as one of the most brilliant critics in the Soviet Union, his likes and dislikes reflect not only his personal views, which are liberal, but also those of the best literary minds in Russia, and contribute insights into the recent developments in Soviet literary criticism.

LASZLO TIKOS
MURRAY PEPPARD

Amherst, Massachusetts
April, 1970

For Freedom of Imagination

On a Collection of Verses by Anatoly Sofronov

❧

The poems of A. Sofronov[1] of the last few years, published in his new book *From All Latitudes,* are for the most part connected with his numerous trips abroad and with the travel impressions of the author. These are works which actually fly "from all latitudes," and they are devoted to India and China, England and Iceland, Egypt and Indonesia, Australia and Japan. From the first glance on they are striking because of their geography, scale, and travel routes of distant journeys, as well as the plethora of rare names and designations: Java, Sumatra, Port Said, Redfort, Jamna, Reykyavik, Akureyri.

Foreign themes are not new in our literature. Many Soviet poets, beginning with Mayakovsky, appear in different countries as ambassadors of friendship and bearers of the new, socialistic culture. Frequently they bring back from their travel excellent poems. And each time one encounters poetry with this theme, one expects more than from "ordinary" verses. Obviously a work of this type presupposes a new view and freshness of conception; it introduces us to a country which we do not know, or know only insufficiently, "not personally," "by our own experience." Together with the poet we, Russian and Soviet citizens, enter a strange country as if we were Christopher Columbus. Not without reason Mayakovsky called his

1

sketches "My Discovery of America." This was not a quarrel with the great navigator. This was "his own," his, Mayakovsky's, discovery.

It is difficult to overestimate the significance of foreign themes for the Soviet reader. In the works of N. Tikhonov, K. Simonov, P. Antokolsky, A. Malyshko, Mirzo Turzun-Zade[2] and many other poets who have created a broad and varied literature on the basis of foreign travel, we not only become acquainted with the life of other countries, but also realize more clearly our own place and role in the world in which we have many enemies, but also infinitely more friends, and in which the Soviet citizen—the builder of the first Socialist state in history—feels himself to be in the front ranks of the fighters for peace, for freedom, and for the happiness of mankind.

In his work on themes from abroad, A. Sofronov adheres to an ancient and good tradition which is firmly established in our literature, our daily life, and in the mind of every Soviet citizen. The motifs of friendship and brotherhood among nations, sympathy for the oppressed classes and nations, and love for one's native region make up the ideational content of the book *From All Latitudes.* And in this lies its merit. The author of the book, expressing thoughts and feelings dear to our hearts, evokes respect as a citizen of the Soviet Union.

But the new verses of A. Sofronov unfortunately do not contain any significant poetic discoveries, because the great ideas appear here mostly in the form of commonplaces. In order to become a real phenomenon of contemporary great art these ideas are in need of a clearly expressed individual treatment, of concrete images, and of an original poetic view af the world.

The author traveled a great deal and saw much; he performed a great and useful work and collected much material about which at least his book of sketches speaks. But in the verses of Sofronov, overloaded with the names of different countries, rivers, seas, cities, and streets, the profile of that specific country, that specific nation is often only hardly noted. The general and the abstract are predominant here, overpowering the concrete and individual, and statement takes precedence over pictorial quality and the idea over the image.

I have friends in the whole wide world,
Count them for a day, a week, and you'll not finish;
And we respond to one another always
And each is good in some special way!

. . . In all longitudes and latitudes of the world—
Wherever fate may take you—
Someone meets and embraces you,
You recognize your friends—there's no end of them!

These are friends "in general," nameless "somebodies" (someone meets, someone embraces), at times, by the way, called by name, but rarely disclosed as living human persons, and it is they who are the heroes of Sofronov's verses. In just what special way each one of them is good the poet does not say. Because of this, despite their geographical variety, his verses suffer from poetic monotony. The same words are repeated, the same formulas and situations. Thus, for example, the handshake of the representative of another nation becomes the symbolic gesture which, passing from one poem to the other, gradually loses its vivid warmth and turns in sum into a conventional, abstract designation of the idea of friendship, into a repetitious literary device, into a cliché.

In Cairo a friend called me simply
Brother, when first we met
And simply shook my hand
Just as soldiers shake hands. . . .
("The Road to Port Said")

I remember the handshake
Above the fjord in the blue silence. . . .
("The Handshake")

We remember friends from Akureyri,
Their handshakes, looks and words.
("The Icelandic People")

Even if you don't know the language,
Come here just the same,
But a hand will squeeze your hand:
Moscow—Peking, Moscow—Peking.
("Song")

You have shaken the hands of honest men,
Have understood without translation.
("On the Bay of Bengal")

For manly handshakes are understood. . . .
("Winter")

Fraternal hands intertwined in handshakes,
And the circle of friendship is broad and firm.
I have friends in the whole wide world,
I feel their clasp in my hands. . . .
("I Have Friends in the Whole World")

The author seems to be captivated by his own phraseology. He marks time, unable to overcome the narrow limits of a vocabulary established once and for all. Instead of expressing his subject matter in words, the poet seems to put a constant verbal mask over it which hides its real aspects and its real appearance. The author became attached to the word "scars," for example, and now the word is used everywhere—appropriately and inappropriately—as though the author were using it automatically and through force of habit. Thus, among the buildings of Plymouth "scars are seen everywhere," and on the body of a Javanese "Under the shirt was a black scar," and the sign board of a London advertisement is "marked with the black scars of letters," and in Nagasaki "not one scar on these people has yet healed" (although, as is well known, a scar appears at the place where a wound is healing).

It is well understood that each poet has his own style and vocabulary. These "scars," however, are not signs of the creative individuality of the author but the result of poetic solutions in the form of clichés.

In the poems of A. Sofronov one may come across evocatory details which open up for a minute a vivid picture. For example, in the twilight streets of London the poet sees some women standing "in the haloes of the neon lights." But there are few such details. The distinctive marks of a foreign country, the so-called local color, the typical traits of national life and psychology, are drowned in the flow of commonplace phrases, which may be all right by themselves but which are not satisfying when applied to everything in general and to no one in

particular. The impression is created that the author looks at
life in the majority of cases from the cabin of an airplane; in
his eyes the earth is covered with fog; its forms and shapes
flow together into one vague spot. In this way the names of
several works take on a self-characterizing sense: "Over
Sumatra," "Over the Bay of Bengal," "Over the Australian
Desert."

> I'm still writing you from airplanes,
> And still at different heights. . . .

The point, of course, does not lie in the travel conditions of
the author nor even in the fleetingness of his observations along
his route. In the poems of A. Sofronov often even the nearest
well-known phenomena appear in the form of cold abstraction,
because the poet replaces their concrete delineation with commonplace judgments. The book *From All Latitudes* is concluded by the poem "A Contemporary," as the hero of which
our Soviet man of today appears. But this again is not a living
person, but a dry, abstract formula deduced by logic and reproducing some attributes of some substance:

> My true comrade, my friend, contemporary.
> Worker, who forges the links of history.
> For all that rang out then in the salutes,
> You know who gave both beginning and end.
> Let us look
> To see who built the great monument of victory
> And who set you among the heroes.
>
> . . . You were a bugler in the Pioneer's brigade,
> You were in the Komsomol, you became a Communist,
> You can be a locksmith, architect, minister—
> All roads of life are open to you,
> If only you have the heart and wings
> And a great desire and a creative mind.
> If you wish you'll achieve much at once. . . .

Before us there is in essence not an image, not a character
but an elastic concept, the schematic idea of a contemporary
devoid of any individual traits at all. In this idea neither a lock-
smith, an architect, nor a minister would recognize himself, but

would find only biographical particulars not of his own, but of
any universal-faceless biography at all. The broad, if you please
too broad, treatment of the theme is developed with unjustifi-
able length. The thought of the author, spreading out in a
welter of words, moves slowly and often gets stuck in one
place:

> You hastened to the factory in your worker's overalls,
> You hurried till the whistle, trampling the grass,
> You were met by the coolness of the courtyard,
> A familiar, intimate coolness belonging to you.

The hero hastens, but the author is in no hurry, since he re-
peats the very same words and phrases; an air of noncommittal
weariness emerges from his enumeration: "familiar, intimate
and belonging to you. . . ."

In the most recent poems of A. Sofronov a feeble form of expression is given not only to concrete traits of the life and the
people which are their subject matter, but also to the concrete
figure of the author and the poet's individual view peculiar to
him and to no one else. These poems often sound like imitations of Yesenin, Mayakovsky, Isakovsky,[3] and other poets. One
must speak here not of borrowing but of a more profound
cause: A. Sofronov does not have his own firm, clearly expressed individual style. Because he writes too "generally," his
muse is easily attuned to the tones of others, ones we know
from other examples.

> I walked above the Alazan'
> Above the enchanted water,
> Grown gray like a legend,
> And, like a song, ever young.

How fresh, how inimitable this comparison of a man with a
story and a song sounded in the poems of N. Tikhonov! But
when A. Sofronov, speaking of Grieg,[4] uses similar comparisons:

> Young as if from an ancient tale
> And at the same time from a song—

they lose in his verses their original clarity and are converted into an ordinary "commonplace," little distinguished from other "commonplaces," and living peacefully alongside such faceless turns of speech that are no one's property!

> He grew into the cliffs, awoke to life in revolt,
> Full of serious simplicity,
> Forever turning into "Peer Gynt"
> Toward immortal life through eternal beauty.

The figure derived from Tikhonov has been somehow blotted out in the new interpretation and lost its character; it has grown old and pale. Of what sort of borrowing or influence can one speak here? Here it is only worth speaking of a loss.

Sometimes in his verses about foreign countries A. Sofronov consciously tries to recall to the reader's memory the figure and verse form of Mayakovsky:

> The Landscape I'll not mention,
>   Nor touch on the weather,
> I'll not excite various people—
>   I wish to dedicate
> The whole given ode
>   With gratitude
> In its entirety
>   To the English police. . . .

Yes, when reading these lines one really recalls Mayakovsky. Still to be discussed is the question of how far and how accurately the author followed this tradition. We wish now to answer another question: where does A. Sofronov himself stand, taken alone, without "commonplaces" and literary reminiscences?

The most successful verses of A. Sofronov in a poetical sense appear to be those in which most distinctly his own personal tonality is heard. These are chiefly poems evoked by love for his native land, longing for his own home, wife—for all that which the poet left at the time of his journey. The personal aspect of a great general theme lends these verses liveliness:

> Like an Australian boomerang,
> Released by your hand,
> Flying across the ocean,
> I fly to you, to you, home.
>
> . . . And if you call, call, call—
> From all latitudes, from distant lands,
> To you, to you, like a boomerang,
> I'll come
>   To your warm hands.

At the same time, among several poems of A. Sofronov which are colored by strong feeling, one also encounters verses with which he would like to quarrel. The quarrel in the present case arises with regard to the author's conception, and the question of the artistic value of the poem is left aside. In any case this very fact itself speaks for the well-known poetic quality of the poem: if it somehow provokes and arouses the reader through the idea contained in it, that means that it possesses its own character and one may either agree or disagree with it (a thing one cannot do with a cliché or stereotype).

A poem which provokes the wish to quarrel, and which belongs to the best works of A. Sofronov, is called "When a Man is over Forty. . . ." In it the poet expresses his own life credo and speaks about himself and deals with those opinions which he had to hear about himself as a man.

> When a man's over forty,
> When he's already grown gray,—
> Behind him there's an obligatory pile
> Of past events and deeds.
>
> And however hard he tried
> To hide from them and go away,—
> He is tied to them forever,
> And there is no other way.
>
> Someone at some time he offended,
> Something to someone he did not give;
> Of someone he caught sight—and didn't see,
> Someone he knew—but didn't recognize!
>
> All are serious transgressions!
> But how shall I fold my hands

> So that these chance opinions
> Permit me to live in my own way?

For some reason the friends of the poet see in this confession an admission of penitence and are distressed that their comrade "gives himself up to the mercy of the enemy," "seeks a quiet refuge," while earlier he "was not a bad Communist." The poet objects to this:

> Yes, for me it was bitter, not sweet,
> But sweetness I did not seek.
> There is no need for sticky syrups
> And songs for the nightingale to sing,—
> I do not need a refined Europe
> With all its psychology,
> With its two-sided vision,
> In which 'pro' and 'contra' are together. . . .

The poem ends with the affirmation of the straight path which the poet wishes to follow in the future, too.

> And if I don't go straight—
> May their looks be taken from me!

Without regard for the danger of the "two-sided vision," one must confess frankly that the expression of the thought here arouses an ambiguous and contradictory feeling. The straightforwardness of which the poet speaks is worthy of all respect, if one understands by it an adherence to principle and a firmness of the soul, and the like. But that is just the point, namely that in the present poem another nuance is added to this understanding, toward which one must come out not "pro" but "contra." "Chance opinions" which are not appropriate to a man of genuine principles are not deleted in the course of the poem but under the pretense of directness are, as it were, confirmed and justified. But does the genuine straightforwardness of a Communist or the implacability for one's enemies consist in offending someone some time, in not giving someone something, in not seeing and not recognizing someone? This is more reminiscent of petty troubles in daily life than of the struggle for one's principles and ideals, and we are astonished at the

fact that the author mixes and mingles such different things under the sole name of "straightforwardness."

A. Sofronov's words about "refined Europe" also call for refutation. We have, as is well known, old and complex relations
with Europe. We reject many things and we accept others. At
the dawn of Soviet poetry, A. Blok, not fawning "on pretty Europe," but rather prophesying a defeat for the old world which
was threatening us with war, at the same time spoke of the
fact that we love and esteem all the best that had been created
by European culture.[5]

> All is understood by us: both the incisive Gallic thought
> And the obscure German genius. . . .

Mayakovsky unmasked the voices of Western bourgeois civilization in a manner that was sufficiently sharp, direct, and in
accordance with Communist principles. But he had a profound
approach to European phenomena and pointed out what was
vital in its complexity and contradictory nature. The famous
Brooklyn Bridge[6] aroused his enthusiasm as a structure of contemporary technology and culture, and at the same time he
wrote with anger and pain of how Americans who were unem-
ployed threw themselves from the Brooklyn Bridge. One must
remember all this because the lines of A. Sofronov lack depth
and in them there appears a simplified hewing to the line:

> I do not need refined Europe
> With all its psychology. . . .

The primitive treatment of the theme makes itself felt in general in the poetic works of A. Sofronov.* In his poems one en-

---

* In this connection it is interesting to note that A. Sofronov's poem
"Little Whip," written in 1944, was printed in his new book which was
recently published, Selected Verses. This poem had already provoked
a quite justified criticism, and it is strange that the author considered
it possible to publish it now in the new edition. "Little Whip" is dedicated to the Cossack nagaika whip, a lash described with unusual care,
love, and admiration:

> And on the right side,
> On the twisted, spiral strap,
> There flowed down, like a rivulet,

counters figures which hurt the ear with their roughness and absence of feeling for meter and good taste. In the poem "To the Icelandic Nation" Sofronov writes:

> We saw a stern Nature,
> Counted the hills on their steep jags—
> They were a match for the Icelandic nation,
> Its poets and its heroes.
>
> We read the national desires
> In its open and simple soul. . . .

A good and correct thought is expressed very clumsily here: in the soul of the nation they read the national desires. . . . This annoying tautology is a result of the insensitivity of the author to the movement of his verse, to its thought content and its resonance.

A. Sofronov's poem "Where do Angels Come From?" has as its basis the very acute, topical subject which is not of first-rate significance—the appearance in England of illegitimate children—and, following this easy path suggested by the subject matter, he began to squander his talents on trifles and to play up various "gay" details connected with the illegitimate children. As a result a great political theme was reduced to the fact that Americans "like to go out with pretty girls," like to "seize by the waist, well, and so forth . . ." as a result of which:

> The delicate stiff little whip;
> Bright yellow, raw-hide,
> Smoothly finished, tidy,
> Woven in three strands—
> You'll never forget it.

Many instruments of warfare and of the soldier's life entered our poetry along with the description of life at the front. The praises were sung of shoes and overcoats and our good old 7.6 mm. rifle. But the Cossack knout evokes completely different associations in our minds which are not connected with the Second World War and which point to our pre-revolutionary past. It was not proper to replace the excellent rifle of the Soviet soldier with it, as Sofronov did, and it was all the more improper to raise a lash to the level of an independent poetic theme and of an aesthetic object.

The publication of this poem in 1958 by the Government Publishing House for Literature is simply incomprehensible.

A little illegitimate "honey" is born . . .
But where is daddy?
But you see, daddy
Has not a trace of shame.
He waves his wings
Over the flying squadrons,
He soars above the shore
And—skips off to America.

The soft consonants of "laponka" [7] ("honey") destroy the tonality of the satiric work and trivialize the figure of the satirist himself.

Unfortunately, in our contemporary poetry there still appear many works written on a rather low level of art, and the poems of A. Sofronov in this sense appear to be no exception. But it is harmful to pass off this level as a high form of mastery. This would mean reducing the general standards which we apply to contemporary poetry, and would confuse and bewilder the readers and poets intending to emulate models which are far from artistic perfection.

Meanwhile in periodical literature there have appeared articles in which the recent poems of A. Sofronov have not only received an exaggerated evaluation, but have been held up as models in regard to their literary quality and placed in the front ranks of our contemporary poetry. Thus, for example, A. Markov asserted in *Literaturnaya Gazeta* (October 7, 1958) that the new book of A. Sofronov, *From All Latitudes,* with regard to its excellence "stands on a good, high-quality level. Here above all it is necessary to speak of the content, and the visual quality of the imagery, and the precision of expression. 'Captivating the sky and earth of Britain,' Sofronov writes of the Americans in England. What an exact word, 'captivating,' and not just anything, but the sky! To put any other word here would be inapposite. . . . There are other examples of such exact, flawless, direct 'hits' of the poet: 'Lest the hangars bunch up on the soil of England': a surprisingly visual quality is in this epithet 'lest . . . bunch up. . . .'"

Strange things do happen! One has only to lend the language some little obvious figures, and immediately this is considered a tremendous achievement. Elementary literary literacy is passed off as a discovery. Naturally in the poems of A. Sofronov there are metaphors and epithets in which A. Markov gets confused (the second example cited by him is not an epithet but a metaphor). Some of these figures of speech are not bad, but with special "content" and "visual quality" not much is gained. By the way, "Lest England's soil be swollen with hangars" is not a great invention, for the poet expresses himself here very clumsily and awkwardly, and one must avoid such conglomerations of words so that it is clear who is "inflating" whom: the hangars, the soil of England, or vice versa.

"But take an important aspect of our trade such as rhyme," continues A. Markov. "I shall cite only one example from the poem 'Where do Angels Come From?' Is this not just what Mayakovsky meant speaking of rhyme as a 'barrel of dynamite': *suzheny—iuzhnymi, Londona—prodano, grokhote—pokhoti* and others. Thanks to this accurate rhyming the verses are memorable and hit their target!"

The examples quoted by Markov are made "in imitation of Mayakovsky." But there is a great difference between them and the genuine Mayakovsky, who in the first place was a tireless inventor of new rhymes and new methods of rhyming (A. Sofronov uses rhymes which are in the best cases based on the type of rhyme used by Mayakovsky), and in the second place never distorted the sense of the words for their sake. As an example of the distortion of the Russian language one must quote one of the rhymes which delighted A. Markov: "American soldiers, captivating England."

> Were accustomed during thunder [*v grokhote*]
> To dream of lust [*pokhoti* . . .]

To dream of lust is just as difficult as to dream of hunger and thirst. One can dream of their satisfaction, alleviation, and satiation, but to dream of the wish itself, to "dream of lust" is impossible.

A. Sofronov was artistically unsuccessful in many poems because he followed Mayakovsky only superficially and tried almost literally to reproduce his figures of speech and intona-

tion, imitating another's style and at the same time violating
some of Mayakovsky's basic principles. In all this it is soon
evident that this violation is not the fruit of new creative
search and not the revelation of the individual character of
the poet, but the result of inability, carelessness, and haste. For
example, imitating Mayakovsky, the poet at the same time
rhymes chance words which are not stressed in the content or
uses "any old rhymes" (*"Kottedzham—Kolledzhei," "Ushlo—
povelo"* and so forth), which, as is well known, Mayakovsky
treated quite ironically.

Also, from the point of view of the rhythmic organization of
language, the poems of Sofronov in the majority of cases approach Mayakovsky only because of the step form. Again
there is only a superficial resemblance to Mayakovsky, because
the verse of A. Sofronov often stumbles, gets stuck, and sounds
attenuated and heavy.

> Here all is still in an earlier memory,
> But an old one,
> The threshold is not obliterated under the foot . . .
> But each
> old
> black stone
> Bursts into sunlight
> and everything stirs a sprout.

Such a heaping up of "everything," which weighs down the
verse and makes it amorphous and sluggish, would not be
tolerated by Mayakovsky.

For this reason we cannot agree either with the judgment
which V. Litvinov published in a review of *From All Latitudes*
in *Znamia* (1959, no. 4): "Sofronov always tended toward a
verse which was melodious and softly orchestrated. But here
the poet has turned to the theme of foreign lands, and in his
new book the 'colloquial' meters of Mayakovsky ring out distinctly." It is exactly the poems of Sofronov that were written
in imitation of Mayakovsky which lack energy, compactness,
and sustained dynamics. The poet's turn to a new theme did
not entail a profound restructuring of his artistic system, for

he assimilated only some external characteristics of Mayakovsky's verse form. This is the source of some stiffness, arti-
ficiality, and lack of conviction on the part of A. Sofronov
which may be noticed especially in those cases where Mayakovsky was "true to himself" and his inimitable tonality rang
out at its best, freely and naturally.

Our contemporary poets who wish to imitate Mayakovsky
often use his "stepped form," but in doing so they forget that
the spacing out of the prosodic line in Mayakovsky's verses is
not the main thing but a derivative and ancillary device, and
that this is only a means of spacing out graphically and underlining the rhythm and intonation. If there is no corresponding
rhythm, it makes no difference how much one spaces out the
verses.

How foreign and organically inapposite the step form à la
Mayakovsky is to the verses of Sofronov may be shown in the
following example:

> . . . Our friend's military columns;
> Our friend's working
> columns,—
> There he is, our brother and our
> friend and comrade,
> There he is, young China!
> . . . The wind sways the yellow leaves
> Broad far-off places call
> to happiness! . . .

If you try to read these verses aloud, pausing at the designated places of the spaced-out lines, as is proper, you will see
that the "traffic signs" are scattered about here as chance would
have it.

Is it worth it to list artistically as "good, high-quality level"
verses which clearly do not achieve such a level? Let us rather
raise our criteria in the evaluation of the artistic quality of new
works. Let us remember Mayakovsky:

> Let there be powerful verse
> so that for a hundred years,

The verse may not waste away
like a puff of smoke,
So that with this verse
we may resound
and boast
Before our times,
before our republic
before our beloved.

This is the high-quality, powerful verse toward which one should strive, and of such verse one may boast.

No Discount

(ON SCIENCE FICTION)

For a long time now there have been complaints in our press about the lack of good science fiction and the lag in this genre. Why are there so few books of this kind, although there is such a great demand for them by the broad mass of readers? This is the contradiction that needs to be solved and which from time to time draws the attention of literary criticism. But instead of accusing the writers, we have to admit that literary criticism itself has not always adopted sufficiently correct, sensible, and farseeing tactics in regard to science fiction, and this was one of the reasons for the serious crisis from which science fiction began to emerge only recently.

This genre, well developed in the 1920's and 1930's, faced great difficulties at the end of the 1940's.[1] It was the time when the perverse opinion was spread and established that Soviet science fiction does not have to be "altogether fantastic," that "cosmic distances and supernatural inventions are alien" to our writers, and that "they can depict only the perspectives of our nearest [I emphasize nearest] future." * From this point of view the writers' interest, for example, in problems of inter-

* S. Ivanov, "Fantasy and Reality," *Oktyabr*, 1950, No. 1, pp. 160, 161.

planetary communication looked like a phenomenon which was contrary to the norm and removed from the present.

There is no need now to prove how mistaken this view was: reality itself refuted it and space flights are by now transferred from the realm of imagination to the sphere of the most palpable and pressing reality. Nowadays, in order to keep up with the times, one has at least to mention space if not write about it.

The barriers that hindered the development of science fiction and even threatened its existence are thus removed by life itself, and this fact could not help but have a favorable influence upon literature. Nowadays our writers, trying to catch up with a reality that outstripped them, can write freely not only about the moon, Mars, or Venus, but even about far-away Uranus and things farther away beyond the limits of the solar system. They can report not only things which are going to happen in science or technology in two or three years (as they were told by the cautious and not very farsighted critics), but also how life might be in a hundred or a thousand years.

The first place in contemporary science fiction is assigned to the topic of space travel and interplanetary communications which, of course, are connected with the remarkable successes achieved by Soviet science in these fields, and also with the generally increased interest in this great task of historical importance. At the same time our science fiction writers also work in other areas suggested by the new problems in biology, radiotechnology, chemistry, etc. There are also works devoted to cybernetics, nuclear phenomena, and other most recent problems of contemporary science. All this testifies to the rise of science fiction, which by now is in a much better position than it was ten years ago.

However, from time to time even today one still encounters the drawbacks of the old mistaken ideas, the attempts to restrain and limit the imagination and channel it into the framework of "moderation and good manners." [2] For this reason we find that the position recently taken by the *Literaturnaya Gazeta* in connection with I. Yefremov's *The Nebula of An-*

dromeda is quite correct as a matter of principle.* The point is not only that Yefremov's book is defended from unjust accusations, but also the fact that Soviet science fiction is presented with the possibility of speaking out boldly, of developing further artistically, and of advancing along the road of inventiveness and artistic variety.

One of the trends in contemporary science fiction is frequently called "the fantasy of the present day," or "realistic fantasy." This trend is represented by writers who, so to speak, work at short range, as for example V. Nemtsov, V. Okhotnikov, V. Saparin, and others. They write about inventions of a kind which in the immediate future may have great practical influence on our lives and our economy (as, for example, especially strong kinds of wool, the perfection of TV, etc.). The utility and necessity of such literature is obvious. It makes the youth acquainted with many problems of contemporary science and technology and infects the reader with the spirit of invention and the rationalization of techniques.†

But sometimes in the art of such writers one gets the feeling of a tendency toward what could be called naturalistic earthiness, toward a certain theory of "triviality." We mean, of course, the unwillingness of certain authors to look into the future, the emphatic lowering of the dream to the level of everyday occurrence. As a result of this, the fantastic story turns out to be less fantastic than our reality.

The novelette *A Splinter of the Sun,* written in 1955, is devoted to the utilization of solar energy. V. Nemtsov, its author, starts it with the following statement which is programmatic for this writer and which has a polemical ring: "This summer no interplanetary spaceship left the earth. On the railways of the country there traveled ordinary trains, without nuclear energy. The Antarctic remained cold. Man

---

* For the polemics which developed around I. Yefremov's novel see *Promyshlenno-Ekonomicheskaya Gazeta* (June 21 and July 15, 1959), and the *Literaturnaya Gazeta* (July 2 and August 29, 1959) (A.S.).

† G. Gurevich's novel, *Bad Weather in Underground,* 1956, is a good example of this type of literature. It deals with the forecast and prevention of earthquakes, with the utilization of volcanic energy (A.S.).

has not yet learned how to control the weather, to get bread from the air, and to live for three hundred years. There were no advertisements for a lunar flight either. All these things did not exist for the sole reason that our story is about the events of the present day, which we like no less than we do the future. And may the reader forgive the author for not wanting to depart from our time and our planet."

Of course each writer, and the science fiction writer too, has the right to pick the time and place for his story as he likes. However, it is curious to note that the characteristics of today, given here by Nemtsov, sound rather archaic. The negative definition of our times, made in 1955, cannot be unconditionally applied to the times of 1959; though there are still no nuclear-powered trains, there are nuclear-powered icebreakers, and nuclear submarines, and also in the field of interplanetary communication tremendous progress has been made. Several years have passed, and the fantastic story of Nemtsov has become obsolete.

In 1959 the same author, in order to catch up with today, was already forced to leave his beloved earth. He did this in his new novel *Halfway Station,* but he did it again rather halfheartedly, with a cautious look, and according to his own expression "controlling the dream" so that it did not fly too far away. And what did happen to the dream with such a cautious treatment?

The new novel is about the fantastic flying laboratory "Union," built for space research. But the heroes, checking out this apparatus, face from the first such insurmountable difficulties that they are forced to interrupt the unlucky mission and give up for an indefinite time all enterprises of such a kind. In simple terms: the author is again too late, for at the time of the successful landing on the moon of a Soviet rocket and of the picture-taking tour of another one, a book is published about the unsuccessful flight of a rocket in the vicinity of the moon.

This is, however, not the main point. In the final instance there can be failures in anything, the more so in such a complicated and difficult enterprise as travel in space. What is strange is something different, namely that the author, taking up such a topic as space flight, during the entire novel deliberately and consistently lowers the level of the topic, deromanticizes it, and tries in every way to convince the reader of the uninteresting features of space flights. His heroes, interrupting the short trip and returning home, tell their colleagues of their impressions and work in the following manner: "We were bored and most of the time we were looking at the Earth. On the big screen you probably saw it much better than we did. As far as I am concerned, I was not very much impressed. Water, deserts, fog. . . . We have not seen the most important things, those which were made by men's hands. We have not seen the cities, the canals, the plowed fields. A dead planet."

Of course the earthly creations of men are worthy of any admiration. But it may be that the heroes of Nemtsov, not satisfied with the heavenly picture, would have done better to take a helicopter for their excursion. Then they would have been saved from the merciless boredom they had to suffer in space. There, beyond the earth, they did not find much that was good—they became convinced, according to the author, "of the naîveté of their childish expectations of something unbelievable in cosmic space," and they understood that "it was much more fun to invent and build that *Union* than to fly in it."

There is no doubt that the building of the *Union* was extremely entertaining. But willy-nilly the question arises: was it indeed worthwhile to guard the space center and build that remarkable *Union* if it was not interesting to fly in it? Even the moon, which Nemtsov's heroes approached so that they could figure out its "geography," gave them no joy: "And again it came to their minds that even the poles of our earth, which lack all life, are much more interesting."

Thus on almost every page the author dampens the reader's ardor and tries to persuade him not to be diverted, not to indulge in fantasy, and thus this book, as far as cosmic flights are concerned, disillusions more than it inspires. "For him the earth is the center of the universe. Around the earth rotate the sun and all the other planets." These words, spoken with rapture about one of the heroes of the novel, express fully the position of the author himself. This geocentric view would even be acceptable to a certain extent, if it did not turn in Nemtsov's hands into a brake or a wall standing in the way of human will, reason, and dreams. Among his heroes there is only one who daydreams: "Show me the thrilling pictures of the future. . . . Discover the secrets of the galaxy," but this person is a negative character and he is sharply rejected by the author. The others, the positive heroes of the book, are not moved by the secrets of the galaxy: they follow strictly "earthly," utilitarian aims. The most romantically inclined among them (according to the assertions of the author), one with the catchy name of Bagretsov, insists upon a "reasonable romanticism," and when he is asked whether or not he would like to be first man on Mars, he answers: "For the sake of discovery or glory alone? No, I don't want to! . . . If I knew that after my return from Mars I could discover new riches on earth, grow some useful plants in the tundra, then I would like to fly."

The conquest of space is also interpreted by Nemtsov's heroes in a narrow sense; with the help of cosmic energy it would be possible to shear sheep in the remotest areas of the country, to milk cows or shave oneself with an electric shaver. These things are, of course, useful, but is it possible to measure cosmic perspectives with them?

It is possible, for example, that future satellites of the earth, or even the moon, will enable us to improve upon the reception of earthly TV stations so that the Moscow TV programs can be received without any trouble, say in Vladivostok. However, we send those rockets into space not because of such relatively small, tertiary goals. We try to decipher the mystery of Mars[3] not just in order to plant a frost-resistant type of turnip from Mars on the Taimyr Peninsula.

In answer to Nemtsov's call for a "reasonable understanding of romanticism" we cannot help quoting Gorky: "The madness of the brave—is the wisdom of life!" And in connection with his "realistic" program of space discovery we remember Mayakovsky, who said that "we are realists, but not on earth."

It is obvious that because of space flights science fiction

should not forget about our planet either, since it supplies other authors working in this field with such rich material. But even under "earthly conditions" there is a great need for books of scientific interest and of high flights of the imagination. Such, for example, is the novel of Y. Dolgushin, *GCh*, published in installments in 1939–1940 and in book form in 1959, essentially revised and enlarged.

The problems of physics, biology, physiology, and psychology are combined in this novel, and they give rise to a whole complex of bright and bold ideas, including the transmission of thought over distance and the elimination of death. People of the most different fields of knowledge will find here ideas for their thoughts and imagination. But the main thing in the book is its profound and universal human sense of scientific-fantastic hypotheses elaborated on by the author, for they tell us of the limitless power of reason and urge our will on to creativity, to the search for the unknown and new.[4]

From an artistic point of view Dolgushin's novel is also an extraordinary phenomenon in contemporary Soviet science fiction. Thought which penetrates the secrets of Nature here becomes the main force that sets the plot in motion. Nowadays in our science fiction the more familiar topic is one of a different kind: the plot revolves mostly around some kind of invention or discovery which is already completed. In addition to this, the novels are frequently burdened with much secondary material which is needed by the author only to build up his entertaining and suspenseful intrigue. In Dolgushin's novel we feel as if we were in the middle of the discovery, and with unfaltering interest we follow the intriguing development of the discovery and follow the process of the searching scientific thinking, which is full of guesses and adventures. Dolgushin's novel *GCh* belongs among the best works of Soviet science fiction. Its publication at the present time in a new, better edition is a very inspiring fact.

Realism in science fiction is sometimes understood as the curtailment of fantasy: the less fantastic a novel, the more realistic it is. However, here obviously different relationships apply, and the degree and amount of fantasy do not mean much by themselves. Historically this genre was composed and developed to a great extent as a phenomenon belonging to and expressing realism. The stories about the "miracles," not motivated by anything besides the will and wish of the author, were replaced by the scientifically founded "generator of miracles." The supernatural received natural argumentation; that is how science fantasy developed, as one of the forms and variations of realistic art.

It is just this predetermined quality of the happenings that makes us accept them as something perfectly believable. In order to achieve this the author is required not only to give a scientific motivation for the phenomena described, but also the development of the plot in accordance with "the truth of life," that is, in accordance with the chosen place, time, characters, etc. The fantastic element does not suffer from this—on the contrary, it is strengthened and confirmed by the course of the story, and acquires authenticity and a similarity to reality of events which do not necessarily happen in reality, but which could happen. A member of the Academy, V. A. Obruchev, said of this aspect of the genre: "I think that the science fiction novel must develop the plot and characters realistically so that the reader is convinced that everything that is described in the novel is possible. The novel must not imitate the fairy tale. . . ." *

The verisimilitude of the fantastic is often achieved by using fantastic means. In order to kill the dinosaur, for example, one must have a nuclear gun. The authenticity of fantasy fiction in many cases is achieved at the expense of consistency in the chosen "course," and if the hero lands on Mars, then the inhabitants of Mars must be kept in "proportion" with the fantastic situation: they cannot, without interrupting the laws of the genre, be similar to our neighbors in the communal apartment.[5]

The authenticity of I. Yefremov's novel *The Nebula of Andromeda* consists, for example, in the fact that the author, in order to depict the people of a distant future, has chosen corresponding criteria and has shown them in further develop-

* *Literaturnaya Gazeta,* October 5, 1954 (A.S.).

ment, in a struggle for an ever more difficult, beautiful, and therefore fantastic goal. Having returned from an interplanetary trip of many years' duration, Yefremov's heroes are already dreaming of even bolder trips to other galaxies. As they advance they wish to top their own achievements again and again. Each new discovery is followed by another, and "the avalanche of new discoveries rolls into infinity, rumbling like a snowball."

From this point of view Yefremov's book differs favorably from the many Utopian stories of recent years in which the ideal society has frequently been described as a ready-made, frozen "perfection" having neither desire nor incentive for further development. The idea depicted in the novel *The Nebula of Andromeda* possesses the wonderful quality of presenting new ideas. Yefremov's book has no ceilings, just as human dreams and knowledge have no limits either. This is what makes his book historically and psychologically believable.[6]

It is difficult to get used to the dimensions of Yefremov's novels. The heroes acting in the book tackle problems which might appear to us to be unsolvable; their scientific knowledge, life experience, education, and psychology are very different from the present twentieth century. But even if the time of *The Nebula of Andromeda* may seem to be far away from our time, even if the heroes may astonish us with the unexpected, still between them and us there is a close relationship. This is a relationship in spirit: as the prototype of the future, doubtlessly, Yefremov has taken our reality—the idea of moral responsibility of each for all and that of all for each, something that we confirm in practice even today. It is also remarkable that Yefremov's heroes, living a thousand years after us, are also storming ahead and are also thinking of their future, of the future of the future, just as we think of it. Those who have achieved, it would seem, all that of which we could only dream, have also inherited from us the passion for the coming day, the thirst for the new, and the readiness to sacrifice themselves on behalf of the future.

Perhaps it is the final scene of the novel that is the most successful: the sending off of the new starship *Swan* on a new trip. While it is being completed one generation takes the place of the other in the ship, and only the children born during the flight will reach the goal. This victory achieved for those who "do not yet exist, who would come many years later" arouses a feeling which could be called one of bodily closeness, the feeling of comradeship, perhaps only with the correction that our neighbors here appear to be the people of the thirtieth and fortieth century. This relay race which we pass on to our children, and the children to the grandchildren, and which continues through centuries, into the immeasurable distances of space and time, unites mankind in one close family.

Perspectives like this could be opened up and could receive artistic form only in our society, in our times—on the threshold of all that beautiful future about which Yefremov is telling us. In this respect his book is modern and very timely. There are, however, passages where the credible pictures of the future created by Yefremov become blurred. It happens in those cases where the heroes in rather simple and everyday (for them) situations start a discussion on abstract scientific questions not called for by the development of the action, or deliver to each other popular lectures on dialectical or historical materialism and make rather frequent excursions into the past —for the sole reason of demonstrating to the reader their high mental and moral qualities. All this has the appearance of a strained effort, just as if a contemporary man sitting in the streetcar constantly raved in conversation about the qualities of electricity by means of which people are moved in the streetcar along the streets, while in the tenth century people walked on foot or used an unwieldy carriage. Such artificial passages which contradict elementary logic prevent the acceptance of the story as a natural flow of life (of course, in fantastic circumstances) and turn living people into mouthpieces who explain appropriately or not what the author thinks of the future of science, art, economics, and life in general.

Here is an example of a conversation carried on at one time by Yefremov's heroes: "I also cannot understand—said Veda —how it could happen that our predecessors could not understand for so long the simple law that the fate of society depends only on themselves, that a society as such is the moral-ideal development of its members, which in turn depends on the given economy." "That the perfect form of the scientific construction of a society is not simply the quantitative accumulation of productive forces but a qualitative level—this is very simple," answered Dar Veter. "And also the understanding of the dialectical interconnections which states that new social relationships without new people are just as unthinkable as the new people are without this new economy." An exchange of platitudes of this sort would sound artificial even under contemporary conditions, and it is all the more painful to hear them from the mouths of people who will live a thousand years after us.

The same feeling of ineptitude also arises in those cases where Yefremov, chasing after beautiful effects, falls into mannerisms and uses images and pictures which belong to the sphere of the superstylish. In such cases the beautiful world of the future is covered with a thin veneer of slightly remodeled old-fashionedness, and unbearable provincial intonations[7] are distinguishable in the book: "'I will obey you, Veter,' Veda whispered the magic words which made his heart jump and caused a slight blush on his pale cheeks."

It is understandable that in the case of I. Yefremov, the scientist who as a writer has an inclination for the artistic formulation of scientific problems, the purely intellectual part of his characters are better drawn. The chapters on space succeed better in the book than the scenes on earth, on "life as it is." One of the tasks of contemporary science fiction is to try to "imagine" the future in a more varied way and to present the man of the future a thousand years from now more vividly, more fullbloodedly, graphically, and less rationalistically. One can only hope for a further development of science fiction in this direction in the near future.

Realism in science fiction, just as in any other literary work, depends mainly on the fulfillment of quite a series of artistic conditions, and is not merely an addition or an appendage to fantasy. Furthermore, the lack of imagination and the passivity of fantasy often turn out to be a hindrance in the sphere of realism. It happens more than once that the author distorts the truth and falsifies exactly because he does not strain his imagination very much and uses ready-made situations "taken from life" and adds them to the fantastic subject matter—and as a result, of course, all kinds of inconsistencies develop. In the novel of G. Martynov, *Kallisto,* the story is about the unexpected landing on earth of guests from outer space who live somewhere near the star Sirius. In the first meeting with the Kallistanians (so the inhabitants of this planet are called) the writer presents us with the following ceremony: "At eleven-thirty everything was ready for the meeting. A hundred meters from the spaceship a company of soldiers lined up in precise order. At a lesser distance there was also an orchestra and the honor guard. At fifty meters from the spaceship a microphone was placed. . . ." Then, exactly at twelve, the state anthem of the planet Kallisto resounded from the spaceship of the unknown guest. "The officers saluted the anthem. The guests get out of the spaceship. The leaders of the Kallistanians embrace our leader of the meeting—a scientist. Then again the orchestra plays, but this time—on our side. The leader of the meeting delivers a short welcoming speech before the microphone. Then before the same microphone the head of the Kallistanian expedition also speaks. . . ."

It is difficult to read this scene without a smile: the official ceremony is so much out of style with the character of the event. It would be perfectly all right in connection with the arrival of some ambassador or other, under normal earthly conditions. But what is described here is the first meeting in mankind's history between us and beings from another planet, and they, according to the author, know precisely our rules of good manners and diplomatic etiquette, which must obviously be the same in all the corners of the infinite universe.

Having made the most fantastic assumption—the arrival of reasonable beings from the system of Sirius (just imagine—Si-ri-us!)—the author then decided not to use his imagination very much and limited himself basically to the statement that there is a great deal of similarity between "them" and "us."

The Kallistanians have black skin. However, "the features of their longish faces were the same as those of the white race, and they were beautiful, very beautiful, from an earthly point of view." In reminding us of the black color of the skin of the space guests the author was in a hurry to give them entirely— entirely!—European features. Such are obviously his ideas about the only possible form of human beauty.

The bodies of the Kallistanians "were little different from the bodies of earth beings. The brain, the nerve system, the breathing organs and the heart along with the blood vessels and the stomach were also the same. According to the books found in great quantity on the ship it was obvious that on their planet there was a rich flora, generally similar to the flora of the tropical zone of the earth. . . . The fish and fowl were astonishingly similar to the species to be found on Earth. Just as the people and Nature of Kallisto resemble the people and Nature of the Earth, so also is their history very similar. In Kallisto not only science but also the social structure was formerly similar to that of the Earth, or rather similar." Also the "scheme of the solar system" of Kallisto turned out to be similar to that of the Earth. The drawing was exactly like that which has been seen many times by Shirikov in astronomy books "where our solar system was depicted," etc.

Thus throughout the book the author gets rid of all the questions which might be asked by a curious reader (what kind of life is there on other planets?) by using laconic references which insist over and over again on the point that Kallisto is entirely a copy of our planet. But by discovering this amazing similarity, the author has put himself in a rather difficult position: what shall he tell about then, on what material shall he build the plot? And he must construct the story like a detective story, telling us about the saboteurs who wanted to annihilate the spaceship of the Kallistanians and how they did not succeed. And the space material, the science, for the sake of which the book was written, could not serve as a basis for an entertaining story: it is gray, monotonous, and it is entirely similar to earthly "data."

It has been known for a long time that fantasy takes its material from reality, that the most astonishing fantasy is always constructed from the elements of our earth. It is also well known that contemporary social problems are not at all alien to the genre of science fiction. In Wells's *The War of the Worlds,* wars on earth are reflected; in A. Tolstoy's *Aelita,* the events of the Revolution find a reflection; in certain episodes of Yefremov's *The Nebula of Andromeda* and in the novel of the talented Polish science-fiction writer Stanislav Lem,[8] the hotly debated issues of our times connected with the danger of a nuclear war found their place. But this similarity of images to the real phenomena of our life will never be literal. In the contrary case there is no need for fantastic fiction, and the writer who is tempted by complete similarity is better advised if he tries his powers in a different genre and turns immediately to the phenomena of the surrounding world.

In G. Martynov's novel *Kallisto,* the similarity of the Kallistanians to us is carried to such an extreme that it raises doubts about the credibility of the story. The author's rejection of the fantastic element in this given case is felt as the distortion of the truth. Such a transfer of our world into a different one reminds us somewhat of the *Weltanschauung* of the distant past, according to which the heavenly hierarchy strictly corresponded to the hierarchy on earth, when the earth stood in the center of the universe and the universe was likened to it. The sad fact is that the novel *Kallisto* almost returns us to the geocentric system of Ptolemy, or even further back to the anthropomorphism of prehistoric man, who tended to populate Nature with his own image. It all turned out this way, of course, contrary to the will of the author, who wished to stay on a strictly scientific basis. But the author plainly lacked imagination, for he did not "think up anything" but took only what he found close at hand: the receptions of the foreign delegates, the features of the black race, etc., and extended them to outer space.

In science fiction space was, for a long time, populated with monsters who were ugly, unintelligible, and hostile to man. The eight-foot men from Mars of Wells became a tradition and soon turned into a stock in trade. In giving up these stereotyped images many contemporary writers must obviously tend to the opposite direction: they stress the similarity to man of the reasonable beings living in space. But they could not get along here either without stereotypes: from now on space is filled with ideal beauties. "Pure classical, ideal forms"— "straight nose and small, curved lips gave him a resemblance to the face of Alexander of Macedonia." That is how the creatures of a far-distant planet are described in B. Fradkin's novelette *The Mystery of the Asteroid 117–03.*

Yefremov could not escape these stereotypes either. In his new story *Cor Serpentis* (*The Heart of the Snake*), a sequel to the theme of *The Nebula of Andromeda,* Yefremov describes the meeting between the people of the future and the ideal beings of another stellar system. Here it is said that these rational creatures, having human bodies and rare beauty, live in an atmosphere where the role of oxygen is taken over by fluorine. "How was it possible to believe," the author exclaims, "that these real people breathe a gas which is the most poisonous on earth and swim in seas consisting of an all-corroding fluid acid?" *

Indeed it is very difficult to believe—not in the fluorine people (a case, by the way, which would be permissible in science fiction), but in the fact that being so radically different from man by their chemical qualities they still retained the external characteristics of a rather banal beauty. The author turned out here to be much more daring in his scientific hypothesis than in his aesthetics. The cosmic beauties of Yefremov remind us strongly of the beautiful princes, and his story—in this respect—calls to mind the fairy tales: a genre, by the way, which is completely permissible in contemporary literature, but is beyond the realm of science fiction.

In this regard Yefremov's old story "Stellar Ships" sounded more credible. There the writer, recreating the portrait of a "stellar being," could do without the stereotype monsters and without sugary charms. The sensible being of the other planet he presented as an actual, living person, neither handsome nor ugly in our eyes, but simply different, resembling man in many

* *Yunost,* No. 1, 1959, p. 61 (A.S.).

ways, although still not his image, but rather something having its own characteristics.

The question of whether the inhabitants of other planets are beautiful or not is, of course, debatable. The defenders of the universality of earthly beauty usually refer to the teleology of nature: ". . . in whatever corner of the universe Nature created reasonable beings they must have been given the most rational form, and the only possible conditions of their existence." * Rejecting this theory of the only possible solution, we wish to recall K. Tsyolkovsky's words: "Life is spread out all over the universe. It has infinite variations. If life has such varied forms on earth, where conditions are relatively uncomplicated, then what kind of other variations might life have in the universe, where all kinds of conditions are possible!" †

We are quoting this high authority, however, not to curtail this or that scientific view. We are, of course, most of all interested in the purely literary aspects of the problem—in how the stylistic, topical, and figurative problems of space and related fields are solved. One must note that in contemporary science fiction one can often feel a heavy-handed way of treating the idea, a slavish dependence on figures and topics in literature which are ready-made, and on the standardization of artistic solutions. Thus, for example, several such schemes became established in accordance with which many interplanetary trips are carried out: 1) the condition of weightlessness, which is experienced by the travelers upon leaving the earth, is described in detail, while repeating with astonishing accuracy all the clever, well-aged tricks of Jules Verne; 2) a boy or a girl sneaks into the space ship secretly and later on provides the travelers with a great many useful services; 3) on the new planet there are either prehistorical animals strolling about, recreating the past history of the earth, or the travelers find a Communist society built up a long time ago, which fore-

* V. Fradkin, *Taina asteroida 117–03* (*The Secret of the Asteroid 117–03*), p. 106.
† K. E. Tsyolkovsky, *Grezy o Zemle i Nebe* (*Dreams of Heaven and Earth*), Moscow, Scientific-Fantastic Works Publishing House, Academy of Sciences of the USSR, 1959, p. 86 (A.S.).

shadows our own future (other, in-between states of historical development for some reason or other are lacking); 4) spies and saboteurs want to destroy the travelers, but it is they who will be destroyed because of their own devices (this method is especially popular, since by using this detective-story procedure the trite plot can be livened up).

Sometimes the authors, enraptured by this latest scheme, succumb to astonishingly bad taste. Such is the case, for example, with G. Martynov in his story *220 Days on a Spaceship*. In this book the enemies (the inventor and a reporter) fly after the heroes, hoping to catch up with them and be the first to land on Mars. On the way up in interplanetary space they drink whiskey for many days and daydream about killing each other: that is how far their feelings of comradeship are developed. But then, when they arrive on Mars—too late of course—the bad-guy inventor, as soon as he steps out of his space ship, is eaten up by a Martian snake (only one foot and his wrist watch remain uneaten). The bad-guy reporter tries unsuccessfully to kill one of the heroes and to kidnap the other, when he himself is taken prisoner and is taken back to earth in order to be delivered to the just judge.

As is well known, in science fiction it is extremely important to elaborate a dynamic plot, rich in action, situations, and ideas—and the individual psychology of the characters can be depicted by means other than those of the usual realistic genre. However, the requirement of clearly drawn, individualized characters is not negligible in science fiction either. In many of the present science fiction books the characters can be distinguished only by their names or professions: the spaceman, the geologist, etc. What can one say, for example, of the following method of characterization used in G. Martynov's book *Kallisto*: "The famous astronomer, director of the observatory, the active member of the Academy of Sciences Stern had always recalled in Kupriyanov's mind the hero of the British author Conan Doyle[10]—professor Challenger." Thanks to this reference to Conan Doyle the astronomer Stern becomes the most colorful figure in the novel: the features borrowed from the well-known literary character can be well "remembered."

But by using the same method the author could easily have characterized the other heroes of his book by giving them a resemblance to Captain Nemo, Anna Karenina, or other VIPs of world literature.

Science fiction also suffers greatly from the dominance of language clichés, and also from that cheap "elegance" which at a certain time swept over petty bourgeois fiction and finally found its last refuge in science fiction. Some authors of this genre consider it their duty to write in such a way that their language sounds, according to Mayakovsky, "elegant" and "aristocratically cinematic." Here are some quotations taken from different authors: The portrait of the hero (the designer and the captain of the spaceship): "His steel-gray soft hair shaded beautifully his high forehead." * The portrait of the heroine (the beloved of the captain): "Liuba had an orange-colored crepe de Chine dress on, the same one which she had neglected for so long. On her feet she wore white chamois leather shoes. The broad-brimmed straw hat suited very well her blue eyes and blond braids." † The portrait of a saboteur (the enemy of the captain): "Nazarov's shoulders started to shake, got narrower, and his eyes sparkled like the sting of a snake." ‡

When one is confronted with such or similar phenomena over and over again, one cannot help getting the impression that the writers of science fiction do not consider binding those general requirements which usually are assumed in a professional writer. As a result of this, deliberately or not, scientific literature is frequently looked upon as some kind of demi-literature which does have to be entirely scientific, but which has the right to be not entirely artistic.

Science fiction is usually published in "special" publications (*Technology—For the Young, Knowledge Is Power*,[11] etc.), but for it to be published, say, by *Novy Mir* or by *Oktyabr*, is

---

* G. Martynov, *220 Days on an Interplanetary Spaceship*, Leningrad, 1955, p. 9.

† B. Fradkin, *Road to the Stars*, Perm, 1958, p. 152.

‡ N. Gomolko, *Following on the Great Road* (translated from White Russian by A. Brushko), Minsk, 1956, p. 187 (A.S.).

an unheard-of case. It is normal for this genre preferred by our youth to be given preference by papers, magazines, and publishing houses aimed at young people: *Detgiz, Trudrezervizdat, Molodaya Gvardiya, Yunost, Pionerskaya Pravda*,[12] etc. But one should not forget that the adult reader is also extremely interested in science fiction, and that it can and must be not only entertaining but also very serious reading—for all ages and professions. We need books for the young ham-radio operators and for young botanists, but there is a great need in science fiction for the general reader, and perhaps even for foreign readers, too. Sholokhov's *Virgin Soil Upturned* is written not only for the kolkhoz members, Prishvin's works not only for hunters, and Leonov's *Russian Forest* not only for forest rangers. Why should one then make an exception for science fiction?

The history of literature knows cases where the idea of the fantasy-fiction writer foreshadowed or even prepared some scientific discovery. However, this is not the only possible and necessary application of fiction, which indeed has the right to pursue broader, general aesthetic goals. The fact of predicting scientific events has in itself no relevance to the artistic value of the work. F. Bulgarin,[13] for example, predicted certain scientific-technical discoveries: TV, radio, gas-heating, and yet his book *Very Improbable Fables, or a Trip Around the World in the 29th Century* is rightly forgotten by everybody. At the same time there are famous science-fiction stories which do not predict anything concrete but which play an important role in literature. The excessively utilitarian understanding of the role of this genre leads to the point where instead of becoming fully accepted art it wanders off somewhere to the periphery, performs the role of a manual laborer in science and technology, and frequently loses its high artistic qualities.

One cannot agree with the statement that was made in our press for a time that we need only a science fiction that is based on those hypotheses and assumptions which do not occur in reality, that the ideas of the science-fiction writers must necessarily develop in parallel with the ideas of the scientists. A number of good books in the past and in the present too cannot be squeezed into such a program. The invisible man of Wells and the amphibious man of Belyaev[14] are impossible from the scientific point of view (or at least in the form in which they are depicted by the writers), but this fact does not lessen the importance of Belyaev's or Wells's characters, because their importance is broader and much more meaningful than just the prediction of this or that scientific discovery.

The present great success of Yefremov can be explained to a large extent by this broad content of real life in the author's books. While working in the field of a certain scientific problem (for example in the field of astronomy or paleontology), Yefremov goes further than the narrow professional interests. The basic idea in his books is usually a great universal human idea, particularly the concept of the great cultural heritage in world-historical dimensions, or what is even more—in the dimensions of the infinite universe.

The development and character of our modern reality, the demands of the modern reader convince us that science fiction does belong among the phenomena of our time which are most viable and full of hopeful prospects. In order to enable this genre to take its rightful place one has to enhance its rights and obligations. It means that one should boldly bring it to the level of the most genuine, the most worthy and greatest literature, and accordingly require that science fiction give no discount to artistic backwardness.

The Poetry and Prose of Olga Berggolts

The poetry of Olga Berggolts[1] is perhaps the most tragic of all contemporary Soviet poetry. The "tragedy of tragedies" has received in her poetry a trenchant and uncompromising expression. The harrowing experience of the siege of Leningrad and the terrible losses of the war period left deep scars in the life of the poetess that will never be healed. They also gave rise to that heightened sensitivity to others' misfortune and to others' suffering which is possessed by people who themselves have lived through great sorrow.

> The old woman said: take off your things,
> Let's drink some tea—there, it's hot already.
> And here: my grandchildren, the daughters
> Of my son Vasily,
> He was killed at Sevastopol.
> And Mike: near Japan . . .
>   The old woman
> No longer wept for her sons:
> In her, sorrow was silent and timeless
> Like blood or breathing—like mine.

But grief which has become the flesh and blood of a person and which remains inconsolable and all-engrossing does not by itself create tragedy in the precise sense of the word. The first condition of tragedy is the greatness of the person suffering. Tragedy appears only in the conjunction of sorrow and strength and awakens not so much pity as admiration, for it elevates the spirit and brings moral enlightenment.

This is the nature of the tragic character which we experience when we read the lyrics of Olga Berggolts. Even in those tormented hours, days, and months when everything, it seemed, spoke to one only of disaster, when "The heart is rent by grief never seen on earth before, without tears, without words," this person shows such lofty and powerful feelings that we have a sense of pride in her and envy for her fate which is both so bitter and so happy.

> Never have I lived with such strength
> As in this very autumn.
> My happiness is unbounded.
> I am happy.
>   And ever clearer now it seems to me
> That I always lived for just these days—
> For this cruel flowering.

We must also keep in mind that all this is associated with the most difficult and terrible time in the life of a person who was not only able to endure and live through the blockade,[2] but also felt with great intensity her own suddenly awakened powers as well as the beauty of those people around her who shared her lot. "Happiness," I would say, is the word Miss Berggolts most frequently employs when speaking about the heroic struggle of besieged Leningrad, for she found in this struggle the source of her spiritual energy. It was a difficult, violent, and cruel happiness, arising in the face of death, and it seems to have the same ring as the feeling of rapturous self-forgetfulness about which Pushkin wrote:

> There is ecstasy in battle . . .

It is not without reason that many verses and poems of Olga Berggolts are so close in mood to these words of Pushkin.

O girl from the heights of Mamisson[3]
What did you know of happiness?
                                        It
Is cold, stern, and sleepless
And attended at times by death.
In its presence even nothingness is happiness,
And joy is but dust.
In its presence the enemy is impotent,
And so are decay and fear.
It soars on swan-like wings
To such undying heights,
So lonely, tender and bare,
That even the gods might envy it.

The verses and poems of Berggolts are not striking because of their wealth and variety of prosodic forms, nor because of the breadth of their lexical ring, nor any special inventiveness in rhyme, metaphors, and the like. And what is more, her poetry is, from a purely formal point of view, rather monotonous and unadorned. Characteristic of her verse is a kind of ascetic restraint in the choice and use of words. In this she follows the language of the people of war-time Leningrad, who, in Berggolts' definition, sounded on the radio like a "solemn pledge, confirmed by life itself; not a word did Leningrad speak in vain, the city backed each word with all it owned: with its blood and life, and therefore there is not a word from Leningrad that would not have come true at once."

Such is the nature of Olga Berggolts' poetic diction: sparing in words, precise and unembellished, and more like a sketch than like a painting. At times her language seems to make do with a minimum of figurative elements, living as it were on the scant rations of the blockade under a stern, war-time regime.

I say: we, citizens of Leningrad,
Are not frightened by the cannonade,
And if tomorrow there are barricades:
We shall not give up ohr barrirade.

The verses of Olga Berggolts, in my opinion, are carried not so much by words as by the intonation with which the words are pronounced. This intonation is a severely tragic and very personal one which comes from the heart and fills the stark verses with passion and ardor. From them arise the contours of a poet for whom art is primarily an outpouring of feeling and an intimate confession. It is not accidental that Berggolts' favorite genres are the diary ("February Diary"), the letter (from "Letters after the Trip"), and intimate conversation ("Conversations with a Neighbor" and others). The position she assumes in her verses is an intrepid one which knows no compromise in its readiness to offer self-revelation, and in this respect one is reminded of the lyrical style of the young Mayakovsky:

> But you, like me, cannot turn inside out
> So that you are nothing but lips.
> This lyre!
> In my hands!
> Just look!
> This is no lyre for you!
> Rent by regrets,
> My heart is torn apart;
> I tear open my veins.

This is the source of the atmosphere of distinctive moral purity which suffuses the poetry of Olga Berggolts. To a great degree it arises from the desire of the author to "conceal nothing," and, as the reader is led into the holy of holies of her soul, the will to find together with the reader that full degree of mutual trust which comes about only as a result of human intimacy marred by no defenses and summed up by the phrase: come share with me!

> From heart to heart.
>   Only this way
> Have I chosen for you. It is straight and terrible.
> It is swift and headlong.

Her prose is similar in nature and is one of the most interesting phenomena of contemporary Soviet literature. *Last Year's Journey* (its subtitle is: *Journey to the City of My Childhood*), and *Walk to the Nevsky Gates* (first printed in *Novy Mir* in

1954 and 1959) are vaguely designated by the author as "Notes" or "Fragments." * These "Notes" are, in the words of the author, preparation for the cherished "main book," that book which is "still to come" and which lives in our mind as an all-embracing composition which is intended to express with the greatest cogency our inner experiences and the "most profound, secret and intimate inner world" of the writer and the reader too. Each writer, Miss Berggolts says, dreams of such a book which summarizes all one's spiritual life. And it is entirely possible that the published "notes"—either as independent chapters or in some other form—will make up a part of the intended book. But apart from any hopes for the future, Olga Berggolts' "Notes" may be interpreted now as being in their own way the "main book" of her life and work.

It is difficult to assign the prose works of Berggolts to a specific genre, since they do not correspond to the customary literary forms. The author herself notes that she did not wish to confine herself "to any form more restricted than the open diary: a form in which past, present, and future, memories of life and its delights, and heroes dead and living may be mingled." But her prose cannot be confined even to the free form of the diary: what sort of diary is it in which the days are deliberately moved out of order and chronological principles are abandoned? Only a few but important features of a diary remain: intimate contact with the reader; the inner world of the writer herself, who reconstructs the past with the same intense immediacy with which the impressions of the passing day are described. Therefore it is difficult to call her prose "memoirs," and the author herself when referring to her past uses what one might call the lyric phrase "resurrection of the past."

Berggolts herself helps us elucidate the specific nature of this work. The "main book," the nearest approach to which she considers to be her prose, the poetess thinks of in the following form: "The writer may not know beforehand in what form the main work will be realized, whether in a narrative poem, in verses, in a novel, or in memoirs, but he does know

---

* Both works published in *Dnevnye Zvezdy* (*Daylight Stars*), Sovietsky Pisatel, Leningrad, 1959 (A.S.).

very well what it will be in essence. He knows that its central point will be he himself, his life, and above all the life of his soul, the path of his conscience and the formation of his consciousness, and all this is inseparable from the life of the nation. In other words the main book of the writer, or in any case my main book, seems to me to be a book filled with the utmost truth of our common existence which has passed through the medium of my heart." As an example of the highest forms of works of this kind Berggolts names Herzen's *My Past and Thoughts*.[4] She asserts that her conception of her "main book" most closely resembles this brilliant "novel of the human soul," the appearance of which in Soviet literature she eagerly awaits.

Without guessing about the future "main book" until it has been given form, one may say that in her present prose Berggolts has to a great extent already fulfilled her intentions. But the novel of the human soul, as distinct from the epic of Herzen's (we are speaking, it should be understood, not of a comparison of levels or scale, but of difference in genre), has been set to an emotional and lyric key. For this reason the sphere of feelings and direct impressions and her feeling for the world have been given precedence, while in Herzen's book the intellect and the *Weltanschauung* of the author and his heroes are dominant. For the same reason Berggolts' prose, which is written from autobiographical material and includes different characters and varying life situations, nevertheless in no way resembles literary autobiographies of the ordinary epic type. In her prose there is no plot in the sense of consistently developing events. There is also lacking the characteristic of the epic, namely the chronological extension of the narrative. Life is described as a whole, concentrated in one instant. This moment may contain infinitely much and may be prolonged for a whole eternity, but it always remains that single given moment which is the symbol, condition, and dimension of lyric poetry out of the living, present moment.

In narrating her first walk to the Nevsky Gates back in October 1941,[5] Berggolts describes the special, inexplicable state of mind which she experienced. It was a state of inspiration, of ecstasy, and of enlightenment, and may be compared with those sudden and impetuous flights of the human soul (a feeling of happiness, freedom, and perilous rapture) about which she has frequently written in her poems. At the same time this scene makes clear to us the structural and artistic principles of her prose. This scene seems to me to be the lyrical focal point of the narrative in "Walk to the Nevsky Gates" and to be so valuable for an understanding of her prose as a unified artistic whole that it is worthwhile to quote the text in full:

He [her father] touched me lightly on the shoulder, did not kiss me, did not squeeze my hand, nor did he embrace me, and almost ran off, going to the right, along Shlisselburg Street, neither stopping nor looking back.

This was neither a pose nor a violent effort on his part, it was simply that he, like me, knew that we could not perish. But I looked after him for a long moment, looked at his billowing and funny overcoat, looked at the depths of the Nevsky Gates at the point where daddy's factory was and Aunt Varin's hospital and the Obukhovsky[6] foundry, the biggest one behind the Gates, and there like a wall stood round, biblically beautiful, freshly formed clouds that rumbled and grumbled louder and louder. I looked over there and suddenly all my life was spread out before me. And with inconceivable swiftness for which no words can be found, there passed through my mind pictures of my whole life and of the life of my Fatherland and memories of things that happened before I could remember.

No, I did not recall, I *lived* that which was, is, and will be. This resurrection of things in my life was sudden, fragmentary, and scattered, and at the same time it flowed into a single, continuous stream; no, it rather flowed into something similar to a powerful southern surf which poured over me with an unendurable, almost painful happiness.

Sometimes they used to say: there will be no more time.[7] Whether or not you believe that this is true, I know it, I know what it means for there to be no time. On that day there was no time: it was all compressed into one radiant cluster in me, all time and all existence. And happily all dividing lines collapsed between life and death, between life and art, between past, present and future. Oh, how fragile these lines seemed, how conventional, how easy it was for me to delight in all of life at once, all its poetry and all its tragedy at its very limits, at the limit of life, standing there at the corner of Palevsky and Shlisselburg streets, between the shadows of absurd constructions of the past, at a moment when the artillery barrage grew silent.

> As if an ethereal stream
> The sky flowed along my veins.

All life was compressed into moments, only moments, but for these moments I need pages. These moments of total life flashed forth suddenly, and I shall not search for any other explanations for them by redating the time of their occurrence. I do not know why, when looking at the figure of my father disappearing in the distance, I thought that there he was going to his factory, and in this factory my first printed verses had appeared, and they were about Lenin. Lenin! And a wave of great warmth and light flowed over me. . . .

We have before us not only the description of a definite psychological moment in the life of the narrator, we have before us the description of lyricism as such, and especially of its distinctive form of appearance as it is present in the lyric prose of Olga Berggolts. The action in it moves with "inconceivable swiftness," passing over barriers in time and space and transporting us to the realm of childhood: to the city of Uglich[8] of the first years of the Revolution; then to the besieged Leningrad of the Fatherland War; then to the remote time of Russian history. One lyric wave follows another: the figure of the father running to the factory gives rise to the thought of her first verses, which were printed in the factory's magazine and were dedicated to Lenin. The story of Lenin and the first verses pass over into the "wave of poetry" which snatches us up along with the heroine and carries us further and further along the "summits" of her soul and the summits of our times. These disjointed sudden flashes of memory and feeling are gathered together into "one radiant cluster," "into a single continuous flow," and the lyric figure of the narrator and hero—his soul turned toward us with its many facets—becomes the central, connecting figure.

At one time Mayakovsky called his programmatic work, the lyric poem "Cloud in the Trousers," borrowing a term from the field of representational art, a "tetraptych," that is, a fourfold, four-part image, each fold of which is a facet of the poet's soul: of the "thirteenth apostle." And thus Miss Berggolts' prose seems to me to be just such an image, not only a fourfold one, but one of many parts. In her prose the figure of our contemporary man does not develop in time, as is usual in narrative genres, but unfolds and opens up in its basic "folds": poetry, Fatherland, Revolution. . . .

Thus we have before us a novel of the human spirit, but also a lyric novel constructed according to special lyric laws. The theme is immense: "The world and I," and "The truth about our common existence mirrored by my heart." How did Miss Berggolts succeed in correlating and uniting her "ego" with this great and differentiated material which passes into the narrative under the name of "our common existence"? For the lyric poet there is obviously only one way: to show universal life as one's own personal experience. Berggolts does not digress for a moment from her "ego," but stretching out her hand now to one side, now to the other, she says: this is mine!

"This is mine" is the title of a section telling about a child's game. "In Uglich, in my childhood, we had a game . . . no, rather not a game, but something serious: if someone sees something that catches the imagination—a handsome person, an unusual house, a surprising nook in the woods, and if you are the first to stretch out your hand and cry 'Hey, it's mine!' then it does become yours and you can do with it what you wish."

In the works of Berggolts it is as if this "seizure" of reality, which is so full of meaning, were continued as "personal use" of the poetess. But the mastering of the world does not now consist simply in calling "mine" everything that is pleasing or striking at first glance. The consciousness that "this is mine" is gained through struggle in life and is acquired by cooperative work and striving as well as by a destiny shared with the nation; it emerges in a "stern and frank feeling of one's living participation in and vital connection with all that surrounds me, with that which is moved and is moving now on the earth and in the water; with those who at different times died for the Fatherland and for Communism; with those who built hydroelectric works in Uglich; with those who are being born or are growing up and working here, in Uglich, in Leningrad, in the whole country. . . ." From this feeling of "participation" in life, in the world, and in the nation the lyric works of

Berggolts arise, so that the poetess, turning to her native country in September of 1941, was able to say:

> Till this time I was your conscience.
> There was nothing I concealed from you.
> I shared all your sufferings,
> As earlier I shared your triumph.

Her prose is formed along the same lines. The idea of the unity of personal and general, which forms the basis of our way of life, has so firmly become a part of our daily life that it often is accepted as a truth which needs no proof and becomes a commonplace in our common judgments. Meanwhile it is evident that in the affirmation and interpretation of this great idea common to all humanity there are possible very different shades of meaning and turns of phrase. In her artistic resolution Olga Berggolts has achieved freshness and originality because, it seems to me, she proclaimed "this is mine" very convincingly with regard to all that which is great and commonly held that surrounds us and forms our life. Thereby all this that is great and common, while not ceasing to be so, passes over into the sphere of the very intimate experiences of the individual soul, and on this account acquires additional warmth, tenderness, and cordiality. A sublime, severe, and immense concept of the Fatherland suddenly becomes so close and intimate that one may say of it:

> Mashenka, but it is: our childhood,
> School, the fir-tree, the Young Pioneer group . . .
> Mashenka, but it is: our youth,
> Komsomol and first love.

"Mine" in such usage means "universal," but "mine" is still something inward, secret, sacred, and especially human. The works of Berggolts are in this respect like those diaries which were kept by the people of Leningrad during the war years and which she closely connects with her composition of the "main book": "I have read through a great number of the diaries from the time of the blockade. They were written by the dim light of wick lamps, in gloves by hands that could hardly hold a pen from weakness (more often a pencil, since ink froze). The entries in some diaries were broken off at the moment of the author's death. Now burning hot, now icily cold, the victorious tragedy of Leningrad breathes from many, many pages of these diaries, in which with complete frankness the author writes about his own daily worries, efforts, sorrows, and joys. And as a rule, 'one's own deeply personal' is at the same time universal, while the general and national becomes deeply personal and truly human. History suddenly speaks with a living and simple human voice."

In Berggolts' prose this translation of universal phenomena into the intimate language of individual life is accomplished that humanization of history, in which a special role is played not only by the seal and stamp of the author's personal understanding, but also by the stamp of his personal achievement. It is not accidental that as a symbol of her theme, her work, and her goal she chose "daylight stars": their reflection, according to a childish and half fairy-tale wish, may be seen only in the depths of a dark well. "Daylight stars," that is, the souls and destinies of contemporaries and fellow citizens, must be reflected in the soul of the writer, open to everyone like a well. "Invisible to the ordinary eye and therefore seemingly nonexistent: let them become visible to all, in all their brilliance, by means of me and in my depths and purest darkness. I want to contain them within me all the time as my own special light and special secret and as my supreme substance. I know that without them, without these daylight stars, I cannot exist as a writer. . . ."

It is not the surface of external events but the spiritual profundity of the author which becames a screen reflecting the life of her contemporaries. For Miss Berggolts this emphasis is very important: the proposal to look into the depths, into the innermost part of the soul and the purest and secret twilight of the author's self. And this depth of the inner, subjective world is the chief content of the book. But in it the reader finds what is "invisible to the ordinary eye," that is, the profound phenomena of his very own soul. Thus "mine" turns into "universal" and the personal property of the author becomes the personal property of all, since it has become "mine" for everyone.

The truth of our epoch and the spiritual life of our contemporaries is presented in breadth and completeness in the prose of Berggolts and in the form of a beautiful panorama that is both historical and psychological. In its creation a special role belongs to memory, for this memory in the works of the author always means active, creative powers and not just the mechanical operation of recalling. Miss Berggolts' creative nature possesses what may be called the feeling of memory, and this feeling is powerful and militant, and is awakened not only by a fidelity to the past but also by a passionate concern for the future. This is, if we may use the definition of Miss Berggolts, an "anticipation in one's own life of the life of those who will come after us, and the wish to leave for them not only a material but also a spiritual heritage, to pass on with uncompromising truthfulness the moral experience of the epoch, and in doing so not only the positive but also the negative experience: here is what is good, go and do likewise, but do not act thus, and do not repeat our mistakes and sufferings!"

It would be no exaggeration to say that all the works of Berggolts are to a significant degree based on this feeling. From this source come her conviction, anger, and the freedom which resounds in her verses:

> And even those who would wish to prettify all
> In the untroubled, timid memory of people,
> I shall not let forget how the people of Leningrad
> Fell upon the yellow snow of the deserted squares.

Most characteristic for her is not the intonation of passive submission to the rush of memories, as for example "I cannot forget," but rather the powerful and proud "I do not wish, I shall not permit forgetting!" This demand arises as a will to live and create, for the memory helps man to be better and purer. The voice of memory sounds like a pledge and a promise.

> Then may the scar, honored and grim,
> Never depart from my soul.
> May my soul never be allowed
> To fill the worthlessness and evil,
> But remember with creative, fiery ardor
> The path it took in the past.

This theme undergoes several variations in the works of Berggolts. It is not only the individual verses and strophes which are devoted to historical relics (the memorial to Lenin at the Finland Station, the sculptures of Petergoff,[9] imaginary monuments which should be set up in honor of the defenders of Leningrad), but also the work of Berggolts as a writer often appears as a means of eternalizing the memory of heroes who fell for the Fatherland. Even the sea, washing the shores not far from Stalingrad, is compared in her verses to a monument ("The Encounter"), to say nothing of the famous house for which the legendary Guard units once fought ("In the House of Pavlov").

In this preference of Berggolts (aside from the fervent wish to maintain everywhere the power and freedom of the memory) there obviously appears in part the local, Leningrad color of her talent. The great city, "inhabited" by so many monuments and converted as it were into a monument-city, was taken up into her works as a central theme and largely determined the character of its picturesqueness.

> The hard light of cannon bursts
> Now lights up the outlines of columns,
> Now statues, standing on roofs,
> Now a bas-relief of stone banners
> And walls—right in the gaps in the salvos.

This is the source in her lyrics of the constant sculptural and architectural comparisons which treat the figure and face of man as a marble or bronze carved image and bring living Nature closer to the city complex. In this respect there is a curious comment in one of Miss Berggolts' articles: "In Leningrad, buildings, complexes, squares and monuments have become Nature, real living Nature, as if independent of man, who at one time created it. The street of the architect of Russia[10] [Peter the Great] is already Nature and not architecture. And our gardens and parks, and the old, St. Petersburg ones and the quite new parks of Victory which were set out by *our* hands: this is already not only Nature, but also architecture, for our parks, streets and gardens were constructed. . . ."

In her poetry Berggolts often constructs landscape, locating it in emphatically decorative forms which are strictly regulated and sharply outlined. She likes to illuminate objects in a similar way, placing them against a background of morning twilight or a sunset, as if suggesting to the reader that he admire their clear, straight contours. One cannot help see behind all this a specifically Leningrad form of aesthetics.

> Surrounded by a ring of mighty hills
> Stood the workshop of Peter the Great,
> And the forest formed snows of the Altai[11]
> Hung on it like a diamond wreath.

Along with her "architecture" and "sculpture" there appears in her writing another peculiarity of style which is even more important as a matter of principle: the tendency to poetic symbolism and the tendency to render concrete phenomena abstract, thereby raising them to the level of universal philosophical categories and emphasizing in them the highest symbolic sense and universal significance. In the poem "Your Path" there are lines which present this side of her work very well:

> In those days everyday life receded, disappeared.
> And boldly
> True existence entered into its rights.

In her works she strives above all to show the true existence of the world and of man, rendering daily life abstract or converting its phenomena into symbols and signs with a broad "existential" content. This does not mean that we do not encounter daily life in her verses, but that it occurs in the majority of cases in a transformed aspect: spiritualized, sublimated, and illumined by the rays of existence behind it. Thus, for example, the simple subjects of life during the blockade are filled in her verses with a great and significant meaning: the paper strips attached to window panes become the "winter of Bartholomew crosses," [12] ashes in home-made little stoves become a "sign of the Great Fire" by which the people of Leningrad keep warm; an ordinary shovel is the occasion for considerations of a highly abstract philosophical level:

> O ancient earthy tool,
> Shovel, true sister of the soil!
> What an inconceivable path you and I
> Have taken from the barricades to the graveyard.

Berggolts is inclined to look at the passing contemporary scene with the eyes of a future historian, interpreting the most prosaic material as gems of meaning in world history. What is private and individual interests her mainly as a manifestation of the universal, and in her imagination things tend to turn into monuments of the time. For this reason, among others, she erects everywhere her beloved monuments. They serve not only as reminders of the past (the voice of an ineradicable memory), but also fulfill the role of symbolic figures and personifications which express some essential aspects of our spirit, history, and existence.

> They came and, as a symbol of completed revenge,
> As a sign of humanity's triumph
> We shall erect anew, in the very same place,
> Samson rending the lion.[13]

It is from the very individualized and vivid features of her poetic gifts, which ensure her a respected place in contemporary Soviet poetry, that there also arise some weakness which can be felt in her poetic works. They are, it seems to me, most perceptible in those of her works which are least lyrical, namely in the tragedy "Loyalty" and in the poem "Pervorossiisk." Without attempting to analyze completely or evaluate these quite powerful and complex works, I wish nevertheless to note that the very same traits of poetic individuality in Miss

Berggolts, thanks to which she achieved success in other cases, have an adverse effect on her form and her verse in places in these poems. The tendency to symbolism and to the abstract-philosophical treatment of concrete phenomena of life and to sublime and inspirational diction is transformed here at times into a geometrical dryness of figurative design, an academic lifelessness and declamatory style.

Obviously the reason for this is that the tragedy "Loyalty" and the poem "Pervorossiisk," in spite of the frequent lyrical intrusions, are constructed to a significant degree out of "objective" material, a subject matter which lies outside the "ego" and does not always possess sufficient poetic power, the power of concreteness.

In the best works of Berggolts, for example in her war poetry, the abstractness of the symbols and the straightforward general concepts—often written in capital letters—(Man, Warrior, Life, etc.) are supplemented by a lyric intonation which is very lively, passionate, and concrete. In the poem "Pervorossiisk" and in the tragedy "Loyalty," however, because of the specific nature of their genre—although such an intonation is not entirely lacking—it does not determine the whole work nor extend throughout it. This lack of a living voice is at times quite perceptible, because the allegorical figures and the oratorical tone begin to become too prominent and to dominate.

We may rejoice in the fact that the lyric diction of Miss Berggolts always has an inspired ring. But when in her descriptive discourse about the people of Pervorossiisk she states outright: "their simple, inspired faces," or "triumphantly the leaders accepted them, and, opening the session with an anthem, Gremyakin cried, full of inspiration . . ." then this sounds bombastic and hurts the ear. The lofty words hang poised in mid-air because behind them there is not sufficiently palpable, living "flesh," either of a lyric or epic kind. The words are taken as a merely verbal declaration of the author, which while very sublime is still of little weight.

But these larger works written by Berggolts after the war are very interesting from the point of view of her further artistic experiments, if compared with her poetry of the war period, and her attempt to broaden the scope of her themes and the boundaries of her lyrics. It is well worth noting in what direction these experiments are tending. In "Pervorossiisk" pure and unalloyed lyricism is replaced by a lyric-epic poem of historical content. On the other hand, Berggolts turns to the form of the tragedy (in respect to content most of her works are like a tragedy, but "Loyalty" is also a tragedy in form), presenting it in an original framework and also approximating to ancient, classical models. The contemporary theme of the Fatherland War[14] is developed here in the form of images and personifications, and in the traditional conflict of inclination and duty, with the participation (in the classical manner) of the chorus of citizens. All this takes place with the proper architectural background of "ruins," a "necropolis," and so forth. This cannot help but give rise at times to palpable contradictions between form and content. At the same time the tragedy "Loyalty" is the most universal and symbolic work of Berggolts, and in it man's existence is so "cleansed" of everyday life that the heroes frequently remind one of talking monuments. Actually the entire poem reminds one on the whole of a marble statue: grandiose, but cold.

Berggolts' prose, continuing in some degree the new tendencies of "Loyalty" and "Pervorossiisk" (the broadening of the lyric possibilities, the close contact with history) is at the same time strikingly different from them, even to the point of contrast: here we are immersed in a sea of concreteness—richly endowed characters, real daily life, picturesque colloquialisms in the mouths of individual persons and so forth. The very fact of the turn to prose obviously opened for Berggolts certain new possibilities which could not be achieved within the limits of her poetry. Thus the rough, tender, and most poetic prose of life, which up to now had been held back in the storehouse of the memory, suddenly burst forth in her works.

The prose works of Berggolts are in a certain way also a

monument, but one which has given a memorable description
of our time not only in symbols but in vivid details. Art is
always striving for immortality and perpetuation. It tries to
stop fleeting time, fix it in words, and on canvas preserve for
the future that life which will not be repeated. To fulfill this
goal the concrete image which recreates man in his uniqueness
is often more suitable than a symbolic monument. It is significant that in Miss Berggolts' prose the theme of memory rings
out in full strength again, but in a new, and for her unusual,
variation. The author is here striving not so much to extol our
epoch and to create grandiose images in honor of departed
heroes and events as to try to give life to the times, and therefore she writes about the past "with a lively memory of the
feeling for events of that time." That memory, Berggolts says,
"connects the discrete memories in a single, unified life, allowing nothing to fade away, but leaving everything forever alive
and contemporary."

In Berggolts' prose everything is alive because everything is
concrete, starting with the trifles that constitute the great
world, which is objective in motion and diverse in form. Let
us take just the most prosaic things of domestic life, behind
which the psychology of a child clearly appears:

"Here there was nothing insignificant and dead. On the contrary, every object lived its own life and had its own personality, voice, and habits.

"In the entrance hall stood a huge tub with deep, dark
water. If, sneaking up on tiptoe, one bends over the tub and
yells, the tub answers with a thick angry voice like an uncle.
Its face was also thick, with chubby cheeks. One could drown
in the tub, and maybe fish lived at the bottom of the water.
Winter began with the tub: on its dark water gathered brittle,
slippery bits of ice like little slivers: Avdotya did not let
anyone catch them with his hands.

"On the kitchen table, which was of a brass color that looked
like edible honey, stood a black tattered lamp-brush, with
which the glass lamps were cleaned. When one took it in one's
hands the handle of the brush angrily squeaked; the brush was

alive, it could bite, and I was afraid of it. Avdotya knew this, and sometimes when I was already very much underfoot, she would seize the brush and cry:

" 'Look out now, or I'll hand you over to Mr. Brush!' And Mr. Brush squeaked in hostile fashion and bristled with malice. We called the sugar tongs Khakha, because they opened up wide like a laughing mouth, grinning with their sharp tips.

"Khakha was also alive and grinned, and was happy when he was biting sugar."

The degree of nuance here is such that we are not dealing with the personification of an object, but with the manifestation of its individual physiognomy and its "Personality" (right to the point of proper names), and it is due to this that the children's understanding and the figure of the heroine also acquire entirely concrete traits. Let us note too that the tub, for example, does not answer simply with a human voice, but "like an uncle," and that the kitchen table is honey-colored, as if edible: the author, following the path of individualization and the supplying of details, always strives to intensify the "personal" characteristics of the object, thus lending the narrative an unusual vividness.

In the same way the broad sphere of history is given body. It appears chiefly in the form of living, directly perceived signs of the times which, scattered throughout the whole text, lend it a varying and historical tonality. The history of our epoch per se arises before our eyes: in the psychological reactions of the heroine, in the responses of the people about her, and in the details of daily life. And in so doing in every separate case it bears the stamp of an episodic detail which is very significant for the content, even though usually apparently not very noteworthy. For example, the passing remark: "I daydreamed about the leather jackets[15] only as a straight 'classical nose' "—a phrase which, it would seem, has no direct historical meaning, but which calls forth in our awareness those vivid associations, thanks to which there arises that which may be called the specific flavor of the time, the atmosphere of the 1920's. Or another detail, involuntarily appearing for a moment in the memory of the heroine, while she was standing on a corner, familiar since childhood, where in far-off times Uncle Grisha, a petty pedlar, traded in toffee:

"Every morning on the way to school I went up to Uncle Grisha and asked:

"'Uncle Grisha, how much is toffee today?'

"'Today it is two hundred and eighty million a piece,' [16] he answered unperturbed."

Again the whole world comes alive. And yet to achieve this the author has employed only a single response, the force of which again lies in its historical concreteness.

Of a similar nature are the frequent details, often at first glance fortuitous, which are often woven into the text as if in passing and which permit Miss Berggolts to preserve completely the naturalness of the narrative: the heroine simply lives and does not concern herself with the investigation of the historical process. Besides this these details establish in her works that vital and historical milieu without which man's existence is not understandable in our epoch. History is present here like the air: it is just as necessary and just as unobtrusive, and people breathe it deeply without any special effort.

With all its great concreteness and factualness the prose of Berggolts, like all her art, is philosophical and does not resemble a collection of fleeting and fortuitous sketches. The author restricts herself to one purpose: to write in such a way that life "can appear before us not in chance episodes, but as a whole, that is, in its essence; not in the partial truth of an isolated event, but in the guiding truth of history." At the moment Miss Berggolts tends toward the depiction of life, but with this difference, however, that compared with her verses this depiction becomes more substantial and beautiful. Architecture is replaced by painting and the symbolic statue by the portrait. The symbol does not cease to be a vivid detail and preserves all its force and the credibility of the fact, person, and object. As the expression of "the guiding truth of history" she makes use not of images and personifications, nor figures of an allegorical kind, but in essence those very details of which the highest demands are made, namely that they embody the main, periodic, and basic phenomena of our life and consciousness.

Many times the nurse Avdotya returns in her tales to her native village of Guzhovo, where her "big brother," who "fears nothing," lived with her. Both "Guzhovo" and "the big brother" (the dream and hope of her whole life) gradually become grown over with life and legends and begin to sound like a leitmotif not only in the speeches of Avdotya, but also in the general structure of the narration by the author.

In our eyes "Guzhovo" and "the big brother" become synonyms of such broad categories as Fatherland and nation. This generalization grew out of the episodic detail which was provided with a general content, while not losing in this process its own concrete and perceptible form. Guzhovo is symbolic and filled with meaning, but at the same time the very idea of the symbol is not in accord with it, since "Guzhovo" is earthbound, individual, and never ceases to be the only village of its kind: "Dunia's Guzhovo." For a symbol it sounds insufficiently abstract and too simple, crude and physical, and is just like the ts-dialect[17] of Dunia. This is daily life in its most concentrated form, but at the same time is the most genuine, authentic reality.

The words and responses used as leitmotifs are of the very same nature. They are at first employed for some particular occasion, but then they are transformed into mottoes of the time and emblems of great spiritual value throughout the prose of Berggolts: "Save the Revolution!" "Anton Ivanovich is angry," "This is mine!" "Flanders chain of happiness," "The Bulge of the Valdai," and so forth. In most cases these designate the "high points" around which the narration is constructed, opening up before us now one side, now the other of human reality. Through them the epoch and the soul of man arise in complete concreteness and individuality, though not in all traits and events without exception, but only basically at the "high points" and the main, decisive sections.

Berggolts renounces consistent and complete descriptions of history, biography, and psychology and makes note only of individual—but the most cogent—landmarks in different spheres of activity and consciousness. This is the path along "the heights" which permits her to create a total picture of "all life at once" and to incorporate a great deal in brief segments of the narrative. The author resembles a man standing on a great height and taking in the whole earth with one glance. As Berggolts wrote in verses which anticipate her prose:

> And I could see all, far, far away,
> Into all four corners of the earth . . .

But the path along the heights is complicated and supplemented in her prose by that which may be called the ascent to the heights, if we may once again use a poetic image of the poetess herself. This second path, difficult and tortuous, is described in detail in her last work in the form of a second walk beyond the Nevsky Gates in February, 1942.[18] Outwardly it is a complete contrast to the first walk made in October, 1941, when, returning from her father's home behind the Nevsky Gates, the heroine suddenly experienced an unusual onrush of spiritual forces, of freedom and of happiness which opened up for her the whole world at once: all the "heights" of her soul and of universal and national life. At that time she possessed a consciousness almost cosmic in its extent and lived all possible lives: in the past, present, and the future, and did not walk but flew along these lives and memories, each one of which was re-experienced anew.

Now, in February, all is different: exhausted, on the verge of dying, with deadly indifference in her heart, she makes her way to the Nevsky to her father along the familiar road (very recently this was the road of the "heights"), and nothing provokes in her either thoughts or memories, or what is even more, fervent and triumphant feelings. The tone and the pace of the narrative change sharply at this point: not world-wide standards, but "micro-tasks" (how to get from one lamppost to another), not headlong flights through the years, decades, and centuries, but a slow path, beyond her strength, along dead streets. All this takes place over several chapters and is described very exactly, implacably, simply, and without emotion. Now the heroine does not think of any "heights" while overcoming fifteen kilometers as if they were a desert of a thousand miles and feeling only "limited and primitive reactions." Slowly she puts one foot after the other, sits down and eats a piece of bread that she had saved. . . . And yet this is the path of ascent, the path to the summit, although the author does not mention this directly. Our consciousness of ascent is composed of minor, hardly noticeable traits at first, up to the point where the heroine, moving forward, meets people who help her and whom she helps. In this she is guided not by any lofty considerations but acts in accordance with the natural and instinctive inclination inherent to man, namely that of love, comradeship, and kindness.

"The very narrow path across the Neva was hard and packed down, but by somewhat unsteady, very light steps: it was notched and winding. The right bank towered up in an inaccessible icy hill, disappearing at the top in greyish-pink twilight. At the foot of the hill women wrapped in shawls and hardly resembling people were fetching water from a hole in the ice.

" 'I won't make the hill,' I thought wearily, feeling that all my terrible, terrifying way was in vain.

"I still went up quite close to the hill and suddenly saw that steps barely cut out of the ice led to the top.

"A woman, quite unbelievably similar to the one who was dragging the coffin, in the same kerchief and with the same brown parchment-like face, came up to me. In her right hand she held a can with about two liters of water, no more, but even so she leaned over to her right.

" 'Shall we climb up, my friend,' she asked.

" 'Let's climb!'

"And on all fours, side by side, staying close to one another, supporting each other with our shoulders, we climbed up, clutching with our hands for the next higher cuts in the ice, dragging our legs along with difficulty from step to step and stopping after every two or three steps.

" 'The doctor hewed out the steps,' the woman said, catching her breath at the fourth stop. 'God bless him . . . makes it easier . . . to go for water.' "

There we have the feeling acquired during the days of the blockade: a feeling of intimate nearness and love for people who share with one another all that remained to them, this support which one receives from known and unknown people, and this is the last height which Olga Berggolts shows us. Her heroine does not arrive at this height by herself, for people help her: the woman who calls her her friend; the doctor who hewed the steps out of the ice so that it would be easier to go for water (it was explained that this was her father); the nurse Matresha who washed her feet when she finally arrived; the fireman who gave her as a gift a "black flatcake," the "generous gfit of a hungry person to another who is hungry," and many other people who were generous not from wealth but from the inexhaustible humanity in their hearts.

Once in 1942 Berggolts wrote in verse about this generosity of the people of Leningrad and their ability to give and help. Her verses were about the ashes from the cold Leningrad stoves, ashes warming the world for many long years to come.

> And each one, visiting these ashes,
> Becomes bolder, purer and better,
> And perhaps the world will warm its soul again
> At the campfire of our blockade.

Again and again she fans these ashes, and returning to her old theme of the blockade, she again tells how the people of Leningrad lived, suffered, died, and fought and how they did not become weary of loving. Besides this the eagerness to make a gift to people—an urge which had become during the last years of the war a passion and a necessity of the poetic nature of Berggolts—is no longer directly connected with the theme of the war or with memories of the blockade. This urge became a general and natural manifestation of a loving soul and of a humaneness which has again appeared and been deeply felt in our time. Of this same nature are her verses about love: "Indian Summer," "Before Parting," and others which noticeably change the tonality of her lyrics and immerse us in an atmosphere of "kindness and light," even if the subject matter is suffering and parting.

But only now did I understand
How to love, pity, forgive and say good-bye . . .

Her prose is distinguished by the same kindly force, especially her latest work "Walk Beyond the Nevsky Gates." The way taken by the heroine with the help of familiar and unfamiliar people reveals to her the highest law of life and the most profound "secret of the earth." Higher than human love there is a different one: love for one's native land, for mankind, for woman, or of a woman for a man . . . one cannot find anything higher than this, "Lialka," her father tells her. And we see how, constricted by cold and death, the consciousness of man, reduced to its most primitive reactions, again begins to live, how it grows and broadens under the influence of human warmth and, absorbing into itself the great human world, it again becomes "of the heights" and all-embracing.

At the end we come back properly speaking to that from which we started and around which the lyric narrative of Miss Berggolts invariably revolves with its central idea, drawing together in one dominant idea all her heights: the idea of closeness, unity, the fusion of the individual soul with the nation's, of personality and community, of man and the world. But in returning for a short time to this same thing, we are enriched each time in our understanding of the idea, and the last height with which Miss Berggolts links us while telling about the terrible winter walk is not a repetition of the previous ones. Yes, this "feeling of merging with universal life" the heroine has already experienced once before when in October, 1941, all that was far off was suddenly revealed to her, and the boundary fell between the personal "ego" and the community "ego." But, as we remember, this truth was revealed then by the power of cognition amounting to enlightenment and at a moment of the highest spiritual flight of which man is capable. Now, however, we approach it through love and action; this is more difficult and longer, but in recompense it is sounder.

The warmth that one receives from people gives rise to the wish to repay them a hundredfold—"to give, to give as much as possible to one's fellow citizens and one's country of the strength and words necessary for their needs." Not only to feel and experience one's complete union with people and with the nation, but to help this union through one's efforts and to dedicate to it the business of one's own life: this, it may be said, is the final moral result toward which Miss Berggolts has been moving. Thus the hands of man become one of the final links in this series of images which goes through her whole book. These are the hands of her father, the surgeon, hands which save people's lives and hew out steps in the icy hill; these are the hands of the nurse Matresha and many, many others—doing good deeds, "shedding light and strength," working hands.

From Olga Berggolts' book we discovered how to look from the "summit" into all the corners of the world, how to reach this summit and how to build it. This book, telling of the ways of the human spirit to the "heights" and along the "heights," is itself interpreted by us as a kind of high point in the works of the poetess. From it the vistas are broad. And we are grateful to the hands which created it.

"Come Walk with Us"

(ON ROBERT FROST'S POEMS)

The Soviet reader's acquaintance with Robert Frost has only just begun.[1] But already the first published materials on him, mostly in periodicals, the first encounters with the art of the American poet allow us to judge the dimensions of the phenomenon opening up before us. Even greater interest has been stirred by the volume *From Ten Books*, brought out by the Foreign Literature Publishing House, presenting Frost's poetry in its long development from the 1890's to the 1960's, in translations by M. Zenkevich, I. Kashkin, and A. Sergeyev. In certain areas the collection includes in full Frost's poetic legacy, and—what is even more important—it evokes the very spirit of his poetic world.

The art of great poets normally has several levels of depth, influence, and comprehension and astonishes us with a diversity of associations, with unexpected affinities which such art establishes with the psyche of various generations. The very nature of art presupposes a varied immersion in the world of artistic images, different for different people, replete with meaning and hiding in themselves infinite possibilities of understanding. Each age reads the classics anew. Even within the framework of our individual perception each of us can notice that the absolute core of what we have read and seen

63

leaves its traces in our soul, with its promise of a further and more astonishing discovery. We are able to return to a book many times, and, parting with it, we feel each time that it is only waiting for another occasion to tell us again of things unheard of before.

Precisely this feeling of being drawn down into the depths, the sensation of being lured on by elusive perspectives arises in us when we enter Robert Frost's poetry for the first time, a feeling which keeps growing as we keep reading and absorbing it. Besides the impressive power which is always present in art—and the more so the more perfect it is—one is given here also the essence of the unique Frostian view of things, his style of presentation. Frost reproduces reality in such a manner that the very scene presented to our view entices us bit by bit, then involves us completely.

His images—one can see this in a good number of the translations—are stereoscopic. They surround the viewer like trees in a wood from behind which now and then other trees—and clearings—gaze at us, creating the illusion that there beyond the next turn the goal will be reached, the goal which we involuntarily keep pursuing until we realize that there is no end to the woods. But by then the original purpose of our walk, strictly speaking, is already behind us.

This analogy of a walk in the woods confronts us strikingly on reading Frost. His lyric poems are not only rich in motifs of this kind (a natural phenomenon for the man living close to nature), but one could also say that they are based on a corresponding "entrance" of the poet (and, along with him, of the reader too) into the world he himself depicts, a world presented three-dimensionally and charged with mysterious, alluring depths and significant happenings. We are fascinated by the close attention paid by the poet to the most ordinary things, by his clear focus upon the actual, the concrete. We are even intrigued by the scrupulousness with which he reports about everything surrounding him. It is a kind of scrupulousness rich in suggestion. And we come to suspect that life's occurrences are not as simple and commonplace as they may

have seemed at first glance. We have only to glance around
and take a good look at the place we have arrived at:

> Out walking in the frozen swamp one gray day,
> I paused and said, "I will turn bask from here.
> No, I will go on farther—and we shall see!"
> The hard snow held me, save where now and then
> One foot went through. The view was all in lines
> Straight up and down of tall slim trees
> Too much alike to mark or name a place by
> So as to say for certain I was here
> Or somewhere else: I was just far from home.

This is how Frost's poem "The Wood-pile" starts. And although the tone at the beginning is kept in such a natural,
unconstrained manner (or perhaps more because of a kind of
unobtrusive way of narrating—duty-bound to nothing, yet
paying thoughtful, unhurried attention to the world), we are
unwittingly permeated by the things we perceive around us,
and having taken the first step, following the poet, we are no
more able to say whether or not we are standing "here" or
"there." We move through the woods, following the pace of
the narration, in the wake of a chance little bird flitting from
tree to tree, leading us on until we come upon a stack of fire-
wood left there by somebody or other for some mysterious
reason. And finally we come upon the idea we were drawn to
by the slowly unravelling, detailed account which in itself
had not seemed at first so notable. Yet at the same time everything, directly and indirectly, seems to have pointed the way
to the poet's intention, seems in fact to have been illuminated
already from afar, long before it is uttered in the form of a
philosophical lament over a pile of abandoned logs and an
absent personal agent:

> No runner tracks in this year's snow looped near it.
> And it was older sure than this year's cutting,
> Or even last year's or the year's before.
> The wood was gray and the bark warping off it
> And the pile somewhat shrunken. Clematis
> Had wound strings round and round it like a bundle.

What held it though on one side was a tree
Still growing, and on one a stake and prop,
These latter about to fall. I thought that only
Someone who lived in turning to fresh tasks
Could so forget his handiwork on which
He spent himself, the labor of his ax,
And leave it there far from a useful fireplace
To warm the frozen swamp as best it could
With the slow smokeless burning of decay.

The actual person whose capriciousness arouses simultaneously the reproach and the pity of the narrator is not present as an acting person, but the action develops with clear reference to him inasmuch as he is responsible for what has occurred and becomes therefore the ideational and compositional focus of the poem.

Such poetic creations are characteristic of Robert Frost. The vivid living source of the action is removed from the center of the stage and put some distance away, whether to the side or the rear, and from that remoteness throws a diffused light onto the front stage of the action. By means of such off-stage illumination the dramatic qualities of the event are compressed. Thereby an impression of depth, of voluminousness, of extension of time and space is created. The figures in the foreground, their faces turned toward the source and illuminated by it, reveal successive changes of attitude in this exaggerated kind of foreshortening and acquire a new, added meaning, from time to time even overshadowing their originally established characteristics.

The substance of Frost's "The Death of the Hired Man" is revealed through informal dialogue between a farmer and his wife arguing whether or not to take back once again an old farmhand returning from his periodic vagabondage, who is no longer of any practical use to them. But this foreground where the central figure and topic of conversation—the hired man—is missing, serves as a screen back of which, behind a wall, the main theme is developed: while they discuss the man and argue about him, he lies dying upstage behind the curtain. Only at the very end of the poem do we learn this definitively, but the tragic conclusion, the thing that happens behind the wall, invisible to us, illuminates the whole progress of the dialogue and lends a totality to everything that is discussed or done this side of the wall.

The ungenerous attitude of the farmer who is disinclined to take back his ailing hired man, the generosity of his wife, the character of the old man who expresses his willingness to work and pay for past and future kindnesses, as we learn from the dialogue, his enforced return, the very "home" to which he drags himself because a man must have, at least at a moment like this, his own corner to crawl into—all this is illuminated and made transparent by the silent presence of death. Nature itself participates in the climax of a tragic event; but nobody knows as yet what has actually happened. And the woman, raising her hand symbolically, bids an unwitting farewell to the forlorn man, unaware that he has died just at this moment.

> Part of a moon was falling down the west,
> Dragging the whole sky with it to the hills.
> Its light poured softly in her lap. She saw it
> And spread her apron to it. She put out her hand
> Among the harp-like morning-glory strings,
> Taut with the dew from garden bed to eaves,
> As if she played unheard some tenderness
> That wrought on him beside her in the night.
> "Warren," she said, "he has come home to die.
> You needn't be afraid he'll leave you this time."

For Frost it is extraordinarily essential to bring different levels together: life and death, past and present, external and internal, spring and autumn, lake and wood. This kind of conjunction may take place in Frost by an exchange of views: "Two had seen two, whichever side you spoke from"—but by such a momentary contact the sought-for fullness and an all-embracing universal integrity are achieved—the internal concatenation of phenomena that may be remote from one another but still appear in the poetic image as a unity. According to Frost, there is "something" in the very nature of things "that doesn't love a wall, that wants it down." For this reason, for example, racial discrimination, social and spiritual segregation, everybody's living for himself alone according to the principle "good fences make good neighbors" found in Frost a definite enemy:

> "Men work together," I told him from the heart,
> "Whether they work together or apart."

In his insistence upon the unity of the world, which in our consciousness frequently appears to be divided and atomized into countless cells, nuclei, poles, lies the ethical and the actual aesthetic program of Frost.[2] He wished he could embrace both heaven and earth ("Birches"). His work, the work of artists in general, consists of building a short bridge from one man to another, of establishing connections between man and nature, body and soul, of demonstrating reality in the wonderful inter-action of its individual parts.

Frost's landscapes and genre scenes—with all their realistic delicacy and liveliness of portrayal—contain something that is more than just a mere imitation of life, a copying of nature. At the same time the metaphysical essence of nature and exist-ence which he abstracts from everyday life surrounding him are always in Frost rooted deep in the soil of reality. Poetry and prose, abstract philosophy and sober everyday occur-rences are so closely interwoven in his poetry that the one be-comes now the source, now the shell of the other. Like his characters, Frost himself, to use his own expression, "mingled reckless talk of heavenly stars with hugger-mugger farming." Physical work he coupled with poetic inspiration and gave himself to philosophy, meditation, contemplation, whether he was chopping wood or gathering hay:

> I thought of questions that have no reply,
> And would have turned to toss the grass to dry.

The favorite heroes in Frost's poetry are working people who know the value of things, who know "what's what on the farm." They are straightforward characters, strong people, with a well-developed feeling of justice and dignity. All this does not interfere with their inclination to philosophize during pauses in their farm work about the final design of the universe, or to plunge into dreams and phantasies. The man with strange features, with oddities, with a tendency toward contemplation is especially close to Frost. Thus, for example, he devotes one of his best poems, "The Star-splitter," to a daydreaming eccentric who burns his farm down and spends the insurance money on a telescope:

> I recollect a night of broken clouds
> And underfoot snow melted down to ice,
> And melting farther in the wind to mud.
> Bradford and I had out the telescope.
> We spread our two legs as we spread its three,
> Pointed our thoughts the way we pointed it,
> And standing at our leisure till the day broke,
> Said some of the best things we ever said.
> That telescope was christened the Star-splitter,
> Because it didn't do a thing but split
> A star in two or three the way you split
> A globule of quicksilver in your hand
> With one stroke of your finger in the middle.

The telescope "christened the Star-splitter," which combined within itself, as it were, the function of wood-splitting with contemplation of the stars—here is an image very much in the spirit of Robert Frost, forever striving toward a unity of contrasting levels in order to arrive thereby, through poetic means, at a conception of the integral unity of universal reality:

> It's a star-splitter if there ever was one
> And ought to do some good if splitting stars
> 'S a thing to be compared with splitting wood.
> We've looked and looked, but after all where are we?
> Do we know any better where we are,
> And how it stands between the night tonight
> And a man with a smoky lantern chimney?
> How different from the way it ever stood?

The Russian reader may find it strange that in the big and all-embracing poetic world of Frost no place is given to the industrial city, to technical subjects and other aspects of con-

temporary civilization, which, to our understanding, are obligatory according to the American way of life. In Frost we do
not see machines nor skyscrapers, but flowers and trees and
souls of living beings. We hear bird-song, we encounter deer,
as if the whole country to which he devotes himself were nothing but woods and fields. The urban motifs interest him less
than antique eclogues. This notwithstanding (and one can see
it unmistakably even in the Russian translation), Frost is a
clearly definable national poet—a very contemporary one at
that. His preference for country life, his regionalism are, however, not accidental. The combined philosophical-aesthetic
tendency in Frost's poetry is closely related to the ideal of the
integral, healthy man, the traditions associated with the struggle for independence in America, loyalty to the democracy of
Benjamin Franklin, Thomas Jefferson, and Abraham Lincoln.

The closeness to nature, to the simple life, to work, and to
the soil served him as a pledge of moral purity, of immediacy
and spiritual freedom, which he would not have exchanged for
any blessings of comfort and technical progress, the last of
which, incidentally, arouses in Frost a somewhat sceptical attitude (see, for example, his poem "Why Wait for Science").
Herein lies also the reason for his appeal to the past, to a return
to "sources," "roots," which, however, does not exclude a free
and open look into the future or an acceptance of life in the
broadest possible sense.

Undoubtedly Frost, the poet-philosopher who preferred to
"walk" through the world in order to observe life closely and
contemplate its origins, goes contrary to modern rhythm. He
looks into the depth of things, not merely at their spectacular,
sparkling surfaces; and consequently his slow and easy, pen-
sive step outruns the field time and again. His whole art sounds
in fact like an invitation to a walk along an old familiar country road where behind every apparent trifle a new miracle is
waiting to be revealed.

> I'm going out to clean the pasture spring;
> I'll only stop to rake the leaves away
> (And wait to watch the water clear, I may)
> I shan't be gone long.—You come too.

The poem from which these lines are taken served as an epigraph to the volume *From Ten Books,* the collection of translations from Robert Frost's poetry. It is a book which is undoubtedly done with great care, selectivity, and poetic taste. One could say so many fine things about the high artistic quality of these translations except that the sense of having been in living communication with genuine poetry and the feeling of elevation that persists after reading it makes words superfluous and wholly inadequate.

We would note only that, along with such well-known masters of translation as Mikhail Zenkovich and Ivan Kashkin, the volume also contains several translations by the young poet Andrei Sergeyev to whom the reader is indebted, in part at least, for the translation of the especially difficult and, perhaps, most arresting of Frost's narrative poems. Finally, one could only wish for a further, more encompassing edition of the poems of Robert Frost. His poetry will no doubt live long and illustriously.

> It's when I'm weary of considerations,
> And life is too much like a pathless wood
> Where your face burns and tickles with the cobwebs
> Broken across it, and one eye is weeping
> From a twig's having lashed across it open.
> I'd like to get away from earth awhile
> And then come back to it and begin over.
> May no fate willfully misunderstand me
> And half grant what I wish and snatch me away
> Not to return. Earth's the right place for love:
> I don't know where it's likely to go better.
> I'd like to go by climbing a birch tree,
> And climb black branches up a snowwhite trunk
> *Toward* heaven, till the tree could bear no more,
> But dipped its top and set me down again.
> That would be good both going and coming back.
> One could do worse than be a swinger of birches.

The Unfettered Voice[1]

(ON ANNA AKHMATOVA)

For many years Anna Akhmatova's[2] poetry appeared to her contemporaries as if it had frozen within the restricted limits laid down by her first books: *Evening, Rosary, White Flock.* . . . It seemed that the poetess, submerged in the past, in the world of intimate reminiscences and in her own tradition of versification, would never tear herself away from the captivity of her beloved themes, familiar images, and established intonations. Even in the twenties critics had written that Anna Akhmatova was doomed to "repeat herself," and, unfortunately, such a view of her poetry is still current even today in her readers' minds.

If one turns, however, to the Akhmatova of today and reads carefully everything that she has produced during the last three decades, then extraordinary, at times decidedly new notes are perceptible, and unexpectedly bold developments and turns are noticeable in a lyrical view which was fully developed long ago and of which we are still quite conscious.

> Like a river, I was
> Turned around by a stern epoch.
> My life was changed over
> Into another river-bed,

> Leaving others unchanged,
> And I do not know my shores.

While not ceasing to be herself, Akhmatova rejects herself, or to state it more precisely, she casts off and broadens the established image of herself which classified her only as a poet of pre-revolutionary times who is locked within her narrow limits, in one unchanged river-bed. Her civic poetry of the thirties and of the war years, so full of tragic power and courage, testifies to this most of all. Akhmatova argues against those who would like to see in her only a "peripheral" phenomenon, alien to the life of her native country, indifferent to the fate of its people. We may refer to her lines about the Yezhovshchina,[3] which became for her a great personal tragedy:

> No, neither under alien skies
> Nor under the safety of alien wings—
> I was then with my nation
> There, where unfortunately also my nation was.

In her lyric poetry during the Second World War the idea of the unity of the poet and the citizen and the high pathos of struggle and sorrow rang out loud and clear. In 1942 she wrote in her poem "Courage":

> We know what is being weighed now
> And what is being fulfilled at this time.
> The hour of courage struck on our clocks
> And courage is not going to leave us.
> It is not terrifying to lie like dead under the shells,
> It is not bitter to remain without a home—
> And we will safeguard you, Russian speech,
> Great Russian word.
> We will carry you onward free and pure,
> And bestow you upon our grandsons,
> And save you from captivity
> Forever!

The very structure, the tonality itself is changed in Akhmatova's lyric poetry. We used to consider it soft, exquisite, womanly fragile, and we used to follow the play of details, of "microscopic trifles," of barely audible and scarcely perceptible modulations. Who would have believed that this "Muse of Tsarskoye Selo" [4] could speak out so loudly, so powerfully, using colloquial language, and all this not about just anything, but about her Tsarkoye Selo, thrice celebrated in songs, which for a long time now has become the symbol of the exquisite poetry of the past? And suddenly:

> . . . There a soldier's joke
> Comes out, not hiding the bile . . .
> The striped sentry house
> And the steam of makhorka.
> They sang at the top of their voice,
> Swore like the wife of a priest,[5]
> Drank vodka till late in the night,
> Ate like the poor priests.[6]
> The crow hailed with a scream
> This unreal world,
> And the sleigh was driven
> By a big cuirassier.

Unlike many of her literary colleagues and contemporaries, Akhmatova was reluctant to use abrupt stylistic shifts, radical changeovers, and was more inclined toward the traditional forms of poetry, toward classical exactness and clearness of language, and toward the harmonious language of Pushkin and Baratynsky.[7] She still favors poetical reminiscences, which again and again perform the function of parallel mirrors, creating in her work a perspective in depth and thus bringing subjects remote from one another into closer relationship. ("Just as the future ripens in the past, so does the past decay in the future. . . .") Names of literary importance, epigraphs, dedications, and gestures of good-bye to the past ("As if I were parting again from things to which I said good-bye a long time ago"), the settling of old accounts with herself and her memory: all this does not impede, but rather facilitates the task of evoking in a small section of poetical text the feeling of great spaciousness, of moving within it with great ease, of exchanging greetings with voices of other epochs and other spheres of existence. Owing to the breadth of her scope the entire world can become the mediator in the author's conversation with her imaginary interlocutor, and the fact that this exchange of thoughts is carried on in a low voice or happens silently no longer presents difficulties. Silence and calm in Akhmatova's poems usually speak not of the absence but rather of the presence of that which is all-embracing and magnificent.

> You and I, just like two mountains,
> Never meet in this world.
> I only wish that in the middle of the night
> You would send me a greeting across the stars.

The new features of Akhmatova's latest lyric poetry force us to take a different view also of her literary autobiography and to reconsider certain traditional ideas about the early stages of her poetry. It is worthwhile to ask a question about her possibilities: is it possible that already in the initial "salon" period of her development there existed potentially and secretly those features which served at first only as a starting point and then later on came to fruition?

Akhmatova has always been the recognized master of the lyric self-portrait, a portrait which recreated the gestures and mimicry of the living face with such ease and clarity that it almost burst the frame of the poem like a relief. In the given case the small format appeared to be unusually spacious. Akhmatova possesses the gift of compressing into the framework of a four-line poem man's fate with all the psychological complications and secrets of the inner life.

> I am happy. But most of all I like
> The gently sloping forest paths,
> The wretched, crooked little bridge,
> And the few days that remained for expectation.

In addition to being filled with ideas and concrete subject matter Akhmatova's early poetry is frequently able to astonish us with the sweep of its intonation, with the power and energy of her voice, which also, as Mandelshtam[8] once wrote in a poem dedicated to her, "frees the depths of the soul." The lyrical voice in this case is borne by such a breadth of spiritual and appropriate intonational movements that the salon genre becomes a great haven for a powerful monumentality. In the most intimate spheres she possesses the art of the exalted, heroic and tragic, both in word and gesture. We all remember her classic tirade:

> Be cursed. With neither moan nor look
> Am I going to touch your damned soul.
> But I swear to you by the garden of angels,
> By the miraculous icon I swear
> And by the ecstasy of our ardent nights—
> That I shall never return.

This invective reveals not only the wounded, insulted, and indignant feminine heart, as is usually assumed, but it also demonstrates to us the genuine possibilities of the personality of the poetess lying behind all these piercing curses.

One could also feel the diapason of her lyric talent rather early in the poems which are permeated with the consciousness of patriotic duty and personal and communal responsibility for the fate of the motherland. Noteworthy in this respect is the poem by Akhmatova written in 1917 which sounded like a reproof to all who intended to leave a Russia caught in the conflagration of revolution. In those circumstances (notwithstanding the fact that contemporary life was presented by her mainly in dark colors) it was the very choice made by Akhmatova in favor of her beloved country that was important. This is why (according to K. I. Chukovsky)[9] Alexander Blok, who loved this poem and memorized it, assigned to it such a programmatic significance. "Akhmatova is right," he said, "this is an unworthy way of talking. To run away from the Russian revolution is shameful."

> . . . I heard a voice. It called me consolingly.
> It said: "Come here,
> Leave behind your remote and sinful land,
> Leave Russia forever.
> I shall wash the blood from your hands,
> From your heart I'll remove the black shame.
> I shall cover with a new name

The pain of defeats and insults."
But indifferently and calmly
I closed my ears with my hands,
So that this unworthy speech
Would not soil my sorrowful soul.

From a barely perceptible whisper to flaming oratory, from shyly cast-down eyes to thunder and lightning—such is the range of her feeling and her voice. It may be that one has to look for the sources of that development which blossomed later on and gave Akhmatova's poetry the possibility of turning into a new riverbed—one which can accommodate between its shores both patriotic pathos, the calmness of high metaphysical contemplations, and the loud, many-voiced arguments of the living and the dead.

Pamphlet or Lampoon?

(ON A NOVEL BY IVAN SHEVTSOV)

A. Laktionov,[1] member of the Academy of Arts, warns the reader in his Foreword to this book: "*Plant-Louse* is a caustic, militant, and angry novel-pamphlet. Very likely it is going to provoke hot debates and even possibly sharp attacks from certain art critics and literati. Well, a fight is a fight. . . ."

Before making an analysis of the novel *Plant-Louse* we would like to contradict the honorable author of the above recommendation: "hot debates" and "sharp attacks" do not seem to be the right expressions here. Although it is true that "a fight is a fight," obviously, various forms and methods can be used. The fight waged by Ivan Shevtsov[2] on the pages of his book is on the borderline—or so it seems to us—of such nonliterary forms as street scandal, a "fight" in the streetcar or quarrel in an apartment. . . . What it requires from criticism is then not counterattacks or disputes, but first of all calmness and peaceful deliberation. To participate in this polemic on the basis of the proposed conditions is somehow shameful and degrading; to refute its arguments with passion is ridiculous. By acting with some forbearance one achieves more useful results, if, as A. Laktionov recommends, one puts oneself in the position of the author and, considering his "unyielding" character, does not attack Ivan Shevtsov, but rather pities him and has compassion for him. . . .

The position in which the author of the novel *Plant-Louse* places himself and his heroes—realists[3] and artists carrying on a fight against all kinds of enemies—is indeed very pitiable. According to Shevtsov, unchecked forces of a "dark, but well-organized and well-trained minority" are at work in our artistic life. They are "not numerous, but astonishingly active," they are "modernists," "cosmopolites," "incendiaries," "aesthetes and formalists of all sorts." [4] They "mock unpunished" at honest artists, giving them advice, in which there is "something devilishly coaxing, intriguing," they carry "the devil's message," they attempt to place everywhere "their people" and to organize "sedition." (All the expressions in quotation marks are taken from I. Shevtsov's text.—A. S.)

The novel *Plant-Louse* is salted and seasoned like a criminal record, or a scandalous exposé. We learn that the well-known artist Lev Barselonsky (the majority of the characters are depicted as if they were quite renowned persons in the world of arts) has barely escaped execution during the Revolution.[5] His further career is marked by wheeling and dealing and shrewdness of a political nature. He received "a gold medal and membership in the Academy of Art" as the rumors have it, for a work which was done by somebody else. The renowned art theoretician and critic Osip Davydovich Ivanov-Petrenko has also achieved glory through doubtful machinations—such as, for example, his doctoral dissertation on Cézanne: "People in the know said that the bulk of this dissertation consisted of unknown material which by chance got into the hands of a smart-alec." "On this Osip—as the positive hero of the story remarks accurately—one could not find a clean spot as big as a postage stamp. He was on friendly terms with everybody, whether S. R.'s,[6] Trotzkyites,[7] or whoever else. What did he care? He lives all right, has his fingers everywhere in the pie and does his dirty tricks."

The biographies of the promoters of "pure art" are filled with theft, forgery, shady deals, and other crimes. Still they are successful and they set the tone in the world of artists. Even of the weather they talk like experienced conspirators, like the confirmed spies of criminal stories: "They exchanged an understanding smile. 'Beautiful weather,' said Ivanov-Petrenko, giving an energetic handshake with his warm hand to Barselonsky. His look was vigorous and resolute. 'Thaw! [8] A good thaw,' repeated Lev Mikhailovich, looking searchingly into the eyes of his companion; Osip Davydovich was familiar with this piercing, soul-searching glance. . . ."

The device used by the indignant author, that is, to heap all the vices upon the opponents of his ideas, and to attach the masks of bloodthirsty criminals to living people, is of course, not a new method. In the novel *Plant-Louse* old traditions are revived which are well known from the yellow press, but which fortunately are not customary in Soviet literature.[9] There is something else in Shevtsov's book that is unexpected: in his blind hatred of people who in his opinion are slandering reality and lowering the level of Soviet art, the author has let himself be carried away and applied black paint to such an extent that willy-nilly, probably unintentionally, he appears in the role of a blackmailer of our art and culture.[10] The criminal elements, the wheeler-dealers, and the shady characters form in the novel *Plant-Louse* a powerful organization, a kind of omnipotent Mafia which legally or illegally directs the aesthetic life of this country. Not only are they living in economic abundance, building luxurious country homes, and drinking cognac—while the realists, in Shevtsov's description, are poor, most of them are even on the level of beggars and borrow money for bread from the charitable aesthetes—but as it turns out, they also have penetrated all corners of society and achieved high and influential positions. To disrupt their net is difficult, almost impossible.

Before Shevtsov's novel *Plant-Louse* was published we naively thought that the review albums at artistic exhibitions serve as one of the forms of expression of public opinion. Of course, we were mistaken. The review albums, according to Shevtsov, are under the control of the agents of Osip Davydovich, who systematically abuse the good artists and publicize the nontalented ones.

We assumed that in the world of art a democracy exists which secures the development of creative possibilities, the justice of judgments, and the freedom of the word. No, democracy in the novel *Plant-Louse* is subjected to the "machine" of the omnipresent Ivanov-Petrenko. "Osip Davydovich has a majority in the committee of exhibitions, they will vote, and that's the end of it." Oh: "Barselonsky and Company succeeded for some reason or other in beating or fooling the MOSKH." [11] Or: "To speak up here is useless: they will hiss you, use catcalls and will spit at you. The hall is filled with the young toughs of Barselonsky and Company." "If, say, I or somebody else of the people not very well liked by Barselonsky ever commits a small error, or says something wrong imprudently, then it will remain forever as a stain on his life. Osip is going to make use of it for all eternity . . ."

"But there is such a thing as the press, the news media?" We won't be kept from countering!

"The press is in the hands of the Barselonskys," answers Shevtsov gloomily.

"Peter Yeremenko carried his article 'To work for the good of the people' to the third editorial office. In two previous offices his article was kept for two weeks and finally refused for publication. In one of the offices a dark-haired, thin-faced woman said in a hostile voice: 'We have already commissioned one article on this theme from an art historian.' And she has returned the manuscript to Yeremenko. She lied, of course, the editor has not commissioned such an article from any art historian. . . . In the other editorial office he was met by an old man who looked like an old crow: 'Your article, Peter Alexandrovich, is interesting. But you see what happened is the following: at the last meeting of our editorial board we decided to publish no articles for the time being on this topic.' This was also just an excuse, since no one in the editorial office had even read the article."

Being convinced of the infection of the press with the poison of formalism, one of the positive heroes of the novel arrives at the conclusion: "The best thing is not to look in the papers and not to switch on the radio to listen to the programs on the pseudo-Repins." [12]

In such an atmosphere it is only natural that the artists' community is paralyzed and is controlled by the savage regime. The novel *Plant-Louse* attempts to suggest to the readers that in our world of art, stupid rumors, gossip, "cynical blackmail, evil inventions and nonsensical insinuations," disseminated by the "salon" of Ivanov-Petrenko dominate the scene. "They crawled out of the 'salon' like acid fumes and spread around among the people with incredible speed, followed by the evil sizzle of the blackmailers." The artists live in a state of moral suppression, make a career by apple-polishing, and in their mutual relations they are guided by personal envy, considerations of career-advancement and nepotism according to the principle: "Birds of a feather should flock together." In this atmosphere honest people feel like "lepers," withdraw into complete isolation, and live a difficult, solitary life. They are not strong enough to stand up against the attacks of the formalistic bandits. So, for example, when a certain Vika Gomelskaya, director of the choir, steals the songs written by the talented kolkhoz member Alexei, the latter asks the progressive artist Vladimir Mashkev for help. "No use complaining, no one would listen to you," said Vladimir with bitterness, pacing the room. "You cannot do anything against her, because she is not simply Vika, but a part of a group which is very strong and which sticks together. You alone cannot take up the fight with them."

The positive heroes of Shevtsov have "black and blue spots in their souls." "He felt as if someone had spit on his soul." Ceaselessly fighting formalism, they live on the verge of despair, of physical and moral exhaustion, lose their faith in the justice of our society, and reach the point where they think of suicide. "I have no more faith, the deep and strong faith I had. Honestly, it has dried up almost completely. Because I can see no progress," confesses Peter Yeremenko. Even the uncompromising Mikhail Gerasimovich Kamyshev, who fulfills in the novel *Plant-Louse* the role of the leader of the realistic trend, changes tragically: "His face was covered with innumerable wrinkles, it became dried-up and smallish, tiredness and sadness firmly got hold of it. His vision began to deteriorate; his eyes lost their sparkle, became dull, and started to hide within themselves the cold flashes of skepticism and spiritual illness."

But what a strange thing: the more you learn of the sufferings of Shevtsov's positive heroes, the less you believe in the genuineness of the grief torturing these heroes. Thus, for example, the author describes the same melancholy Kamyshev as a person who "could not forgive anybody anything." "He enjoyed the confidence of the best Soviet artists as a first-class authority, but he was even more considered an authority among the simple Soviet people and their leaders." Why, one may ask, since he has such authority, has he to hide skepticism in his eyes? Or is the recognition of the people, of the leaders, and of the best artists not the most important thing for Kamyshev?

Shevtsov tells us about the fate of his heroes in the Epilogue: "And how do Mashkov, Yeremenko, Okunev, and Vartanian live now? Well, just as they did before. They travel much in the country, see people in the villages, at the construction sites and in the factories. They write according to the old style, which brings them neither noisy glory nor money. But they are stubborn people, and remain true to themselves and to their public—millions of mortal toilers who haven't yet learned to understand the 'new' art. But never mind, this is just a question of time, Vinokurov and Ivanov-Petrenko will teach them and will indoctrinate them. They have already published several books on contemporary Western art[13] and on the new trends in Soviet painting."

It is difficult to say what there is more of here: playful boldness or an unjustified minor key? And why is it so that the followers of the "old style" have no "money or glory" although they work ceaselessly and are successful with the general public?

Similar questions of misunderstanding appear in the text of the novel *Plant-Louse* repeatedly. They result from the fact that the author has not made both ends meet on the pages of the book, and apparently he himself does not have much faith in the picture he has drawn. The terrors depicted are made up, and the characters, even if they are cleverly tailored after real prototypes, are distorted to the point of incredibility. The exaggerations which Shevtsov uses so liberally have not much to do with the hyperbolic nature of the satire. They can be better described by the everyday saying: fear has big eyes. For this reason, among other things, the positive heroes of the novel also appear in a somewhat unexpected light and reveal characteristics which are not appropriate for simple good people, and even less for progressive artists. Although their high moral values are declaimed by Shevtsov, their psychology and general behavior contradict their beliefs. In words they are fighters—but in reality just cowards. In words they are firm, self-assured, of strong principles, but in reality they are wavering, pathologically fearful, revengeful, and envious. They think only that they are not appreciated (although it is said that the people love and honor them). Their conversations when among themselves are spiked with sensational rumors aimed at their neighbors. They feverishly collect information and compromising material meant to annihilate their enemies. Their speeches are colored with such phrases as: "As long as Varyagov [a responsible functionary in the ministry of culture] is in the saddle, Osip has nothing to fear." Although they are outstanding artists, Osip's hope and future, they are too stomach-conscious and are dominated by ideas about the distribution of merit increases, jobs, and petty insults. They differ but little from the negative heroes of Shevtsov, and with their conspiratory bustle, allegations, and threats stamp upon the novel that heavy atmosphere of mutual suspiciousness which returns us to the mores which disappeared into the past under the name "The Cult of Personality." [14] Here is an example of this unhealthy psychological agitation of the positive heroes of the novel: "On the third day of the exhibition Pavel Okunev called Vladimir in the morning.

"'Have you seen today's issue of "Soviet Art?"'" he asked enigmatically.

" 'No, why?' Vladimir asked with unconscious restlessness.

" 'Well, read it. Unbelievable things are happening in this world . . .' and hung up the telephone.

"Vladimir ran barefoot to the mailbox in front of his apartment door and with shaking hands took out the paper. . . . "

This atmosphere of suspicion, of conspiratorily nervous gestures and of the fear of spies serves as the impelling force of the unlikely fears of Shevtsov and also of those illicit methods he is using. The complex problem of our contemporary artistic development is placed upon the level of a kind of military or intelligence operation, and every aesthetic debate is turned into combat smelling of blood. The strategic and tactical operations, maneuvers, and battles are closely connected with the psychology of the author and that of the heroes of *Plant-Louse* who prefer military vocabulary to artistic: ". . . the apologists of *l'art pour l'art* were pushed back into the second line of defense. All these Vinokurevs, Yakovlevs, Ivanov-Petrenkos, like cockroaches hid themselves in the slit trenches and did not show much activity. In the silence of their private villas they carried out a regrouping of their forces, worked out new tactics, and made reconnaissance and observation trips."

The "reconnaissance and observation" is followed by "reconnaissance with combat contact"—as befits a war situation: "The watercolors of Barselonsky were a good beginning," said Ivanov-Petrenko, "and they all understood that this actually was already the reconnaissance with combat and that the time of decisive attack upon realistic art had come."

In such situations in the already excited consciousness of the positive hero Peter Yeremenko the preparation of the artistic exhibition is clothed in the colorful images of hand-to-hand combat borrowed from *Taras Bulba*:[15] "And that's how they went into the battle."

This rattling of the saber is very far from the ideological battle facing Soviet art. The military terminology itself does not decide anything. On the contrary, in certain cases it can be harmful. The atmosphere of military alarm and gloomy tension, artificially sustained in the novel *Plant-Louse,* time and again results in panic, hysteria, and bragging, when the author's and his heroes' nerves give in and they start to "cut 'em" to the right and to the left, not distinguishing between friend and foe. The amassing of suspicions, the creation of sentimental complaints, denunciations, and pasquinades appear not as a defense of the realistic tradition from aesthetic attempts, but rather as an evil parody of this defense and of the very tradition itself.

The psychology of fear is based exactly upon the idea that man loses the feeling of reality and starts the battle in a fictional world, threatening himself with new and increasing numbers of fantasies. The accusatory tirades of Shevtsov's heroes are built on the basis of such autosuggestion; they are obsessed with a mania of persecution and are ready to provoke any phrase of the imagined enemy in order to turn him inside out and find in him the "diversion" of the day. It is enough if someone speaks up about the diversity of art of Socialist realism for the Bacchanalia to start.

" 'I know, they are also in favor of Socialist realism, for its unlimited variety, for the freedom of art!' exclaims Kamyshev. 'I know what kind of freedom they want! They need the freedom of a pogrom against the people who think differently, the freedom of dictatorship in art so that they may produce any trash they want and then call it a masterpiece, in order to create their own "geniuses" and "classics." They are in favor of the freedom to prohibit Socialist realism in art. Do you understand? Freedom for prohibition! We are not going to give them this freedom. The party won't allow it. . . . In one of the second-rate magazines they have published an article, in which they requested the opening of a museum of so-called contemporary Western art in Moscow, that is, they wanted a museum of aesthetic-formalistic distortions. There was a time when there was such a museum in Moscow,' explained Kamyshev. 'The snobbish merchant Shchukin[16] opened it. But what de we need such a museum for? . . . Here I think to myself: well, let's give them their "freedom," and let's open the museum of Siniak and Cézanne, but do you think they will be satisfied with that? If you give them your finger they'll bite off your hand. The Tretyakov[17] Gallery, maybe, they will not dare to close, but on the other hand they surely will throw out Shishkin and other artists of the people from the exhibition halls. . . . If you give them a little breathing time, they will close even the Art Theater. . . .'" [18]

Why should "freedom" mean "prohibition," "diversity" mean "pogrom," why "to open" a museum mean "to close" a theater? . . . It is useless to ask: Kamyshev won't listen. It is all the same to him to turn white into black, and vice versa. It means nothing to him that the "snobbish merchant" Shchukin, just like the merchant Tretyakov, left for us a tremendous artistic heritage, of which Russians are justly proud before the entire world, and that Shchukin's collection of "great European masters, mostly French artists of the end of the nineteenth and the beginning of the twentieth century" is a "unique one" and "as far as its high-quality artistic values are concerned it has nationwide significance and contributes thus to the education of our people." This was said in a government decree signed by Lenin, and this was the decree which was issued on the occasion of the opening of the Museum of Contemporary Western Art.[19] What does he mean "French"? For Kamyshev and his sort everything that is foreign is suspect both morally and politically, and all French art, beginning with the impressionists, is but "distortion." It was the French, after all, they say, who "were the first in destroying art"! By the way as far as aesthetic ideas expressed in the novel *Plant-Louse* are concerned they may just as well be left unmentioned. Although the characters are well-versed in intergroup intrigues, in the field of aesthetics they are innocent children. The level of I. Shevtsov's aesthetic ideas can perhaps be characterized by one detail. The room of one of the characters, Boris Iulin, a no-good and sentimental fellow, is decorated with "colored reproductions of naked women: Rembrandt's *Danae*, Giorgione's *Venus, Susanna* of Rubens, the *Virsavia* of Bryullov[20] and of course, the young lady by Renoir in a sitting pose, with her back to the onlooker and with a slight turn of her head." Enumerating these masterworks of universal geniuses, Shevtsov explains to the reader that they helped Boris Iulin to seduce young girls.

Let's also mention in passing the author's inclination to understand works dealing with unvarnished nature, to put it mildly, in an extremely utilitarian way. Kamyshev himself, as it turns out, was guilty in this respect (however, what has been described as the sign of sentimentality and formalism in the case of the aesthete Iulin, turns out to be the sign of physical strength and healthy realism with Mikhail Gerasimovich). Here, however, the author turns nostalgic, because old age came and "it took away with it the young models." Maybe that's how it was with Mikhail Gerasimovich; we do not want to doubt Shevtsov's words. On the other hand, and we say this to console painters, "the young models" do not go away with old age. Old age is no hindrance in this matter, provided, of course, that one approaches nature with the most direct, i.e., artistic intentions.

Shevtsov's interpretation of realism leaves us dumbfounded, too. In his opinion realism means the careful depiction of details right up to the very point, where, to quote an example, in the genre painting *In the ZAGS* (marriage registration bureau), presented here as a realistic masterpiece, the bridegroom's mood "can be recognized from his long, shivering eyelashes"; on the table one sees an "empty registration form," above which the pen "froze" before it would register the marriage. If one also considers that all this, together with a mass of other details, is depicted on a "canvas of rather smallish size" then it becomes clear that the artist must have worked on every trifle painstakingly. And this is what is considered here the genuine art of realism. Also the other heroes of Shevtsov work very hard depicting "how the eyelashes shiver," and in a landscape study they find it especially important "to depict the diamonds of dew sparkling on the little fir-trees."

Is it necessary to explain that all these diamonds of dew, etc., are limiting and vulgarize the aims of art, pretending to be realism? The main trouble, however, is that in the novel *Plant-Louse* only such an art is allotted the highest authority and all other types of painting are the subject of sharp criticism and are categorized as formalism or aestheticism.

There is a sufficient quantity of everything in the novel

Plant-Louse as far as abuse, illiteracy, and crocodile tears are concerned. This is understandable: that which is now excluded from circulation by our life tries at some time to take revenge for its bad luck and all means are proper to achieve this. However, one cannot understand or grasp the news awaiting us at the end of the book, where we learn that the publishing house "Soviet Russia" has published this book in 100,000 copies as "an addition to the thematical plan for 1964," that is, by a nonstop method, above the plan and in overtime, as a happy surprise. . . . The papers *Literaturnaya Gazeta* and *Komsomolskaya Pravda,* and the magazine *Ogonyok* have published critical comments on the novel *Plant-Louse.* The book has been subjected to a definite and unanimous condemnation. Such unanimity is pleasing, although we have the impression that sometimes the tone of criticism of *Plant-Louse,* especially in *Ogonyok,* is lowered to the level of the criticized novel and gives the author a recommendation which reminds one of his art. However, the point is not that one has to antagonize Shevtsov publicly or abuse him even more. It is more important to contemplate whether it is only Shevtsov who preaches ignorance under the disguise of realism and who smears with mud the intelligentsia of the arts. Especially because the man who is classified now in the *Ogonyok* as "apple-polisher," "opportunist or careerist," not long ago enjoyed recognition in certain circles, and has been given encouragement. "He knows our reality very well and is at home in the ins and outs of our artistic life," A. Laktionov[21] wrote about the author in his foreword to *Plant-Louse.** And the previous novel of Shevtsov: *The World Is Not Without Good People* has been accompanied by a sympathetic Foreword of A. Gerasimov. . . .

Reading the reviews on *Plant-Louse* we come to ask another sort of question. It looks as if all the reviewers, like

---

* *Literaturnaya Gazeta* of September 17 published a letter by A. Laktionov as follows: "I had not read the novel when I signed the Foreword to it which was prepared in advance by the author himself. . . ." Our issue was already in print when this letter appeared and for this reason we could not take into consideration this sensational announcement by a member of the Academy of Art of the Soviet Union (Editor of *Novy Mir*).

conspirators, fell upon one man. Does this not mean that the novel *Plant-Louse* proves by its sad example after all—in an indirect way—the very version of the grievous story of the fate of a hero who is attacked by evil enemies, who in addition are getting away with insulting him, too? Would not the insulted author exclaim that he was right when he wrote about the witchhunt against realistic art and that now everything happens in life as he described it in his novel and that he has been accused in vain of falsehood and slander?

And would not he again give the call to arms, brandishing quotations from Gogol and Hugo, Repin and Chaikovsky, from Dal and Karamzin,[22] or is he going to write a new book on this theme,[23] spicing it—just as he did in the novel *Plant-Louse*—with irrefutable epigraphs? In order to avoid similar misunderstandings I shall also permit myself to use a quotation, which in my opinion explains fairly well the trouble that happened to Ivan Shevtsov. This quotation is taken from a very old book dealing with various wonders of nature and human disposition. Among the many similarly interesting topics there is the scientific explanation of hail which falls upon the earth in the form of "hard and icy balls." I beg to be forgiven for the long quotation: the style of this old book is incomparably beautiful, but it still harmonizes with the human passions storming forth from Shevtsov's book. The quoted text can also serve as an afterword to this novel sent upon us as unexpectedly as hail:

"These balls, being either square or round, depending on whether they are polished to a lesser or greater degree by the air and winds, fall upon the cities and fields with the terrible whistle of ferocious winds. . . . The animals, surprised by such unexpected blows, which they cannot escape, howl and roar, gripped by fear and anxiety. The people in the fields and haystacks caught by the hail cover their faces and turn their heads and not so sensitive backs to it; however, the fierceness of the hail frequently makes them fall down and the balls, hitting them like death-bringing lead in a battle, throw them down to earth. . . . He who abuses you can be compared to such a storm. His eyes sparkle with envious and all-consuming fire, from his ferocious jowl a hail descends upon his friends and foes, full of abuses and slander; they hit and wound one terribly and one cannot hide anywhere from them. But luckily the abuser also destroys by his abuses his own happiness, and being despised disappears just as the hail does when it falls upon the warm earth. It causes fear, wounds you, sometimes even kills you; but as suddenly as it came, it disappears just as quickly." (*The Light Visible in Faces; or the Greatness and Diversity of Creative Intentions as They Are Revealed in Nature and Morals Explained Through Physical and Moral Examples, and Illustrated with Words Very Worthy of These Objects For the Benefit of People of All Social Strata, But Especially For Young Orators, Poets, Painters and Other Artists,* St. Petersburg, 1789.)

There Are Such Verses

(ON YEVGENY DOLMATOVSKY'S POETRY)

In recent years the level of poetic technique has risen appreciably. In respect to quality verses have become more varied in form, more interesting and more subtle. Poets who have appeared with new collections as a rule demonstrate better preparation and greater artistry compared with what was the case ten years ago or fifteen years ago, when illiterate verse was customary in print and many authors lacked even elementary skill, good taste, and a professional attitude. For most poetic production crude formal miscalculations are no longer characteristic, rather one notes knowledge and ability in the sphere of versification. The time has come to settle accounts with verses of medium-level quality.

There are such verses "of medium quality," and one cannot deny the author thoughts and feelings in regard to experience or inventiveness in the means of depiction, composition, or in garish aphorisms and the like. What is lacking is precisely poetry in the great and sublime sense of the word, and that is something which is not always subject to exact calculation, but is clear to the ear and to the soul, before which suddenly open up "both divinity and inspiration." In verses called "of medium quality" all the virtues of form and content cannot overcome the kind of internal barrier which divides this apparently quite correct production from great poetry. Too distinctly felt in such verses are the limits, the rules, and boundaries within which the author confined himself, the "ceiling" above which (in a manner of speaking) he decided not to rise, and his attempt and capacity and the ability which leaves an imprint of "preconceived intent" and of "coy invention" on the verses—lines which may well be quite correct and even successful in regard to their idea and literary expression.

The new book of Yevgeny Dolmatovsky,[1] *Verses About Us,* evokes a similar mixed feeling of relief (insofar as everything is sufficiently smooth and professional, and the author, as the saying goes, "is in command of his verse") and of annoyance because he did not rise higher than the "average level." The book does not contain any serious defects or errors of style. At the same time something prevents it from going beyond the limits of "the common run" with all its positive attainments and all the consequences of a widespread standard of common usage. But our conversation would be pointless if it were reduced to the "irrational" nature of poetic art and to distressing sighs because of the lack in this case of "inspiration" and such things. Let us try to approach this book rationally and practically and see what lends it a relative harmony and symmetry, and what it is that keeps the author from taking flight and fetters his creative freedom.

The lyric hero of Dolmatovsky is designated as our contemporary and as possessing a long series of positive traits. They are enumerated in the "ABC"[2] before us:

Attack.
Brotherhood.
Inspiration.
Heroism.
Duty.
Unity.
Longing.
Star.

Quest.
There is meaning
In this alphabet for each letter . . .

This very list of virtues arranged according to the alphabet
scares one off: the hero is not visible behind the sum of "symp-
toms" which are supposed to establish the author's ideal, but
in fact replace the integral personality and the human person
with a kind of questionnaire and diagram. "F stands for people
with fantasy," the author affirms, but these people with fantasy,
under the letter F, show little imagination. The letters set in
an exalted typography do not fit together into "a unifying
word" but hang in midair. Here, in our opinion, lies the first
barrier dividing this verse from reality (and at the same time
from poetry). In Dolmatovsky's poem man looks the way he
would if looked at with binoculars that were not in focus.
Concrete traits are lost and only general contours remain
visible: "To live and believe: that is remarkable! Before us lie
untraveled paths. . . ."

In *Verses About Us* there is not enough of "us"—neither
with regard to the sharply outlined and distinctive "self" of
the poet. It is possible that in such obscurity of figurative
portrayal ("The beloved town is hidden in blue smoke. . . .")
old tendencies of the songster Dolmatovsky have reappeared.
As is well known, in song and in living melody great concreteness and clarity of depiction are not required, as, for
example, when during the Second World War Dolmatovsky
wrote: "We shall win the victory, to you I shall ride on a hot
black horse." This symbolic promise sounded like a traditional
song-like formula which by no means demands that the soldier
at the front actually return home mounted on a horse. But
what is apposite in a song cannot always be transferred to
verse constructed like a stage and drawn from nature. And if
now Dolmatovsky in the poem "My Acquaintances" tells
about his own telephone conversation with a little boy whose
daddy is flying in space and will return "in an hour," and
"mama went to the market in the morning and will come back
only who knows when"—we recognize at most an anecdote

widely spread in our time and not invented by Dolmatovsky but simply arranged—in a worse form—by him in rhyme.

The reader must not think that the author of the present review is an opponent of conventions of art and that he demands of poetry a rigidly factual accuracy. It is rather a question of the artistic authenticity of the image and of seeing the living face of a contemporary and not his fashionable symbol ("daddy is in space") or title: "Your contemporary and your ancestor, coeval with the revolution. . . . "

Besides the well-known abstract quality, the lyric hero of Dolmatovsky is tied down by other fetters which prevent him from growing before our eyes to his full stature and taking up the role which the poet ascribes to him, the role of the town-crier of our turbulent epoch.[3] There where he is actually given the right to be "his own self" and to display his living individuality (but not to set forth a list of attributes) he acts as if chained, under duress, indistinctly. It is not that he is a modest or shy person. He has rather a distinctive exalted feeling of his own worth and his positive characteristics: "I simply need too much to become happy. . . . I despise those who seek quiet. . . . But with good and noble feelings I can tell a man with half a glance. . . ." All this would be wonderful if the lyric "self" of the poet possessed a strong and consistent character, passion, ardor, and if Dolmatovsky fulfilled in his verse his declaration:

> O that I may never become an egotist,
> Jealously complaining of my fate.
> I shall not drink life like hot tea with sugar
> From the dish, fearing to burn my lips.
> Let my drink
> Be bitter, sour and salty.
> But I shall drink with one gulp, to the bottom.
> With twisted and singed mouth
> I shall tell of our times.

But it is exactly this bitter taste, acidity, and salt which is insufficient in the verses of Dolmatovsky. He talks about everything not "with a mouth twisted and singed" but quite calmly, insipidly, and soberly, and it is strange for us to hear that someone calls his hero "frivolous" ("All my life I've been considered frivolous"), since in the poems before us a character is portrayed who is praiseworthy but in general ordinary, and if you please too sober, one-sided, and always looking around to catch the opinion of others and inclined to lectures, declamations, and philosophizing. Although he considers himself frivolous, he obviously does not notice his own reasonableness when, for example, right after recalling the front lines and attacks which he had lived through, he suddenly bursts out with the crafty question:

> How shall I proceed?
> Narrate or be silent,
> Bow my head or strike a blow,
> While the central press is silent
> And dully the lobbies whisper.

And although, in the words of the poet, the proper decision comes to him "with the speed of cybernetic machines," the very posing of such a question on the same level with a martial deed makes us feel a cold blast and forces us to think that the hero, set forth by Dolmatovsky as a brave man, is at the moment not so very daring and bold.

Naturally it is not obligatory for everyone to be a desperate romantic. Solid, rational heroes are possible too. Poetry that is didactic and rational is permissible: on the one condition, however, that it does not pass itself off as a very daring deed and does not appear under the label of impetuous genius. Inconsistency in character portrayal, a tendency toward psychological compromises (he is both frivolous and sensible), and a passion for reservations (the constant "but" is a correction to these verses) and as a result—inconsistency, and ambiguity in the poetic intonation which mixes cold and hot and confuses propriety with tragedy:—this is the chief reproach which we make to the hero and to the lyric verse of Dolmatovsky.

Is it possible, composing and printing verses about love without any visible limitations, to declare coquettishly and in refutation of oneself:

Again death drones over the earth,
Again they aim at the future.
Therefore about love
I speak rarely and little.

Is it worthwhile recommending oneself as an indefatigable traveler who has gone around half the world, only to complain here about the absence of interest in all that is foreign? ("Only for two weeks no news from Home, Venice," and others.) (By the way, the motif of a tourist's nostalgia has recently become a cliché in our poetic practice. Once they have been away from home for two weeks the poets do not weary of writing about how they long for home and how sad and gloomy they are on the journey. One may ask: would it not be better to give up these depressing trips and not spoil one's nerves?)

We know great poetry that is also full of contradictions and bold ventures. But in these very contradictions which have become the subject of the creative effort, there must be consistency and a line of development in order for the literary image to live like a human personality. The law of selectivity works more decisively, probably, in art than in life, the law expressed by the biblical formula: "O that thou wert cold or hot! But . . . thou art lukewarm. . . ." Turning to more recent sources, one may supply a similar thought with the words of Mayakovsky: "Poetry begins where a definite tendency exists."

Verses About Us consists of lukewarm verses of medium temperature, with an obscure tendency; they are verses which avoid extremes and pungency and tend toward a golden mean. For that reason in part the poet did not completely succeed in achieving a frank and direct conversation with youth, with the "children" (on behalf of the "fathers")—a conversation which makes up the main and striking part of the book. The mixture of excuses and curses ("That sincerity was the basis of all bases for us—do not doubt that") with threatening outbursts ("The deceased swearing terribly, came to himself, he owes history, but not you!") and allusions which serve at the same time as a measure of educational prophylaxis ("And sometime

I'll give you a thrashing, simply so that you'll not put on airs"),
and over all this a tone of condescending superiority ("I have
a great advantage over those who are merely young in years")
—that is the way this communication of the "contemporary
and predecessor" with the young generation appears up to
now. "No, no, I don't feel like becoming like one of your
tutors" the poet affirms, while not ceasing to reprimand. Even
the jokes he drops while talking with youth have a kind of
playful-critical character:

> And having met a grown-up girl,
> I may, having embarrassed her a bit,
> Relate how I changed her diapers,
> And if she cried, I gave her a spanking.

Meanwhile Dolmatovsky has other verses which treat more
profoundly and humanely the problem of the different generations, the "fathers" and "children." We have in mind his poem
"To the Memory of a Mother," written in 1959 and not included in this collection. In it are genuine words of love and
sympathy for the past and for what has been lost ("Repent,
disobedient son, you have not made your mother happy"),
words that re-establish with the dying mother the former,
severed bond which is closer now after the bitter and frank
confessions than any sworn protestations of friendship between
children and parents.

> Today for the last time
> I spend the night here by right of a son.
> And the room, like my pain,
> Is light, spacious and empty.

But how quickly the roles changed and the repentant
speeches of the "son" gave way to the complacent reasoning
of the "father"! Will the "children" not say, when they hear
the reproaches and admonitions in the new verses of Dolmatovsky: "But you yourself, papa, acted that way when you were
a son?" And then will not the best answer of the "father" be
not to exalt himself and exaggerate his services to his fatherland, and not to flatter youth nor threaten them as "recreants,"

but rather this sad and tender poem "To the Memory of a Mother"?

The lyric verse of Dolmatovsky is by far at its best in those cases where it is filled with personal experience and biographical details, and passes from the sphere of speculative judgments and global generalizations to the field of life, suffering, and the fate of a concrete person who appears in this real condition more natural and attractive. Then we really recognize in him both the brave soldier (until the front lines turn into a conventional allegory or a fruitless symbol), and the loving human being ("Once More in Uman," some verses about love). When we compare this position drawn from life with the doctrinaire pose which the poet assumes when he rises on his toes and tries to act important and strong as is proper for "a contemporary of great events"—then one wants to say to him: don't write "about us," write "about yourself"—you will have better success and it will be a better tale about us.

We would not like to dwell on the specifically formal virtues and faults of Dolmatovsky's verses. Both the former and the latter are connected with the central lyric character of the book and fluctuate within the permitted limits of "medium quality." A deviation toward poorer quality is seen in the poem "The Old Drummer," the poem which opens the collection and plays a crucial role in the aesthetic program of the poet—we quote in excerpts:

> The young drummer, the young drummer,
> Beats away like the heart—tuck-tuck-tuck.
> The Pioneer's camp raises its banners,
> The young drummer—there he is . . .
> They beat him, but could not kill him, they burned him,
>   but he didn't die,
> Why did you become gray so soon?
> In distant countries with the good drum
> We passed, leaving a good track.

> Such are the times—seek no rest,
> Grown-up drummer, adult age.
> Raise the world, my friend, from its smoldering ruins,
> Deliver the planet, oh man!
> With the roll of a drum or with a march

We shall still discover beauty for old and young.
Old drummer, old drummer,
Old drummer at your post.

The splendid tradition of Heinrich Heine has been caught
up by the merry beat of the drum, coming to us here from the
comic "Ballad of the Drummer" of Ilya Selvinsky[4] (which
probably in turn was influenced in tone by the comic verses:
"Old drummer, old drummer, the old drummer has long been
sleeping, he woke up and turned around" and so on). Right
away this text sounds like a parody of Dolmatovsky, although
it was composed long ago and with regard to "The Old Drummer" plays the role of a primary source. In order to evaluate
this similarity in sound, let us listen to Selvinsky, especially
since he sounds more entertaining and sonorous:

> The peasant woman stole the grapes,
> The peasant woman stole the milk-agaric,
> She stole the beans and peas.
> And in the grass were lonely bachelors
> They took the woman under fire . . .
> The peasant woman was pockmarked.
> But she was afraid:
> "Ah, that God
> Might help me here!"
> But instead of God
> There wandered in this age
> A poor little fellow
> With the drum on his shoulder
> He was wounded, pariah
> On the field of battle.
> He slept on his drum
> And walked to the dressing-station.
> Suddenly he noticed from the bushes,
> That someone was arrested—
> And not by our command . . .
> What is that? A revolt?
>
> . . . .
>
> Drums on both sides
> Beat the drums for glory
> Beat-beat the drums
> As loud as can be. Ours. Rage.

Neither
In Provence
Nor in Brabant
Are there such
Drummers. Like. Ours.

We, of course, do not believe that Dolmatovsky deliberately imitated anyone: the theme is too serious for the author for him to have decided on such a cheap paraphrase. It is simply that a catchy verse, overheard at some time and then happily forgotten, supplied his memory with an unexpected refrain, and the poet inadvertently submitted to a rhythmic inertia which plays a joke on him at the main entrance to his volume. This unconscious submission to another's rhythm, which he took for his own discovery, is nevertheless an indication of the insufficient clarity and lucidity of the lyric "I" of the poet, which lacks a clearly expressed personality and a firm originality.

In conclusion it must be stated for the sake of fairness that *Verses About Us* by Dolmatovsky is no worse and no better than many other collections of verses which are printed nowadays. The critical faultfinding displayed toward his book was evoked by the desire to call to mind once again the responsibilities demanded of poetic art, demands which should not be replaced by ones of medium magnitude. To one of them, perhaps the decisive one, we have already referred: "Poetry begins where a definite tendency exists."

Sometimes a fateful significance is ascribed to these words, applicable only to the art of political agitation. But let us remember that Mayakovsky, when speaking about a definite tendency, cited as a classic example Lermontov's "If I go out alone on the road." Tendency in its broad sense is a living, formative, and creative principle in verse, a movement which breaks down dogmas and clichés, and does not permit compromises and wishes to live in a new way, an individual way. It maintains itself both by means of the style and genre and the very life of the artist, who has a horror of mediocrity and does not even let himself think that he could be confused with anyone else once he has mastered his own idea. Tendency is both source and supply, it is the soul of poetry in its real sense and in the maximum, always maximum demands on oneself. Because genuine poetry in any of its manifestations invariably strives to become higher and greater than itself.

The Poetry of Pasternak[1]

⚜

The creative work of Pasternak has been well known for a long time to a comparatively narrow circle of connoisseurs and lovers of poetry. The literary isolation and uniqueness of Pasternak were noted by the critics over a period of many years and can be explained in part by the difficulties in understanding his poetic texts which the reader encountered on first opening his books. "Readers meet a poet of a very special kind," a critic wrote at the end of the 1920's. "In order to understand him, it would be necessary to make a special effort and, in a certain sense, recast one's accustomed manner of understanding. His manner of interpreting the world and even his vocabulary seemed at first unacceptable and astonishing, and troublesome questions of "incomprehensibility" and of "how can that be" for a long time accompanied the appearance of each book." *

The compact metaphorical nature of Pasternak's works in his early period often was interpreted as pretentiousness in form behind which one could vaguely sense a profound content. At the same time his first books created an impression of almost complete remoteness from contemporary life. With the

* K. Loks, "Boris Pasternak. Poverkh baryerov" ("Boris Pasternak. Above the Barriers"), GIZ, 1929, *Literaturnaya Gazeta*, October 28, 1929.

103

name Pasternak there became firmly associated the reputation of a poet far from the great, general questions of the time and completely immersed in very intimate experiences.

But along with this negative and at times even impatient attitude toward Pasternak, there was Mayakovsky, who as early as the beginning of the 1920's was claiming that Pasternak's works were among the examples of "the new poetry which has a wonderful feeling for the times." *

It was then also that V. Bryusov[2] noted: "Pasternak has no special poems about the Revolution, but his verses, perhaps without the conscious intent of the author, are nourished by the spirit of the times; Pasternak's attitude of mind is not borrowed from old books; it expresses the essence of the poet himself and could only be attained in the conditions of our time." †

In regard to the nature of his talent and to his understanding of the tasks of art, Pasternak did not belong to the tribunes and heralds of the Revolution. Abstract ideals of moral perfection determined his attitude toward life and his approach to reality, which did not always respond to the demands of a concrete historical situation. There predominated in the creativity of Pasternak a conception of life based on "eternal" categories of good, love, and universally human truth.

However, in a series of the poet's works, written in various years, the Revolution and the new Soviet reality are clearly delineated, and they are shown (as is generally characteristic of him) from the point of view of moral changes introduced into world history by our time and our nations. In 1957, in his declining years, he wrote about this very fact in his New Year's message, addressing himself to his foreign readers: "And something else for which you may thank us. Our Revolution, however great the differences may be, set the tone for you too and filled the current century with meaning and content. It is not only us and our youth, but even the son of one of your

---

* *Teatralnaya Moskva*, No. 8, 1921, p. 6.

† V. Bryusov, "*Vchera, segodnya i zavtra russkoy poezii*" ("The yesterday, today and the tomorrow of Russian poetry"), *Pechat' i revolyutsiya*, No. 7, 1922, p. 57.

bankers who is entirely different from what his father and grandfather were. . . . And thank us too for this new man, even in your old society, and for the fact that he is livelier, subtler, and more gifted than his clumsy, bombastic predecessors, because this child of the century was delivered in a maternity home which is called Russia. Is it not better if we congratulate each other on the approaching New Year and extend to each other the wish that the peals of thunder of war will not be added to the popping of wine corks at the New Year's coming, and that they may never resound in the course of the year nor in the years to come? If it is fated that there be thunder with unhappiness, then remember what events brought us up and what a stern, tempering school they were for us. There is no one more desperate than we and more ready for what is unrealizable and incredible, and any call to arms will turn us all into heroes, just as in our recent ordeal." ✻

Pasternak's nature poems are replete with serious content necessary for people of today as well as yesterday, and these poems belong probably to the best that he wrote during a half century of literary activity. Pasternak's landscapes, because of their life-affirming pathos and fresh view of the world, are in keeping with the frame of mind of contemporary man. Not for nothing did the poet himself connect the writing of his book *My Sister Life*, which was completed in 1917, with the feeling for the world born of this new epoch: "I saw the summer on the earth as if not recognizing itself, as natural and prehistoric as in a revelation. I kept a book about it. In the book I expressed everything that one could find out about a revolution of what was most fantastic and elusive." †

✻ *"Druzyam na Vostoke i na Zapade. Novogodnyee pozhelanyie"* ("To Friends in East and West. New Year's Wishes), *Literaturnaya Rossiya*, No. 1, 19.

† Unpublished Afterword to his book *Safeguard*, 1931 (Archives of B. L. Pasternak).

1

Boris Leonidovich Pasternak was born on the 10th of February (29th of January) in 1890 in Moscow. His father was the well-known artist L. O. Pasternak, and his mother the pianist R. I. Kaufman. The childhood years of the poet were spent in an atmosphere of art, music, and literature. The many-sided cultural interests and connections of the family exerted an influence on his inclinations at an early age. Thus even during the time of his childhood and early youth the German poet Rainer Maria Rilke, Leo Tolstoy, and Skryabin made an indelible impression on him. Later he assigned decisive significance in the formation of his own spiritual cast of mind to just these first contacts with the world of great creativity and artistic genius. To these contacts were added later the equally personal and intensely biographical conception of lyric poetry by Blok and his acquaintance with Mayakovsky.

The first creative passion and enthusiasm of Pasternak was entirely directed to music. Under the strong influence of Skryabin[3] he devoted himself, from his thirteenth year on, to musical composition and learned the theory of composition under the guidance of Y. D. Engle and R. M. Glier.[4] After six years of constant effort he gave up music forever. In 1909 Pasternak entered the historical-philological department of Moscow University and took up the serious study of philosophy. In order to complete his philosophical education he went to Germany in 1912 and studied for a semester at Marburg University. During this time he undertook trips to Switzerland and Italy.

As early as the years 1908 to 1909 Pasternak's interest in contemporary poetry was awakened, and friendly relations were established in this area. He participated in the poetical circle of Y. P. Anisimov and tested his skill in literary work. But his true calling appeared finally only after his stay in Marburg. Pasternak grew cool toward philosophy and devoted himself completely to the art of poetry, which from 1913 on became for him the chief and constant concern of his life.

The same sharp breaks and abrupt transitions from one sphere of ideas and occupations to another (music, philosophy, poetry), dissatisfaction with himself, attempts to create at maximum capacity, and the readiness to sacrifice years of work in order to experience a "second birth"—all these also characterize the literary biography of Pasternak. He developed by boldly wiping out his own past. The initial period of his poetic quests, marked by the conflicting influences of symbolism and futurism (at that time he entered, together with N. Aseyev and S. Bobrov, the group of moderate futurists of the "Centrifuge"),[5] was later thoroughly revised. A great deal of what he had written before 1917 Pasternak did not include in later editions.

The appearance of the book *My Sister Life* in 1922 put its author in the ranks of the prominent masters of contemporary verse. With this book one can say that Pasternak begins to exist as a completely original poetic phenomenon. That which preceded it in the works of the young poet, that is, the books *Twin in the Clouds* (1914), and *Above the Barriers* (1917), bore the stamp of first attempts, or practice, and of tuning up, and was connected with the search for his individual voice, his own view of life, and his place in the wide variety of literary currents. A series of poems which were in the collections *Twin in the Clouds* and *Above the Barriers* was later so rewritten that it was hardly recognizable in its new form. Although as early as the second book some significant distinctive signs and firm tastes of the poet (the striving for liberation of spoken expression, for the authentic establishment of tableaux, and for impetuous and dynamic imagery), he considered it necessary to rework them completely when he was preparing *Above the Barriers* for a new edition in 1929. The poetic clichés, characteristic of his early collections and derived from the Symbolists, the abstractness and deliberate obscuring of speech, the futuristic "children's rattles," as he later expressed it, which lent the verse a "strange pungency" at the expense of its sense and content—all these disappeared.

In considering the development of the stages of Pasternak's creative activity, one may designate the period from 1912 to

1916 as a time of learning, of gathering experience, and the establishment of a poetics that was neither mature nor completely independent. The most significant landmark in Pasternak's literary career was the composition of the book *My Sister Life* in 1917. Work on the book proceeded in an unusually concentrated, turbulent, and intense fashion, and bears witness to the flight of poetic inspiration and the sudden, powerful burst of poetic energy thrust into this book. Later, after the appearance of the collection *Themes and Variations*, which was published in 1923 and which is in many ways a continuation and offshoot of *My Sister Life*, there begins the period of intense epic efforts on the part of the poet during the years 1923–1930—the work on *Sublime Disease*, the historico-revolutionary poems *1905*, *Lieutenant Shmidt*, and the novel in verse *Spektorsky*.

During the 1920's Pasternak joined the literary society "Lef" [6] (V. Mayakovsky, N. Aseyev, S. Tretyakov, O. Brik, N. Chuzhak, and others). The aesthetic tendencies of "Lef" toward an emphatically tendentious and agitational art and its preaching of utilitarianism and technicism were remote from his own views. The temporary and very loose connection of Pasternak with the members of "Lef" was strengthened by his friendship with Mayakovsky and Aseyev and some degree of common striving for prosodic innovations and for a renewal of contemporary poetic language. But Pasternak felt that he was a foreign body among the members of "Lef," and he stated this openly in 1928. We should note, by the way, that Pasternak took no part in the group regimentation, the adherence to a sort of school, or to the clearly defined literary platform. Even in the early, pre-Revolutionary period, when he was in concert with the Futurists, he reinterpreted futurism in a different, rather impressionistic way and was irked by the narrowness of the group to which he belonged.

When he had finished the larger part of the work on the historical poems, Pasternak turned at the beginning of the 1930's to lyric verse (the book *Second Birth*). He visibly changes his lyrical tonality and manner of depiction, and develops in the direction of greater clarity and classic simplicity of poetic language. The process continued and was accompanied in his work by a temporary loss of energy and by long interruptions in his activity.

The 1930's were the most difficult and critical years for the poet. During this period he produced few original works and devoted most of his energy to translating, which from 1934 on became quite regular and continued to the end of hs life (translations of Georgian poets, of Shakespeare, Goethe, Schiller, Kleist, Rilke, Verlaine and others).

Not until the beginning of 1941, on the eve of the war, did the poet overcome the crisis and enter a period of upsurge in his creative activity. A series of first-class verses appeared in the book *On Early Trains* (1943). This book has direct connections with the lyric poems of Pasternak from the 1940's and 1950's which crown his career (Pasternak died May 30, 1960).

During the 1920's and 1930's and later right up to the last years of the poet's life we observe his constant attempts to reconsider and re-evaluate his literary past. Well known, for example, is the statement he made in 1956, namely, that he did not like his own style until 1940. Similar self-evaluations, not always fair to himself, lay in Pasternak's nature, for he preferred not to accumulate but to get rid of early things for the sake of further achievements. In his understanding art is a constant dedication, movement, and concern not with results but with discoveries.

> Creativity's goal is self-devotion,
> And not sensation and not success.
> It's disgraceful to know nothing
> Yet be a saying in everyone's mouth.
>
> One must leave gaps in one's fate,
> But not in one's writings,
> Marking off on the margins
> Passages and chapters of a full life.

The persistent tendency to reshape his views of art and style, observable throughout his whole life, does not preclude, however, a great internal unity in his works from 1917 to 1960. It is an integral part of his dominant ideas and stylistic tendencies. Right after *My Sister Life,* which established the aesthetic and life credo of the poet, Pasternak underwent a change, but without destroying the basis of his lyrics. He filled out and developed what took shape in this book which had the ring of being his original discovery.

In drawing the outlines of Pasternak's poetic development, let us try to enter the individual world of the artist, devoting meanwhile great attention to his philosophy of life, to the texture of his language, and to the metaphorical structure of his poetry. In order to do this we shall not stay with a consistently chronological exposition of his works and we shall turn directly to poems written at different times and often in varying styles, but belonging together and corresponding in various basic stimuli and resolutions.

2

A central place in Pasternak's lyrics belongs to nature. The content of his nature lyrics is broader than the usual descriptions of landscapes. In writing about spring and winter, or about rain and dawn, Pasternak tells about the nature of life itself and of the way of the world, and preaches a faith in life, which, it seems to us, predominates in his poetry and constitutes its moral basis. In his sense life is something unconditional, eternal and absolute, an all-pervading element and a great wonder. The sense of wonder in the presence of the miracle of existence—this is the stance in which Pasternak persevered, always struck and spellbound by his discovery: "it is spring again."

> Where have I already heard
> Snatches of speech of yesteryear?
> Ah, it's once again, I suppose, today that
> The brook came forth from the grove at night.
> And it is, as in earlier times, that
> The mill-pond swelled and
> Thrust out its ice-floes.
> It is truly a new miracle,
> That it is, as before, once again spring.
> That's what it is.

There is a fresh and healthy quality to his landscapes. O. Mandelshtam correctly noted that "to read the verses of Pasternak is to cleanse one's throat, to strengthen one's breath and refresh one's lungs—such verses should make one immune to tuberculosis." *

> The dawn swings the candle wildly
> And sets aflame the martin.
> I search my memory and say:
> Let life be ever new again!
>
> The dawn is a rifleshot into the dark.
> A bang—and there dies in flight
> The flame of the rifle's wad.
> Let life be ever new again.

From day to day, from verse to verse Pasternak does not weary of repeating this vital, salutary, all-conquering quality of nature. Trees, grass, clouds, and streams are in his verses invested with the right of speaking in the name of life itself and of forcing us onto the path of truth and good. ("On earth there is no grief such that the snow would not cure it.") The most valuable and beautiful thing may be contained in a willow tree:

> When Desdemona's time for singing came—
> And little time was left for her to live,
> Not of love, her star, she sang—
> But of willow, willow was her sobbing song.
>
> When Ophelia's time for singing came,—
> She'd had enough of bitter dreams,—
> With what trophies did she fade away?
> With a wand of willow and of celandine.

Landscape in Pasternak's works is often not an object of depiction, but the subject of activity and the chief hero and motive force of events. All the fullness of life in the variety of its phenomena is placed in a bit of nature which, it seems, is capable of performing acts of feeling and of thinking. The

---

* O. Mandelshtam, "Boris Pasternak," *Rossiya,* No. 6, 1923, p. 29.

comparison of nature with man, peculiar to poetry, reaches such a degree in Pasternak's verse that the landscape appears in the role of mentor and moral model. "The forest lets fall its crimson dress"—this is the firmly established, classical formula in Russian poetry. With Pasternak we often meet the reverse course of thought: "You throw off your dress as the grove throws off its leaves. . . ." "Your meaning is unselfish, like the air . . ."—thus the poet addresses his beloved. Man is defined by means of nature and in comparison with nature finds his place in the world. This power, or more accurately this intercession of nature does not belittle man, because in obeying and becoming like her, he follows the voice of life. At the same time nature in the works of Pasternak is so close to man that, while he is being pushed aside and replaced by landscapes, he comes to life again in her. The degree of personification of the word is here such that, walking in woods and fields, we are concerned basically not with the pictures of these woods and fields, but with their characters and psychology.

Of his stay in Venice Pasternak recalls: "And thus this happiness fell to my lot too. And I was happy to discover that day after day one can have a rendezvous with a bit of built-up area just as if with a living person." * In his poetry a similar kind of rendezvous with landscape took place, a landscape understood as an inimitable, independent personality:

> And here you enter the birch wood.
> And you and it look at each other.

With Pasternak nature takes on all the traits of an individual person. We are accustomed to the fact that "it rains," and now we find out: "The rain tapped at the doors, more from sleep than from the roofs, more forgetful than timid . . ." Pasternak's landscapes have their own disposition, sympathies, favorite amusements—the clouds play catch, the storm is busy photographing, and the brooks sing a song. His landscape is also endowed with portrait-like features:

---

* Boris Pasternak, *Okhrannaya Gramota* (*Safe Conduct*), Leningrad, 1931, p. 81

> And the forest is shedding and
> Sweat flows off in many drops.
> And they shine, shine like lips
> Unwiped by human hand,
> The willow wands and leaves of oak,
> And the footprints by the pond.

"The face of the blue," "the face of the river," "the face of the storm tearing off its mask"—such is the world of nature, an assemblage of many people and faces.

The poetry of Pasternak is metaphorical through and through. But the metaphorical character of all these comparisons often is not so much intellectually perceived as it is an action taking place right before our eyes. Not in an allegorical sense, but quite literally "The garden cries" or "the thunderstorm runs," and thus are present in all the verisimilitude of an inimitable act, shared by all:

> A storm at the gates! Outside!
> Transforming and frolicking
> In the dark, in peals of thunder, in silver,
> It runs along the gallery.

A metaphor in the poetics of Pasternak fulfills above all the task of connecting. It binds together, instantaneously and dynamically, into a single unit the different parts of reality and thereby personifies, as it were, the great unity of the world and the interaction and mutual interpenetration of phenomena. Pasternak started from the notion that two objects, placed side by side, will closely interact and penetrate each other, and therefore he connects them, not by their resemblance, but by proximity, using the metaphor as the connecting link. The world is written "as a whole," but the work on its reunification is carried out with the help of the figurative meaning of words:

> It's spring, as I come from the street,
> Where the poplar's amazed, the distance trembles,
> And the house fears its collapse, where
> The air is blue like a bundle of laundry
> Of a person dismissed from the hospital.

The last line lets us understand why "the distance is afraid" and "the house is afraid of collapse"—they too were just discharged from the hospital, like the person from whose bundle the air turned blue.

Landscape and the broader, all-encompassing world acquires with Pasternak an intensified sensitivity. It reacts acutely and instantly to changes taking place in a human being, not only by corresponding to his feelings, thoughts, and moods (as is frequently the case in literature), but by becoming the complete double, the continuation, and alter ego. The mechanics of these transformations are revealed in the prose work "The Tale" of Pasternak. The infatuated hero suddenly remarks: "Of course, the whole street in its compact darkness was entirely Anna. There Seryozha was not alone, but knew this. And it is true, such a thing had not happened to him. Only the feeling was even broader and more precise, and there the help of friends and predecessors was at an end. He saw how hard it was for Anna to be a morning in the city. . . . She silently stood in beauty before him and did not know how to help him. And, dying of grief over the real Arild . . . he saw how, closed around by poplars as though with icy towels, she was engulfed by clouds and slowly tossed brick, Gothic towers." *

Let us be alert: the feeling taking hold of Seryozha was broader and more precise than similar phenomena experienced by other people such as friends or predecessors. The point is that here Pasternak is talking about himself and about his differences from his predecessors and contemporaries. His "correspondences" are distinguished from the traditional ones (landscape as an accompaniment to the experiences of man) by the very breadth and precision of the image which arises: everything—round about and entirely—is transformed into Anna Arild.

In doing this Pasternak is moving very close to the metaphorical ventures of Mayakovsky, who compared the world to the passion and suffering of his hero ("From my laughter and

* Boris Pasternak, *Vozdushnye Puti* (*Air Ways*), Moskva, 1933, p. 134.

my weeping the ugly face of the room was mowed down with horror. . . .") But with Mayakovsky the extension of an emotion to reality is motivated by an anxiety carried to an extreme degree of tension ("I cannot be calm"), and by the force and grandeur of the psychic experiences of the poet. Pasternak is "calmer," "quieter," "more restrained" than Mayakovsky; this kind of dislocation is in Pasternak's case evoked not so much by the exceptional nature of the passion as by the subtlety of the feeling for reflexes and resonances and the sensitivity of everything for its neighbor. The corresponding reaction here does not attain such hyperbolic dimensions, rather each drop casts a reflection; all objects, even the most insignificant, influence each other and imitate the other's characteristics. In Pasternak's poetry one must not separate man from his environment nor living feelings from dead matter. By means of the metaphorical "cursive writing" reality is depicted as a single unity in the blending of the different components and in the intersecting of boundaries and contours.

Pasternak was captivated by the task of establishing within the limits of poetry an all-embracing atmosphere of existence and life and of the poet's transmission of "the feeling of intimacy with the universe." In his poems the lyrical narrative is not developed consecutively from one statement to the next, but jumps "above the barriers," tending toward broad sketching in and bold pictorial vividness of the whole. With the aid of allegories and the figurative meanings of words, things are displaced from their long-occupied places and enter the stormy, chaotic movement which tends to impress reality in its natural disorder.

> I want to go home, into the vastness
> Of my room which inspires sorrow.
> I enter, doff my coat, collect my wits,
> And am illumined by the fires of the streets.
>
> Through the thin-ribbed partitions
> I pass, pass through like light.
> I go through like form entering form
> And like an object cleaving an object.

The distinctive position in this transparent space cut across by metaphors is occupied by the image of the poet and artist. With the exception of a few works, he is not marked off and displayed as a completely independent and distinct character. In contradistinction to Blok, Tsvetayeva, Mayakovsky, or Esenin, the lyrical part is comparatively rarely done in the first person. Then the personality of the poet was the central focus, and his works, extended by a diary kept over many years, prolonged by a narrative "about the times and about myself," constituted something experienced and a dramatic biography which was enacted before the eyes of the readers and was surrounded by the halo of legend. Pasternak avoids this concept and terms it "romantic," "the biography of a poet for the sake of show." * He tells little about himself and carefully removes and conceals his "ego." When reading his poems the illusion can arise that the author is not present at all and that he is also absent as the narrator or witness who sees everything that is depicted. Nature is explained in its own name:

> The clouds through the open windows
> Sat down on their needlework like doves.
> They noticed: the fences were lean
> From water, noticeably, the crosses, barely.

It is not the poet but the "clouds which noticed," just as in another place it is not the poet who remembers his childhood, but "the snow remembers in passing: naps they were called, with a whisper and syrup the day sank behind the cradle. . . ." In one of Pasternak's last poems, "Frosts," we encounter again a somewhat unusual picture in which the landscape and the observer seem to exchange roles and the picture itself looks at the man standing in front of it:

> The cold morning's sun stands in foggy air
> Like a pillar of fire in the midst of smoke.
> I too, as in a bad photograph,
> Am completely invisible to it.

* Boris Pasternak, *Okhrannaya Gramota* (*Safe Conduct*), pp. 111–113.

> While it does not emerge from the mist,
> And shines upon the meadow behind the lake,
> The trees can barely see me
> On the distant shore.

If Mayakovsky or Tsvetayeva wish to speak for the whole world in the first person, then Pasternak prefers for the world to speak for him and instead of him: "not I about spring, but spring about me," and "not I about the garden, but the garden about me."

> At the wattle-fence
> Among wet branches with a pale
> Wind an argument went on. I
> Stood still—'t was about me!

Nature itself appears in the role of the main lyric hero. But the poet is everywhere and nowhere. He is not a detached glance at a spread-out panorama, but its double who becomes now the sea, now the woods. In the poem "The Weeping Garden," for example, the usual parallelism "I and the garden" is replaced by the inverse equation "I am the garden," and Pasternak with the same words tells about "it" and "himself":

> It's horrible!—it drips and listens:
> Is it then the only one in the world
> That pushes a branch at the window,
> Or is somebody watching . . .
>
> I shall lift it to my lips and listen:
> Am I then the only one in the world,
> Ready to weep on occasion,
> Or is somebody watching.

This identity with nature, without witnesses or onlookers, lends Pasternak's verses a special intimacy and genuineness.

A garden also appears as the hero of his well-known poem "The Mirror." The garden, reflected in the mirror and living as it were a second life, is seen from a secret depth of the mirror: "The huge garden, is given no peace in the hall in the mirror —and does not break the glass!" It is interesting that in an

early publication this poem was emphatically called "I Myself": the story about the mirror which absorbed the garden
was also for the poet a story about himself. By means of just
such a mirror which, like him, has a relation to life, Pasternak
achieves self-awareness. And in the poem "A Girl," which continues the figurative pattern of "The Mirror," the opposite connection is established—the mirror recognizes itself in the
branch which runs in from the garden, and the poet sees in
nature his own likeness and repetition:

> Beloved, great one as big as the garden,
> By nature sister! A second mirror!

3

Such is the nature of Pasternak's artistic procedure in a book
with a title which sounds like a poetic declaration—*My Sister
Life*. In this way the unity of poet and nature is confirmed and
this unity is the first and basic tenet of the poet.

> It seemed the alpha and the omega—
> Life and I were made alike;
> The whole year through, with snow or not,
> She lived like my alter ego,
> And I called her sister.

It is the profound conviction of Pasternak that poetry is both
the direct consequence and creation of life. The artist does
not invent images, but rather gathers them on the street, helping the creativity of nature but never replacing it with his own
meddling.

> It happened that snow brings abruptly that
> Which just now comes to mind.
> With its twilight I paint
> My house, and canvas, and daily life
> All winter the snow writes sketches,
> And in sight of the passers-by
> From here I transfer them to the poem,
> And steal and hide and copy them.

The origin of art in the bosom of nature is a favorite theme of Pasternak. Presented in different variations, it is unchanged in one respect: Life itself is the primal source of poetry, and the poet is at the best her partner and co-author, for whom there is left only the task of observing and wondering while collecting his willing rhymes in his notebook. This is the reason for the prevalence of literary terms in Pasternak's landscapes:

> As epigraph for this book:
> Hoarse deserts . . .
>
> . . . .
>
> The remnants of the downpour lie dirty
> In clusters, and long before dawn
> They'll scribble their acrostic,
> Leaving bubbles in the rhyme.
>
> . . . .
>
> Call this as you wish,
> But all about the forest, dressed,
> Ran like the plot of a tale,
> And recognized its interest.
>
> . . . .
>
> And now come the days of blossoming,
> And lindens at the waist of the fences
> Scatter, together with the shade
> An irresistible aroma . . .
>
> He composes in these moments,
> When he touches deeply,
> The theme and content of a book,
> And park and flowerbeds are the binding.

This identification of art and life, of poetry and nature, and the transfer of the author's rights to the landscape serve in general one single goal: in presenting for our attention verses composed by nature itself, the author convinces us so to speak of his integrity. But integrity and authenticity of an image appear as Pasternak's highest criterion for art. His views of literature and his poetic practice are filled with the concern: "to succeed in not distorting the voice of life which resounds within us."

"The inability to find and tell the truth is a defect which no

amount of skill in telling what is not the truth can hide," *
said Pasternak. Realism, in his understanding of the word (the
intensified sensitivity and sincerity of the artist in the convey-
ing of real life, which, like the personality of a human being,
is always integral and unique), is inherent in any true art and
reveals itself in the works of Leo Tolstoy and Lermontov, of
Chopin and Blok, Shakespeare and Verlaine; whereas Romanticism for Pasternak was rather a negative term, because it
tends to let the imagination run free and easily ignores the
veracity of what is being depicted.

This side of his aesthetic views is all the more interesting
since Pasternak for a long time was connected with a group of
Futurists, and later with the "Lef" group, among whom the so-
called formal method had great currency, a method which
treated an artistic work as the sum of technical devices. "Contemporary trends," Pasternak wrote at the beginning of the
1920's, "imagined that art is like a fountain, whereas it is really
a sponge. They decided that it should gush forth, whereas it
should dry up and become saturated. They figured out that it
should be assigned to the means of its figurative nature,
whereas it is composed of the organs of understanding. It must
always be present in the observers and see most purely, recep-
tively, and truly, but in our days it got to know make-up
and dressing-room and it lets itself be shown from the
screen. . . ." †

The same image, "poetry-sponge," recurs in one of the early
poems of Pasternak, who considers a heightened sensitivity the
decisive factor in his work:

> Poetry! Be thou a Grecian sponge
> Among sucker-fish, and amid the sticky greens
> I'd set thee on the damp plank
> Of the garden's green bench.
>
> Grow luxuriant branches and farthingales,
> Absorb clouds and ravines,
> And at night, poetry, I shall
> Wring thee out on the thirsty paper.

* Boris Pasternak, "Neskol'ko polozheniy" ("Some positions"), Sb.
Sovremennik, Moskva, No. 1, 1922, p. 6.
† *Ibid.*, p. 5

Upon becoming acquainted with the literary views of Pasternak one is struck by the insistence of his warnings: do not interfere, do not frighten away! These misgivings are for the most part directed against a biased attitude toward nature, against thinking in borrowed, ready-made or stereotype formulas, and against cliché in the broad sense of the word. The power, purity, and immediacy of comprehension he affirms as the necessary condition of art, and for him innovation coincides with the search for the greatest naturalness and veracity of portrayal. For this reason he remarked in his article on the works of Chopin that Chopin's work was "thoroughly original not because of its lack of similarity with his rivals, but because of its similarity to the nature about which he wrote." *

Understood in this way art presupposes a new look at the world, which is as it were understood for the first time by the artist. Pasternak considered that the initial moment of the creative process consisted in our "ceasing to recognize reality" and endeavoring to speak of reality with a lack of constraint and with the artlessness of the first poet on earth. This is the source of the accents and tendencies peculiar to his lyric poetry: the exceptional and fantastic quality of ordinary phenomena, which he prefers to all fairy tales and fictions, and the morning-fresh view (the characteristic stance of a person just waking up—"I am waking up. I am wrapped up in discovery . . ."), and the feeling of first creation and the novelty of all that is going on round about ("The whole steppe, as if before the fall. . . .").

It is remarkable that stylization has no place in his poetry. His style and his view of the world preclude any kind of imitation except the imitation of nature. When dealing with a historical person, as for example Balzac, he creates an image closer to Rodin than Balzac in its distinctive features:

> He dreams of freedoms like a lackey,
> Like an old bookkeeper of his pension,
> But the weight in this fist
> Is that of a bricklayer's hammer.

* Boris Pasternak, "Shopen" ("Chopin"), *Leningrad,* No. 15–16, **1945,** p. 22.

A poem dedicated to Anna Akhmatova begins with the claim:

> I believe I am selecting words
> Like your original creation.
> But I'm wrong—that's all the same,
> I still won't part with my error.

Further on, while revealing the essence of Akhmatova's lyric poetry, Pasternak nevertheless remains true to himself and does not write "in imitation of Akhmatova." Unable to part with his "error," he selects words which do not recall another's style but the creation of the world. Just for this reason Pasternak is not afraid to come very close at times to the classics and runs the risk, without lapsing into banality, of choosing as epigraph such verses from anthologies as "A golden cloud spent the night on the breast of a giant rock," or he risked beginning a poem with the well-known "On the shore of the desolate waves he stood, full of great thoughts." Such encounters with classic images were not dangerous for him: he was insured against literary reminiscences by the freshness of his view and the novelty of his manner and could permit himself, as in *Themes and Variations,* to take deliberately traditional images as the basis of a work while giving it a profoundly original treatment.

In his poetic activity Pasternak came into contact with the very broad sphere of artistic phenomena of both the past and the present. Because of the very individual character of his view of the world and of his manner, he did not tend to sever his contacts with his cultural heritage, but rather to maintain constant contact with it and an affirmation of the idea of connection with it and the historical continuity in the growth of art. These tendencies also separated him in the 1910's and 1920's from the Futurist group which was imbued with the spirit of the destruction and rupture of artistic traditions.

In a questionnaire explaining the relation of contemporary authors to classic literature (1927), Pasternak wrote: "I believe that there is now, less than at any time, a basis for departing from the aesthetics of Pushkin. By aesthetics in the case of an artist I mean his notions of the nature of art, the role of art in history and his own responsibility to it." Here also he explained what concrete influence Pushkin had had on his work: "Pushkin's aesthetics are so broad and elastic that they permit different definitions at different ages. The impetuous imagery of Pushkin means that he may be understood impressionistically, as I understood him 15 years ago in harmony with my own tastes and the trends then current in literature. Now I have broadened my understanding so that it includes elements of a moral nature." *

Indicative in its own way is also the fact of Pasternak's literary biography that he arrived on the scene during the early period of the Futurists in the group "Centrifuge," where, in contradistinction to the most aggressive tendencies of cubist-futurism, there prevailed a more tolerant attitude both to the poetic tradition of the nineteenth century and to the nearest teachers, namely the Symbolists.†

As to the "precepts" of Russian symbolism, Pasternak's sympathies belonged to I. Annensky,[7] A. Bely, and especially to Blok, in whose works he sought first and foremost the same "impetuous imagery" of a poetic picture, understood in an impressionistic spirit, that was characteristic of his own style of the period, in which an "instantaneous picturesqueness that indicates motion" was dominant. Many years later, in a biographical sketch of 1956, Pasternak confessed that of the various qualities of Blok's verse it was the "Blokian impetuosity," the "rambling intentness" of his view, the "fluency" of his observations and sketches that were closest to him and that made the greatest impression on his style. "Adjectives without nouns, predicates without subjects, games of hide-and-seek, agitation, briskly sparkling figures of speech, and abruptness—thus this style suited the spirit of the times, which was concealed and secreted, underground and hardly emerging from the cellars,

* "Na literaturnom postu" ("On Literary Guard"), No. 5–6, 1927, p. 62.
† V. Bryusov notes that futurism "was combined with the attempt to connect their activity with the creative art of preceding generations," and that they were "more closely connected with the pledges of the past." (A.S.), *Russkaya Mysl*, June, 1914.

and explaining itself with conspiratorial language which had as its principal person the city and as its chief event the street . . . This St. Petersburg of Blok was the most real of the St. Petersburgs painted by the artists of recent times . . . At the same time the image of the city was composed of traits chosen by such a nervous hand and infused with such inspiration that the whole was transformed into a captivating phenomenon of the most uncommon inner world." *

It is not difficult to note that Blok receives here, so to speak, a typically Pasternakian christening. This very distinctly expressed individual point of view of the works of predecessors and contemporaries is displayed in the interpretation of Shakespeare, Verlaine, Rilke, Tolstoy, Chekhov, Mayakovsky, and other authors close to the poet. Pasternak was always biased and at times paradoxical in his aesthetic evaluations and treatment of others. Here especially there appears the profound originality of his artistic nature, which combines a taste for the traditions of world art with the spirit of the boldest innovating. He wrote of his own youth in poetry and the influence of his nearest predecessors in *Safe Conduct*: "What was that art?" It was the young art of Skryabin, Blok, Komissarzhevskaya,[8] Bely —an outstanding, captivating and original art. And it was so striking that not only did it not evoke thoughts of change, but on the contrary for the sake of the greatest durability it wished to repeat from the very beginning, only more quickly, more ardently, and more wholeheartedly. It wished to retell at one stroke what was unthinkable without passion—passion was a deviation—and in this way something new was achieved. However the new did not arise by abolition of the old, as is customarily thought, but quite on the contrary in the delight in reproducing models." †

In the attempt to look at reality and poetry with new vision, to refresh the aesthetic understanding of the word and, in harmony with this, refashion an artistic system, Pasternak had much in common with a number of poets who, on the eve of the Revolution and afterward, were struggling for the libera-

* Archiv B. L. Pasternaka (Archives of B. L. Pasternak).
† Boris Pasternak, *Okhrannaya Gramota* (*Safe Conduct*), p. 91–92.

tion of literature from the old forms. In this broad movement, which included all spheres of art in the twentieth century, there was a price to pay and there was some empty striving for originality, but the movement also contained the healthy and refreshing strength without which the growth of a truly contemporary art is unimaginable, and the demand was made for life itself, which does not submit to depiction in the language of outmoded canons and clichés. Mayakovsky said of this:

> And suddenly
> Everything
> Rushes along,
> Rending the voice,
> To throw off the rags of worn-out names.

The same cry is heard in Pasternak's lines:

> What does it mean, what in the universe—a mask?
> What does it mean that there are no such latitudes,
> Which would not be called upon
> To close one's mouth with putty for the winter?

> But things tear off their masks,
> Lose both power and honor,
> When they have cause to sing,
> When there is occasion for a downpour.

As is generally true of Pasternak, the renewal of poetry presupposes here the liberation of things from their literal lack of personality and the mask of literary clichés.

In searching for new words capable of returning to the world its individual face, Pasternak turned to living, conversational speech and took part in the resolute democratization of poetic language which during the 1910's and 1920's concerned many poets and which proceeded most violently in the works of Mayakovsky. But if the broadening of the lexicon proceeded in Mayakovsky's case chiefly at the price of the language of the loud-voiced street, where vulgarisms were mixed with the jargon of political speeches and where the change was dictated by the expansion of *the* theme, namely, that of including the city, the war, and the Revolution, then Pasternak for a long time remained within the circle of traditional themes worn out by poets of the past and the present. But he spoke in a new fashion of the traditional springtimes and sunsets and told of the beauty of nature not with the language of conventional poetic banalities, but with the distinctive words of our everyday life and common prose. At the same time he returned to this language its lost freshness and its aesthetic meaning. A trite subject in his reworking turned into a living event.

In introducing into the high style of poetic language the language of ordinary living and of urban contemporary times, Pasternak did not shun officialese, colloquial expressions, and conversational idioms. In their new application these forms, worn down in our ordinary life like coins, sound fresh and unexpected. For this reason the cliché of general use becomes a weapon in the struggle with the literary commonplace. Pasternak tended to express himself on the most lofty themes without beating about the bush and in a homespun style, and he conveyed the agitated grandeur of the Caucasus quite simply in the tone of an unceremonious ordinary talk—"be not quite oneself," or "The Caucasus was all there, as if in the palm of one's hand, all there like a rumpled bed. . . ." His originality consists in the fact that he poeticizes the world with the aid of prosaic phrases which introduce into his verse the truth of life, and therefore they transport the verses from the sphere of invented fiction into the category of genuine poetry.

In the tale "The Childhood of Lyuvers," when tracing the inner growth of the heroine in her encounter with reality, Pasternak remarks: "Upon ceasing to be a poetic trifle, life strayed from the stern, gloomy tale so much that it became prose and transformed into fact." * The prose of a real fact serves in his works as the source of what is poetic, because through it the credibility of the real course of things is communicated to the images. In this connection Pasternak's paradoxical remark becomes understandable: We drag everyday life into prose for the sake of poetry. We introduce prose into poetry for the sake of music." † Later, referring to Shakespeare's *Romeo and*

---

* Boris Pasternak, *Vozdushnye Puti* (*Air Ways*), p. 20.
† Boris Pasternak, *Okhrannaya Gramota* (*Safe Conduct*), p. 22.

Juliet, he once again declared that prose in poetry was the champion of life: "This is an example of the highest poetry which, in its best examples, is always saturated with the simplicity and freshness of prose." *

Prose constructions and a colloquial vocabulary lend Pasternak's images a very concrete quality, give substance to abstract concepts, and bring them closer to us. The syntactical and rhythmic structure of his verses is directed at the same goal: to establish such a flexible poetic system that it will, by its own tonality, remind one (be it understood, only remind) of conversational speech and permit one to speak in the language of poetry just as unconstrainedly as we speak in ordinary life. He develops a poetic phrase in all its complexity of composition, interrupts himself, drops a few connecting links, as happens in everyday practice, but the main thing is that he strives for free, unfettered poetic speech which possesses a broad "breath" and which is based on the development of large and integral intonational periods. In the works of other poets Pasternak especially esteemed the ability to think and speak in verse not in separate lines but in strophes, periods, and locutions, and in particular he praised highly in this connection the verbal art of Tsvetayeva, which he considered related to his own.

But Pasternak did not reduce this problem to a simple approximation of verse to conversational forms. Naturalness and lack of constraint in intonation were correlated in practice with the more general aesthetic demand which he set himself, namely, the demand for breadth and integrity of an artistic understanding whose mission it was to create in verse some unified panorama or atmosphere of life. This may be clearly felt, for example, in the poem "The Death of a Poet," dedicated to Mayakovsky: the life of a genius in the ages, his sudden death, rumors and the confusion of the witnesses of the catastrophe, and the noisy spring street presented at the same time as a fragment of the explosive drama and as its wretched accompaniment, and all this collected into one lump and set in mo-

---

* Boris Pasternak, "Zametki k perevodam shekspirskikh tragediy" ("Notes to the translations of Shakespeare's Tragedies"), Sb. *Literaturnaya Moskva,* Moskva, 1956, p. 198.

tion by the irresistible force of a voice which bursts forth right
after the event, embraces and surrounds it and embeds it in
powerful, resonant periods which tumble over each other:

> They didn't believe, said he raving,
> But recognized him from all others,
> They equated his final time
> With the houses of officials and shop-women,
> With flats, trees and on them
> Rooks that cry from noonday heat
> Angrily at rooks for the fools
> To mind their business and let him be.
> Only on their faces a moist motion,
> As if in the folds of a broken dragnet.
>
> It was a day, a harmless one, more
> Harmless than ten previous days.
> They crowded about in the hall,
> As if your shot would scatter them,
> When, flattening them, there would splash
> From the flow of bream and the flash
> Of the pike, heaped up in the sedge,
> Like the sigh of empty riverbeds . . .

Pasternak gladly resorts to apparent digressions (for example, the rooks on the trees at the beginning of the poem)
which do in fact speak of the broad stops and turns of the intonation and involve in the action all the surroundings, thereby
leaving no neutral background in the poem. Often he seems
to lose his footing and seems to return to what has been said
and begins from the beginning, so that, by going round and
round, he makes forward progress, fitting the complete picture
in the involuntary course of his speech. In spite of the great
verbal effort and the high degree of mastery, his verses do not
produce the impression of elegantly polished baubles. On the
contrary, his is rather an awkward language, at times even im-
pacted to the point of being tongue-tied, with unexpected interruptions and repetitions, a language "breathless" and "explosive," replete with cumbersome words that get in each
other's way. Later his language becomes light, winged, and
transparent, but preserves the same immediacy. In this naive,
artless effusion of words, which at first glance is not directed

by the poet but carries itself, Pasternak achieves the desired naturalness of the living Russian tongue. The characteristic which he ascribes to the poetic method of Paul Verlaine may in many respects be applied to himself:

"He gave to the language in which he wrote that unlimited freedom, which was his discovery in lyric poetry and which is met with only in masters of prose dialogue in the novel and the drama. The Parisian phraseology in all its purity and captivating accuracy flew in from the street and took its place in the poetic line entire, without the least effort, as the melodic material for all following construction. In this progressive lack of constraint lies the main charm of Verlaine. The turns of French speech were for him indivisible. He wrote in whole locutions, not in words, and he did not hone them down nor rearrange them.

If compared with the naturalness of Musset, Verlaine is natural in an unexpected way, that is, he is simple not in order to be believed but in order not to interfere with the voice of life which issues forth from him." *

In Pasternak's poems special significance is attached to the tonal organization of the verse. This is not identical with the rhyme, although this side of his poetics is also thoroughly new and varied (not for nothing did Bryusov consider him the founder of a new rhyme to a greater degree than Mayakovsky). In Pasternak's verses it is not only the ends of the lines which rhyme, but essentially any words within the text. Characteristic of him is the tonal similarity of words which are next to each other or at some distance from each other:

> Paris in golden corpuscles, in particles,
> In rain, as if in revenge, long-awaited . . .

This phenomenon is broader than onomatopoeia and more meaningful than the usual melodic regulation of language in poetry. The phonetic connections appear as the expression of semantic connections, and the similarity of sounds strengthens

* Boris Pasternak, "Pol Mari Verlen" ("Paul Marie Verlaine"), *Literatura i Isskustvo,* April 1, 1944.

adjacent images and speaks, in the last analysis, of the con-
sonance of different interrelated and interwoven aspects of
life. The phonetic instrumentation aids the transference of
thought from one object to another, and this is realized by
means of the metaphor and the poet's striving to demonstrate
and emphasize the inner unity of the world. In Pasternak's
exemplary definition rhyme is not "the repetition of lines" but
immeasurably more: "In it is heard the rumble of roots and
the buzz of bosoms," and through it "Dissonance enters our
world as the truth."

Such intense attention to the "tonal quality" of words and
their selection according to their phonetic-semantic appropri-
ateness reminds one of Khlebnikov.[9] But the latter made
phonetics logical, connecting each sound with a definite abstract concept and with an exact "power instrument" which
calculated the laws for its poetic cosmogony. The a priori element, the compulsion of meanings for sounds, the linguistic
rationalism as well as the wholesale insistence not on the concrete sense of a word but on its hidden, abstract content were
foreign to Pasternak. In his verses bridges are thrown among
words of similar sound that are not abstract-logical but metaphorical and associative, and they are motivated by the ad-
jacency of nearly related phenomena or by similarities which
simply arise by chance.

> The boat beats in the sleepy breast,
> Willows hung down, kiss in the clavicles,
> In the elbow, in the oarlocks—, o, wait,
> This might well happen to anyone!

Here *uklyuchiny* (oarlocks) appears beside *klyuchitsami*
(clavicles) for the same reason that willows kiss and the
boat beats in the breast, that is, before us Pasternak has
displayed his usual mutual correspondences of nature, man,
and objects, underlined here by the tonal analogy.

In the movement of his poetic language frequent tonal harmonies arise unintentionally and as if involuntarily. They do
not destroy that everyday and conversational intonation which
forms the basis of the verse. Just like his metaphors these

tonal harmonies are optional and fortuitous, because "the more fortuitous the truer the verses are composed."

In Pasternak's verses Y. Tynyanov[10] noted "the fortuitousness turns out to be a stronger tie than the closest logical connection." "We do not possess the connection of things which he gives, it is fortuitous, but when he establishes it, it reminds us of something, it was already there somewhere—and the image becomes obligatory." *

The explanation for this fact must be sought in the peculiarities of Pasternak's language. We believe in the connections which he offers (metaphorical, tonal, and so forth) in spite of all their unexpectedness, just because they are expressed colloquially, naturally, "without pressure," as something quite self-understood. What is fortuitous here only helps the naturalness. The naturalness of intonation serves as a guarantee of the veracity of the lyric narrative which is being told.

The poetic language of Pasternak of the 1910's and 1920's is often very complex and difficult to understand. On the one hand the oversaturation with images was an obstacle, an oversaturation which arose from the author's attempt to take into account and convey with linguistic means all the manifold interrelations of life. Pasternak knew only too well that two objects, placed side by side, in their combination result in a third object. He tenaciously refused to divide the world into pieces, and wrote a whole, where everything was whimsically and chaotically intermixed, where the poet did not forget for a minute "what the visible thing becomes when people begin to see it." † Complexity, therefore, was the consequence of too many items. At the same time, having plunged nature into the stream of conversational language, Pasternak dislodged many concepts from the channel of customary associations and provided them with new ones, which, although adopted from our immediate surroundings, were unusual because they were not used before in such combinations. The simplest and most natural means of expression then became incomprehensible for

* Yuri Tynyanov, *Arkhaisty i novatory* (*Archaicists and Innovators*), Leningrad, 1929, p. 566.
† Boris Pasternak, *Okhrannaya Gramota* (*Safe Conduct*), p. 85.

an ear accustomed to the fact that in poetry people do not talk the way they do in real life.

In one of the tales of Edgar Allan Poe experienced detectives go astray when seeking a stolen document, while the thief had hidden it by putting it in the most obvious spot. It is just the very obviousness, the author explains, that frequently escapes our observation. Something similar takes place at times with the images of Pasternak: they are "incomprehensible" because they are too close to us and too obvious.

When, for example, in the poem "The Death of a Poet," it is said of the dying man:

> You slept, pressing your cheek to the pillow,
> Slept—at topmost speed
> Rushing again and again with a swoop
> Into the ranks of new legends . . .

the immortality of Mayakovsky, which is the subject of narration here, strides into the future so realistically and not figuratively because it is described with words taken from our daily life, from conversation and business accounting ("into the ranks"). In normal practice these words have become familiar, but to encounter them in verse is a great unexpected rarity, and all the more so in a solemn and sublime poem long since tending toward verbal piety. The destruction of the piety, the lack of canonical form and the freshness probably evoke in the reader the deceptive feeling of some "complexity," although in fact the example cited is not complex in a formal sense, and one needs only to get rid of one's literary blinders and accustomed conventions in understanding a poetic text in order to feel its straightforward incisive content.

Pasternak's linguistic innovations were to a great degree dictated by the search for the greatest state of freedom and naturalness of verbal expression. This is fully disclosed and confirmed in his works of the 1930's and especially of the 1940's and 1950's, and we shall return to this topic. Then those tendencies which earlier were hidden under the cover of the unrestrained Pasternakian imagery became evident and greatly increased. At the very first they were not noticed and were only latently active, completely acknowledged by the author, but far from being available to the reader of Pasternak's verses. In this regard the poet wrote at the beginning of the 1930's in a lyric cycle "Waves":

> In kinship with all that is, believing
> And knowing of the future in life,
> At the end we cannot help but fall, as into heresy,
> Into an unheard-of simplicity.

> But we shall not be spared
> If we do not conceal it.
> Men need it more than anything,
> But understand the complex better.

"Complex" here does not mean what is banal or stereotyped in poetry. Simplicity is asserted as the inner basis, stimulus, and final goal of poetic efforts and quests as yet not concluded.

4

In the poetry of Pasternak the primary place is given to the description of nature (the soul of man, the feeling of love, etc., are also frequently expressed in Pasternak's poetry by means of landscape description). Let us see now how his artistic system could leave its imprint upon his pictures of contemporary history. For dealing with this theme, the poet had all the necessary prerequisites: a sensitive ear for the "voice of life," and freedom from pseudopoetical canons, which forbade him to express himself in the humble language of everyday reality. As is well known, many poets of the first years of the post-revolutionary period ran into great difficulties precisely in this respect and remained limited in their language because of their poor selection of generally used clichés about the "beautiful." Mayakovsky mocked these poets when he wrote: "nightingales—yes, *forsunka* [(1) carburetor, (2) playgirl]—no." What Mayakovsky had in mind was the right of poetry to the use of contemporary vocabulary.

In this respect Pasternak had no problems: the "nightingale" did not exclude for him the "carburetor," and the poisons of aestheticism did not affect his ripe poetry. Another factor might also have prevented him from taking that road and probably did, namely, the understanding of the role and the tasks of art and the fact that he belonged to a poetic type which by its very nature gravitates toward a contemplation of life rather than to its decisive, revolutionary change. Pasternak's attitude toward art as an organ of perception, and his understanding of the role of the artist as an attentive and sensitive observer (but not an immediate participant in the changes) made it possible for him to express directly and adequately the devastating pace of our age. In this sense, both according to his views and character, he is the complete antithesis of Mayakovsky, who once said something to the effect that he and Pasternak seemed to live in the same home but in different parts of the house. The Pasternakian way of understanding poetry as the organ of perception, as an effort to suck in and to drink up the colors of living nature, is completely alien to Mayakovsky. Mayakovsky, entirely absorbed by historical events, affirmed the active poetry of the struggle and did not see in nature anything else but just a material in need of refinement. ("If the Kazbek[11] hinders us—blow it up!") He approaches nature with contemptuous condescension and considers everything created by human hands higher than all the "ant hills" and "grass leaves." In Mayakovsky's definition poetry is a weapon, a gun, production, the primitive weapon of the rebel or if necessary a bayonet, a factory, a uranium mine. Pasternak, on the other hand, ascribed to poetry rather "natural" attributes: "It is an abruptly emitted whistle / It is the cracking of pieces of ice . . ." and so forth. Mayakovsky puts the poet on the same level as a worker, an engineer, a politician, while Pasternak usually is more selective and sometimes even contrasts these functions.

This differentiation of the functions of a poet and those of a politician has been formulated with the greatest clarity and straightforwardness in a prerevolutionary article of Pasternak: "The Black Goblet." The poet and hero, lyrics and history, eternity and time are designated here as categories of different, irreconcilable levels. "Both of them are a priori and absolute," and paying his due respect to "soldiers of absolute history," the author upheld the right of poetry not to be intertwined with time and not to take up the task of "making the history of that tomorrow." *

It is true, though, that Pasternak did move away from these considerations expressed in his early and still immature period. However, echoes and variations of these ideas, in different forms, recur in the later period of his art. He is ready to bestow all the high titles on history, on a hero, or on an active person, but still he sets them apart from the "realm of the poet."

In his relationship to history, just as in his relationship to all natural phenomena, the poet is an absorbent sponge, and not a hammer, crushing the stone. This sponge sucks up the surrounding environment, becomes heavy with the characteristics of the times, but does not become a part of the social-historical existence to the same extent that it is part of nature. In Pasternak's treatment of history one feels a certain detached view of events which one does not find in his treatment of nature. This view is usually very observant, but it still belongs to an observer recording the events meticulously and not to a participant acting in these events.

Pasternak called art the "extreme limit of the epoch" (and not its resultant force) and related the creations of art to the events of history as congenial phenomena on different levels. Thus, according to this idea, Leo Tolstoy is congenial to the revolution. Similarly Pasternak considered his own book of poetry *My Sister Life* as being parallel to the revolutionary times, and he even thought it to be about the Revolution, although there is nothing there about the Revolution or social upheavals, but rather about the most ordinary thunderstorms and dawns, and it would, indeed, be stretching the point too far if one wanted to interpret those poems in an allegorical sense. Nevertheless, history entered Pasternak's art and it did so far back in that period when the poet demonstratively re-

* Boris Pasternak, "Chorny bokal" ("The Black Goblet"), *Vtoroy Sbornik Centrifugy,* Moskva, 1916, p. 42.

fused to be in contact with it and pretended that he did not understand "what kind of thousand years stand here, my dear friends, in our yard." Repercussions of the war and Revolution rolled past like an echo in quite a few of his poems about landscape, and the images of nature bore the stamp of history. As early as 1915–1917, images appeared in his poetry like "heaven on strike" and charging cavalry's tracks on the ice, in order to recall the year 1905, the spirit of "soldier's rebellions and summer lightnings" filled the air, and the clouds reminded him of recruits and POW's:

> The clouds moved over the dusty market places,
> Like recruits marched on the field in the dawn,
> They moved not for an hour, but for eternity

> Like the Austrian POW's
> Like the quiet whisper
> Like a whisper: "Give me some water, lady."

Nature acquires strange characteristics, since it draws them from the world of social storms and class conflicts. The penetration of historical reality into the realm of nature was a natural phenomenon for the poet. He drew the landscape as it appeared in the perception of the contemporary city dweller who, while taking a walk in nature, carries with himself not just the world of his private life but also a whole chain of social-political associations and thus involves the meadows and the forests in the circle of those events amidst which his life is being lived out.

After the Revolution these historicized landscapes in Pasternak's art undergo a special development. Sometimes they even develop into the symbols of revolutionary Russia, just as in his poem, "The Kremlin in the Snow at the End of 1918." The snowstorm coincides here with a figurative storm which breaks out over the vast areas of the new era and bears it relentlessly into the future. This is not just a storm, but the elements of time, the weather of the Revolution perceived with enthusiasm and depicted with the brush of an experienced landscape-painter:

Last night the Kremlin, the incomparable,
And somehow strange, all covered with foam,
In the rigging of so many winters,
Vented its fury upon the present winter.

And the grandiose building, all covered with the past
Like the visions of a prophet
Is hurled, terrible and stopping at nothing,
Through the unspent part of the year, into the 1919th.

In a chapter that was intended by Pasternak as a part of an autobiographical sketch, Pasternak recalled the events of 1917: "Forty years have passed. From such a distance in the past the voices of the crowds are not carried to us any more: the voices of the people who met day and night in the summer squares under the open sky, as they met in the old *veche*.[12] But even from this distance I still see these meetings, like soundless spectacles or frozen tableaus. . . . The simple people opened up their souls and talked about the most important things: how and for what one should live and what means to use to establish the only meaningful and worthwhile existence. The infectious and all-embracing quality of their enthusiasm tore down the barriers between man and nature. During the remarkable summer of 1917, in the interlude between two revolutions, it appeared as if not only the people participated in the discourse, but together with them also the roads, the trees, and the stars. The air, free and unlimited, carried the ardent enthusiasm through thousands of versts and seems to be a person with a name, appeared to possess a clear sight and soul." *

The Pasternakian pictures of that stormy period, with their cleansing rainstorms, thunderstorms, and snowstorms, were intended to transmit that "all-embracing sense" of the upheaval that was going on. The theme of the Revolution is felt here as a strong pressure, as the emotional disposition of the images, which united the language of the crowd with the meetings of the roads and the trees. In Pasternak's lyric poetry

* Arkhiv N. V. Bannikova (Archives of N. V. Bannikov)

of the revolutionary period it would be difficult to separate this theme into a special paragraph under a title such as "Poems about the Revolution." This theme is omnipresent and is as indefinable as air, and its existence could be compared to the omnipresence of a higher, spiritual concern, such as the meeting place of the eternal and of the temporal, which has always been the main concern of the artist. Although many of the poems of Pasternak are not strictly poems about the revolutions, still many of them were written, if one may say so, in the presence of the Revolution, and therefore are colored by the loud music of that period.

> We were people. We are the ages.
> They beat us and rush us along in the caravan,
> Like tundra, under the deep breath of the train
> And the train pistons and the rush of the ties.
> We fly together, burst in and
> Whirl with the crow-black storm
> And—we're past! You'll catch it later.
> They, having piled straws in a heap in the morning,
> For a moment they're swept together,
> A trace of the wind lives in the talks
> Of the stormy meeting
> Of the trees on the shingles.

In the twenties, the poet's direct turn to history is connected with an unexpected awakening of epic tendencies in his art. In 1923, in his volume *Sublime Malady*, he sends a "scout into the epic." This is followed by the poems *The Year 1905* and *Lieutenant Shmidt* (1925–1927). In 1930 Pasternak finished his *Spektorsky*. The epic forms fascinated Pasternak so much that he, who until recently had been the most convinced lyric poet, now declared: "I think that the epic is suggested by the times, and for this reason in my book *The Year 1905* I switch from lyrical thinking to the epic, though it is not easy." * This was also the time when Pasternak said: "Lyric poetry almost ceased to exist in our time." † This orientation toward the tastes and requirements of the times was very significant, al-

---

* *"Na literaturnom postu"* ("On Literary Guard"), No. 4, 1927, p. 74.
† Molodaya Gvardiya" ("The Young Guard"), No. 2, 1928, p. 199.

though of course lyricism did not cease to exist, as Pasternak's own poetry and that of other authors testifies. Besides this contemporary interest in epic works, which arose everywhere in other literatures, one also has to take into account a characteristic feature of Pasternak's art, namely, that he always worked in an extremely concentrated fashion, with consciousness of his goal, and he considered it to be his duty to establish the very genre of poetic narrative itself as a complete and compact unit. He measured his artistic career usually by books and not with individual poems. These books acquired in his biography the meaning of individual periods, or turning points, which frequently then changed the further direction of his work. In the middle of the 1920's Pasternak's preferences were for epics, and he worked on them intensively, finishing one poem after the other.

All these canvases are devoted to the revolutionary period. It is in the volume *Sublime Malady* that Pasternak gives for the first time "an epic, outside of the subject-matter, as a slow swaying, a slow growth of the theme—and its realization at the end." * The language of the poet is deliberately complex and formal and collects in itself the "Moving Rebus" of the events: the pictures of the Revolution, of the war and destruction, but they are presented not in the form of a consecutive narration, but rather revealed in the freely flowing movement of the poem. The epic "grows" to the extent to which the narrator plays his role, "drags his feet and mumbles," transmitting the pattern of life through the different modulations of the flow of the language:

> Altho, as before, the ceiling
> Serving as support for a new closet,
> Carries the third floor to the fourth
> And the fifth to the sixth portage,
> Suggesting by a change in the state of affairs
> That all is as before in the world
> Only this was a forgery
> And in the water supply

* Yuri Tynyanov, *Arkhaisty i novatory* (*Archaicists and Innovators*), Leningrad, 1929, p. 579.

The empty, suctioning scream
Of the turbulent times
The stench burned in the fires of the newspaper
Of laurel and Chinese soybeans.

The *Sublime Malady* of Pasternak is an attempt to approach the writing of epic by means of language itself. What we have here is essentially the form of an extended lyrical digression which starting from certain data of the period makes an effort to present it broadly like an epic, and to discover the aspect of the times by means beyond the subject matter, such as, for example, metaphorical imagery, syntactical constructions, and changing stress patterns. The poem that was finished in 1923 was taken up again several years later, and the final lines of it were then dedicated to Lenin. These lines, which recreate the unfettered energy of Lenin's ideas, belong to the best presentations of the leader of the Revolution in the whole of Soviet literature. Confused and retarded at the beginning, the language of the poet becomes strongly accented toward the end of the poem and is filled with the strength and tension of the will which appears as if taken over into the poem directly from Lenin's podium:

He was like a thrust of a foil.
Chasing after what had been said
He shaped his own course, opened his coat
And stared at the tops of his boots.
The words might be about black oil
But the bend of his body
Breathed with the flight of naked essence
Breaking through the stupid layer of husks.

In the poems following the *Sublime Malady* Pasternak changes to more direct forms of epic narration. But even here the characterization of the individual human fates and characters does not occupy much space. Even in *Lieutenant Shmidt* Pasternak's main concern is the recreation of the very atmosphere of the period and the unfolding of a broad historical panorama. The sketchy ramification of the images, the colorful background which unites everything and simultaneously washes away the silhouettes of the individual characters, and on the other hand becomes in itself important and meaningful —these are the characteristic features of Pasternak's prose and poetry.

> Is there anything living in the contours of that picture,
> Does he believe in the reality of the individual person

the author asks his readers, whom he keeps reminding in *Spektorsky*:

> One cannot talk of individuals, of course,
> It is better to put crosses over them now.

Therefore, even the main hero of the poem, whose name is the title of the poem, does not, strictly speaking, interest us very much.

> I started to describe Spektorsky, obeying
> Blindly the force of the objective.
> I would not have been interested in the hero himself
> And would not have thought about him,
> But I was writing about a bundle of light,
> Which kept looming before me.

For Pasternak the broad presentation, the general perspectives are important; not Spektorsky but the spectrum in which he is placed, the piece of history torn away from the past by a ray of memory. In the structure of the poem a particular role is given to the course of memory and only its logic connects the individual figures, episodes, and parts and restores the grandiose historical picture.

This unfolding of the theme of breadth also becomes obvious among other things in the manifold meaning given to the motif of space in Pasternak's poems. There one finds the wideness of the horizon, the great expanse of times and distance, and the attempt to look around oneself and grasp with a glance everything that can be seen. "Space sleeps, being in love with spaciousness"—such is the world that opens up to the poet; the world of history, which is transformed into the plane of geometrical measurements. Space becomes the stimulus of his art ("Even the sight of the expanse was enough for

me to form a poem . . ."), the motivating force of the subject-
matter ("We take upon us the views of the beloved distance
and we can fill stories with them for a whole year. . . ."), and
the hero of the work and a force that creates its own chosen
heroes. Lieutenant Schmidt himself found out how "lovingly
endless space is."

Stretching the framework of narration to the very limit,
Pasternak fills the space thus created with images from the
most different levels. One finds here people sketched only by a
few lines, or landscapes that take upon themselves the human
passions and the characteristics of the time, or entire classes
and levels of society and stories about actual historical events.
The same method that was employed by Pasternak to paint
nature is applied here to history too. History is presented as a
whole, where the different glittering parts of the whole appear
in their kaleidoscopic mutual connections, and the stress is
put on the general picture of life. In the poem *The Year 1905*
the figures of the fathers and sons, of the peasants and sailors
and students appear like successive figures on the screen. The
storm at sea is transformed into the uprising on the ship
Potyomkin, and during the battles at the Presnya[13] in December "the sun looks into the fieldglass and listens to the gunfire."
From individual episodes lines lead to the general situation, to
the fate of the state itself:

> With each turn of the wheel of the gun
> Someone fell
> From among the gunners,
> And with each
>
> Prestige was falling.

Subjects and ideas different in their nature are brought
under one common denominator:

> Snow lies on the branches
> On the electric lines
> On the branching section
> On the insignia of the dragoons
> And on the ties of the railroads.

Pasternak likes to list and enumerate, likes to list objects and to connect objects taken from different spheres of life and to put them on a common level. Thus in a few lines he is able to draw a summary picture, full of details, which gives the reader the impression that it was created with one motion of his hands. This cursory sketch evokes the momentary unity of the impression. In a similar vein he treats the broad historical characterizations, also the individual episodes, as for example when describing the scene of the courtroom in his *Lieutenant Shmidt*:

> Benches, swords, the coats of the gendarmes
> Faintings, shouts, fits and spasms
> Reading, reading, reading, regardless of
> Headache, regardless of
> Jets of ammonium chloride and the spicy
> Drunken smell of the tears and valerian drops,
> Reading without singing of the hymn,
> A frame, and veteran-gendarmes
> Wide trousers and the sash of the tsar
> And an eight-fold ray of light under the chandelier.

In the description and the very conception of history Pasternak is close to Blok. This closeness consists of the ability to catch the basic rhythm of the period, and not only with respect to the obvious course of events that are all in one dimension, but in all areas of life; it is also the poet's effort to find a general historical equivalent for all the things that are going on around him, and thus present the world in the total unity of its components—be they the Revolution, earthquake, or love. In the introduction to his "Retribution," Blok combines varied phenomena such as the trial of Beiliss[14] and the development of the French wrestling in the circuses of Petersburg, the heat of a summer and the strikes in London, the development of aviation and Stolypin's assassination.[15] "All these data, although they seem to be of very different character," explains Blok, "for me have one musical meaning. I got used to gathering facts from all areas of life that were available to me at the given moment. And I am convinced that all of them taken together will always create a unified musical effect." * As is well known, it is precisely the collision of such facts, seemingly contradictory but internally connected, that forms the great historical panoramas of Blok, especially his characterization of the nineteenth and twentieth centuries in his poem "Retribution."

Pasternak has a similar sharpness of vision for the characteristics of the time. These characteristics are scattered everywhere and it is they that give to each object a particular, designating meaning. Pasternak also hastens to single out the common denominator of human behavior, of sunsets and city streets. And if, for example, *Lieutenant Shmidt* is about the period of the Russian-Japanese War, which was on the eve of the Revolution, then everything, even the hippodrome at Kiev, speaks of that anxious condition of world affairs. History enters all the cells of life, turning even the smallest details into history's likeness.

The fields and the distance lie flat like an ellipse,
The silken umbrellas breathed the thirst of the storm.
The hot day took aim with the bottomless sky
At the tribunes of the hippodrome.

The people were sweating like Kvass on ice,
That appeared by magic due to the cloud of the distances.
Galloping in the sandstorm of the hooves and leg-covers
The horses were churning the distance like butter.

And behind the measured beats of the gallop
Of some sort of underground beginning
The war year was following the jockeys
And the horses and the spokes of the carriages.

No matter what they talked about, or whatever they were drinking
The year of the war was growing everywhere, crawled over the gates
And interrupted the conversation and clung to the
Waters like a pinch of ash.

The turn to a historical theme and to the description of objective reality contributed to the clarification of the com-

* Aleksandr Blok, *Polnoye sobraniye stikhotvoreniy v dvukh tomakh* (*Collected Works in two volumes*), t. 1. Leningrad, 1946, p. 530.

plex poetic imagery which is especially perceptible in the poem *The Year 1905*. Gorky, who was rather critical of Pasternak's poetry, wrote to Pasternak after receiving the book: "The book is excellent, it is one of those books that won't be appreciated according to its worth immediately, but such books are destined to have a long life. I do not want to keep it a secret: until this book I have always read your poems with a certain irritation, since I found that they were excessively full of images which sometimes were not clear to me. My imagination had a hard time embracing all the capricious complexity of the images, and the unfinished nature of your images. You know yourself that their richness frequently forces you to speak and draw in a rather sketchy way. In your *1905* you are more sparing and simple, you are more classical in this book, which is filled with pathos, and which infects me, as reader, quickly, easily, and tremendously. Yes, indeed, this is an excellent book, there is the voice of a real poet and of a poet with social interest at that, in the best and most profound meaning of this word." *

As is clear from the correspondence between Gorky and Pasternak, they did not have a complete and mutual understanding. As an adherent of classic poetry, Gorky preferred even in contemporary poetry the more traditional forms. In a letter to E. K. Ferrari he remarked in 1922: "Khodasevich[16] is immeasurably higher than Pasternak in my opinion, and I am convinced that the talent of the latter, in the final instance, is going to put him on the hard road of Khodasevich—the road of Pushkin." † Several years later in a dedication to a volume of his *The Life of Klim Samgin* given to Pasternak, Gorky admitted that the Pasternakian "chaos" was alien to him and that he wished the poet had "greater simplicity." Pasternak answered: "You have the wrong impression of me: I have always been striving for simplicity and I shall never stop doing so." ‡

---

* "Gorky i sovetskiye pisately. Neizdannaya perepiska" ("Gorky and the Soviet writers. Unpublished correspondence"), *Literaturnoye Nasledstvo,* t. 70, Moskva, 1963, p. 300.
† *Ibid.,* p. 568
‡ *Ibid.,* p. 307–308.

His later evolution indicates how much of this striving was realized.

The correspondence with Gorky testifies to the fact that the first part of the novel *The Life of Klim Samgin* had a great influence upon Pasternak; he was especially astonished by the art of recreating the historic atmosphere. In Pasternak's evaluation of the novel, which deals with the recent past, it is impossible not to see Pasternak's own interest and the taste of an artist who at that time himself was working on a historical-revolutionary theme. The distance, sketched "with moving colors," the "crowd of details" coiled up like a spring, the "way of writing that embraces all latitudes with one swoop" the essence of history, consisting of the chemical transformation of each moment of it: caught and transmitted with "the forcefulness of a suggestion." * In these remarks of Pasternak about the character and structure of an epic canvas we also recognize the characteristics of his approach to history.

5

The saturated nature of the Pasternakian images which give the general atmosphere of reality results in a situation where it is impossible to distinguish in his poetry between the "main" and "secondary" images, or to extract the basic thread of the narrative, and to separate the action from the background upon which the action is developed. The background itself is a source of action to a great degree and time and again it turns out to be the primary level of the poem. What is accidental in the fate of his heroes has a providential character and is given a climactic importance in developing the narration. Thus, in *Spektorsky*, the sudden encounters and discoveries of the heroes, the interruptions in the speech and the unfinished sentences which appear not to be motivated deliberately, but rather overheard, by chance, unaware, as if by the will of chance, play an important role in the presentation

* *Ibid.*, p. 304–305.

of the intelligentsia, which reacts to the revolutionary events and which is dispersed over the world and the roads and cross-roads of history. As the plot moves ahead everything is mixed up and tied together: the direct continuation of the story about the phenomena of great historical importance may be achieved by means of an interior, or a landscape, or may reveal itself in a kind of everyday episode, in an unexpected acquaintance-ship with some private person.

Here is, for example, the way Pasternak established connections in *Spektorsky* between the phenomena of "sky" and "air," although they may have different levels of existence but are connected by and filled with the theme of the Revolution which either appears in the landscape, or is presented in the form of a broad symbolic generalization, or the action is transplanted from Moscow to the Urals, and the Revolution is presented in the concrete image of a woman-revolutionary. For the sake of brevity we leave out several stanzas and ask the reader to pay attention to the "aerial way" of the heroine personifying for Pasternak the Russian Revolution in its moral beginnings and world-historical significance:

Spektorsky

It happens: having burst forth in declarations
Time in November comes forth with snow
And the day slides secretly by like an exile,
And this day—is a blank in the calendar . . .

Suddenly there's the cry of a girl in the pantry,
The door is smashed, there's a movement, tears, a clatter,
And the yard lies in the smoke of suppressed desires,
And in the bare footsteps of high-borne banners.

And she, worrying about what she hid in the apron,
Now possessed by intense shame,
Flies into the gap of the revealed advantages
On the crest of the endless steps . . .

And now the dawn loses the daughter's shame,
Shattering the window with a blow of its heel,
It flees into the hands of the mob
And in its hands beyond the clouds . . .

The house on the corner glides over the corner house,
From where it stretches its hands into our field.
There it was tormented, there thrown into the galleries
There the Urals were mocked by the mines.

There in open places are clusters of corpses,
There they zeroed in, books burned to ashes,
And ran up to the woman in the Circassian coat,
Who was surveying the scene from the saddle.

Before and behind her, round about and in back,
Crawled, smoking, the civil war
And you would recognize the fugitive in the horsewoman
Who was thrown from your window.

On the whole earth there lay a hoarse sea of sorrow,
Filled with smoke the news of it rumbled and was spread,
Of [Marusya] of the quiet Russian remote places
That shook the earth in ten days.

Who is this "refugee woman"—the dawn? Is she a sudden burst
of time and space? A people's revolution? Woman, whose social
and spiritual liberation was interpreted by the poet as the
most important achievement, as the moral imperative of the
Revolution? Obviously she is all these things taken together:
Pasternak's imagery is always trying to combine different levels
of reality in one poetical world-view that is not broken down
into individual parts. The poetical requirement of Pasternak
expressed in the same *Spektorsky* is the basis of his epic constructions: "Poetry, do not waive your rights to breadth."

Pasternak will often tell the reader about the weather in this
or that historical moment rather than explain the whole chro-
nology and the order of the events. The content of the event is
disclosed through areas lying on the borderline, close to the
event, or through the atmosphere surrounding it, following it,
or preceding it as in the manner of a prelude. In illuminating
the most varied phenomena and processes Pasternak is inclined to proceed in a roundabout way and to write Forewords
(which by the way, upon close examination, turn out to be
the story about the main problem), and frequently the poet's
gaze wanders around, not focussed on the most important
object that he is describing, but on its prehistory, on its de-

velopment, or on its broadest environment. He likes to define a
thing through the borderline that divides it from other things.
In poems about cities he would write about the suburbs and
the poems about the first of May he would note with the 30th
of April:

> I do like very much its first days,
> When there is only talk about the spruce tree.

In the lyric poetry of Pasternak during the period of the 30's
and 40's (when the epic efforts disappeared in his poetry but
developed in his prose) this feature of Pasternak's artistic vision became especially noticeable. Thus, the cycle of lyrical
poems "Waves" which opened the book *Second Birth* (1932)
is constructed wholly as an introduction to the theme; the introduction then keeps unfolding until it becomes clear that
the introduction itself is the actual theme. There the poet tells
us what it actually is that he wants to write about and this intention itself, this promise turns into the story about our world
rolling away from us into the future like waves. The promise
is unfulfilled and it hides in itself the kinds of new possibilities
that inspire the poet, but on the other hand they are spelled out
only half-way, and fade away into the future. Thus the form
of the introduction appears here to be extraordinarily capa-
cious, meaningful, and in harmony with the idea of the bio-
graphico-historical and poetical development that is contained
in its basis.

In the following books by Pasternak—*On Early Trains*
(1943), *Terrestrial Space* (1945), *When the Skies Clear*
(1957)—we again observe the particular character of the sub-
ordination of his poetry to the historical realities. Direct
references to historical events are not too numerous here. And
the main thing is that Pasternak's work, which had appeared in
the form of direct reaction to historical events (for example,
some of his poems about the Second World War—"Terrible
Tale," "Victor") noticeably yields, as far as its artistic quality
is concerned, to poems written on the same topic in his formerly characteristic form of landscape painting, or in an intimate, lyrical key ("Gates," "Winter is Coming," and others),

and not in a pathetic and journalistic style. It is worth noting that his best poems, filled with an atmosphere of history and contemporary reality, frequently sound like an introduction or foreword to the future, and in the majority transmit the condition of the epoch through imperceptible movements of nature and the soul of the poet, or through everyday details and the characteristic features of the trivia of the present. Thus, for example, in the poem "Spring" (1944) the atmosphere of the end of the war is in the air, and the poet attempts to catch the voice of the time, as the voice of everyday life, which is particularly meaningful and promising:

> Everything is so special this spring,
> The noise of the sparrows is livelier
> I do not even try to express
> How bright and quiet I am in my soul.
>
> Thinking and writing turn out differently now,
> And like a loud octave in the choir,
> One can hear the gorgeous earthly voice
> Of the liberated territories.

If in Pasternak's art of the period of the Revolution and of the 1920's landscape took over the characteristic features of historical existence, and was filled with Kremlinesque storms and the noise and speech of the garrulous trees, in his later lyrical poetry history itself takes on the features of nature, so that in history a process of growth and ripening takes place, amazing in its final result, but still hidden and untraceable, just as the process of growing of grass or change of the seasons of the year ("Grass and Stones," "After the Storm"). This, of course, is connected not just with the evolution of the style, but also with a change in the artistic interest of the poet, and with the changes in the surrounding world which opens up new viewpoints to him.

Pasternak is preoccupied with the phenomena of a moral nature, concentrated not on the foreground of life, but in its depth, expressed imperceptibly, softly, in the habits of everyday life, in the simple events of the life of the nation and that of the individual, and it is they, from Pasternak's point of view, that make up the core of historical existence.

He has always been attracted to a life "without pompousness and parades." Beginning with the 1930's Pasternak gives more and more preference to themes that lie somewhat on the periphery of society's life, but which are filled with hidden historical meaning (see, for example, the poem "On Early Trains"). As he said once in one of his speeches, everything that is "laboriously elevated and rhetorical appears to be of secondary importance, useless, and sometimes even directly suspect from a moral point of view." * From now on the poet is especially charmed by small villages, peasant huts, the ports and ferries of the Russian province, the simple feelings and the modest people who do simple work, and nature itself is looking for correspondences in its environment: the good-smelling tobacco is compared to a relaxing stoker, the spring puts on a padded jacket, and finds a friend for herself in the barnyard. Prosaic and colloquial phrases that have served him formerly, too, as the source of poetry, receive now an additional, ethical motivation, underlining the democratic sympathies of the poet, his dislike of a pompous and boasting style.

Simultaneously Pasternak's views on fate, of man's place in history, and of his calling are also formulated and find expression in his lyric poetry. The human personality appears as the bearer of high moral values, although the personality is unobtrusive from the outside (the ordinary and the genial are closely connected for Pasternak, and every person is potentially a genius, and the genius is simple and unobtrusive). He lives a life not for ostentation; he lives a profound inner life and is committed to the victory of the voluntary sacrifice, self-denial on behalf of the victory of life, and in a fuller and more general way of history and the world spirit. Between the "microcosmos" and the "macrocosmos" in Pasternak's way of thinking, there exists a profound connection, and therefore

* "O skromnosti i smelosti. Rech tov. Borisa Pasternaka" ("About Modesty and Bravery. Address of Comrade Boris Pasternak"). **Literaturnaya Gazeta,** February 16, 1936.

the individual possesses an absolute meaning, not in animosity and separation from life, but in harmony and unity with it. In a letter to the poet Kaisin Kuliyev (November 25, 1948) he presents his views on man's fate and on the calling of a gifted person as follows:

"It is amazing that the born talent is but a child's model of the universe, implanted from our childhood in our hearts, a school educational device for the comprehension of the world from the inside, from its best and most charming side. Talent teaches us to be honest and fearless, but it discloses the fabulously rich qualities of honesty and of the generally dramatic reason of existence. The talented man would know that life gains tremendously if it is totally and correctly illuminated, and that it loses much in a half-darkness. A feeling of personal involvement inspires a feeling of pride and striving for truth. That such an advantageous and happy life in reality can turn out to be a tragedy is of secondary importance."

The idea of the sublime historical destiny of the individual human personality was developed in Pasternak's poetry. From *Lieutenant Shmidt,* where the moral ideal of man is made concrete in the hero of the poem (Shmidt sacrifices himself, committing the heroic act of historic renewal and accepting as unavoidable his tragic fate) through the lyric poetry of the 1930's and the war period there is continuity with the most mature works of Pasternak's later period. Their philosophical content helps us to understand Pasternak's remarks made in connection with Shakespeare's *Hamlet* which he had translated into Russian: "Hamlet renounces himself so that he can carry out the will of Him who has sent him. Hamlet is not a drama of a weak character, but rather a drama of duty and self-renunciation. When it turns out that the external appearance of things and reality do not coincide and are divided by a precipice, it is unimportant that the reminder about the falsity of the world enters the play in a supernatural form, and that the ghost demands revenge from Hamlet. What is more important is that Hamlet, by the will of chance, is chosen to be the judge of his time and the servant of a more remote one. Hamlet is a drama of high destiny, of ordered victory and assigned predestination." *

The lyrical poetry of the later Pasternak discloses for us the position of the poet in relation to the world and time, in a somewhat different perspective from that evident in the earlier periods of his art. The idea of a moral service supersedes everything else, although Pasternak never ceases to emphasize the perceptive powers of poetry, its ability to recreate the living world of reality (and the moral element in his artistic perception of the world was also important for him in his earlier works). If in his earlier aesthetic credo the central place was given to the image of the "poetry-sponge" then now, without changing this, another motif becomes dominant: "The aim of art is self-sacrifice." Simultaneously, toward the end of Pasternak's life, the recognition of his completed historical predestination becomes completely clear and is voiced with full power. This is the source, in particular, of the unusually bright coloring of his latest lyric poetry, disregarding the tragic notes of some of the poems, and of the dominating feeling of trust in the future.

Also in his moral-historical understanding, in the understanding of the tasks of art, characteristic features, views, habits become visible that bring the poet closer to his contemporary world, but which simultaneously also question some of its demands and premises. "You are the beginning of a city and not that of a song," Pasternak said about poetry. Poetry embraces reality and is closely attached to it, like a suburb to a city, but in Pasternak's understanding poetry does not sing out everything literally, does not reproduce trivialities of the generally accepted truth. A similar analogy, which by its very structure corresponds to the Pasternakian images, also explains, to a certain extent, the character of his connections and differences with his times.

The particular understanding of the problems of art (in its

* Boris Pasternak, "Zametki k perevodam shekspirovskikh tragediy" ("Notes to the Translations of Shakespeare's Tragedies"), *Literaturnaya Moskva*, Moskva, 1956, p. 797.

relationship to nature, to reality, and to the original) defines Pasternak's vision to such an extent that we discover analogous habits and notions even in his work as a translator. His translations contributed a special chapter to his literary biography. But the features which are characteristic for the art of the poet also appeared in this secondary field of activity, which occupied an important place in his life and activity from the beginning of the 1930's. Pasternak the translator strives to recreate above all the spirit of the original text, leaving details and literal exactness aside. Just like actual reality, the works of geniuses do not need a literal, but rather a congenial transformation, which in its principles and in its ideals is inspired by the orginal, departs from it, and becomes harmonious with it in its "own particular uniqueness." The translator, in Pasternak's conviction, does not have to make a mould from the object which he is copying, but he is obliged to transmit its essential and poetic force, and thus transform the copy into an original work of art which lives along with the original in a different language system.

It is not difficult to notice that Pasternak's ideas about the art of translation are akin to his ideas about art as such. He achieves "more than anything else" that "deliberate freedom without which there is no approach to great things." *

Comparing his principles of translation with those of others Pasternak remarked: "We are not in competition with anybody as far as individual lines are concerned; the debate is about the entire structure, its rendering, and with faithfulness to the great original we enter into a greater and greater dependency on our own language system. . . ." † Or: "The relationship between the original and the translation should be the relationship between the bases and derivation, or the stem and the branch. The translation must be done by an author who has experienced the impact of the original long before he

---

* Boris Pasternak, Ot perevodchika ["Predislovie k perevodu *Gamleta* Shekspira"]. (From the Translator. ["Foreword to Shakespeare's *Hamlet*"]), *Molodaya Gvardiya*, No. 5–6, 1940, p. 16.

† Boris Pasternak, "Novy perevod *Otello* Shekspira" ("A New Translation of Shakespeare's *Othello*"), *Literaturnaya Gazeta*, December 9, 1944.

starts his translation. The translation should be the fruit of the original and its historical consequence." *

Pasternak worked for years over his best translations, preparing himself for them by the very process of inner development. In a certain sense these translations are of an autobiographical nature. Thus, for example, Pasternak's translations of Georgian poetry are connected with his trips to Georgia in the years 1931 and 1936, with his friendship of long standing with Georgian poets, and finally with that appreciative love of this area and of the people and the culture which permeates many of his original poems. One could call them "branches" of Georgia in the life and art of Pasternak.

Hamlet in his translation was published as a single volume in 1941, and it became the starting point for the translation of a whole series of Shakespeare's tragedies. But already in a poem of his from 1923 we encounter the idea which was developed in his activity as a translator: "Oh! The essence of Shakespeare may be in the fact that Hamlet talks plainly to the ghost." "Just talking plainly," that is, speaking on the most elevated subject freely, in an everyday way, is as we know, one of the main rules of Pasternak, who has also some other features that relate him to Shakespeare's realism, freedom, and power of depiction. "The impact of the original" (of course, not always in a direct way, but sometimes in a rather roundabout way, refracted in the different phenomena of world culture) has started here long before his immediate work on Shakespeare's tragedies and to a certain extent coincided with the particular interests and intentions of the artist. That is why Shakespeare has taken root in his poetic soil, and the work of a translator, having received the impact of the individual tastes, preferences, and manners of Pasternak the poet, also influenced in its own turn Pasternak's original creations. Through this close and yet extremely free communication with Shakespeare, whose greatness and force Pasternak has tried to transmit "in his own particular uniqueness," Pasternak practically realized his own principal assertion that "translations are meant not to

---

* Boris Pasternak, "Zametki perevodchika" ("Remarks of the Translator"), *Znamya*, No. 1–2, 1944, p. 166.

be means of acquaintance with individual works, but rather
the eternal communication of cultures and people." *

6

The meaning of existence, the destiny of man, the essence of
the world—these are questions that interest Pasternak during
the course of many years, especially toward the end of his life,
when, one may say, he devotes his entire lyric poetry to the
search for the basic problems, for the unriddling of final aims
and first principles:

> In everything I want to get
> To the very essence of things;
> In work, in the search for ways,
> In the confusion of the heart.
>
> To the essence of past days,
> To their cause
> To the basis, to the roots,
> To the core of everything.

An inclination to the philosophical consideration of life is characteristic of the entire poetry of Pasternak, of the poet-philosopher, gravitating toward the art of broad generalization and
greater spiritual content. He has always been close to that
"bottomless exultation without which there is no originality, to
that infinity which opens up before us from any vantage point
of life in any direction, without which poetry is just a great
misunderstanding, temporarily inexplicable." † In many works
of Pasternak belonging to the most various periods of his art,
one senses the persistent desire to dig down to the roots, and
when telling about things, not just to present them as they are,
but to lay bare their original nature.

> My friend, you ask who orders
> The speech of the Idiot to burn?
> In the nature of the lime-trees, in the nature of the flagstone,
> It was in the nature of the summer to burn.

* *Ibid.*
† Boris Pasternak, *Okhrannaya Gramota* (*Safe Conduct*), p. 100.

It was not "the summer was hot," but "to burn was in the nature of the summer." This is the typical poetic approach of Pasternak.

This care about the essentials and about the nature of things puts the poet into a very interesting and ambiguous position in relation to impressionism, traces of which are discernible in his art (especially of the earlier period) and for which official critics have frequently scolded Pasternak. The simplicity of the immediate perception, and the pathos of impressionability and response relate Pasternak to the Impressionists. The images of Pasternak remind us sometimes of the canvases of Monet, Renoir, Pissarro, and Vuillard. Like these painters, Pasternak also frequently tries to create by using the impressions of the moment and by hiding his previous knowledge of the world, and tries to describe the objects as they appear to him in the given moment. Here, for example, is a sketch made in the impressionistic manner:

> The dishes of the bartender were clattering
> The waiter was yawning, counting the crockery
> In the river on the level of the candlestick
> The fireflies were swirling in a swarm.
>
> They were trailing like a sparkling thread
> From the streets close to the shore. The clock struck three.
> The waiter endeavored to scrape off the melted candle
> From the copper, using his napkin.

The fires on the shore, their reflection on the water, the waiter on the boat, all this is embraced with one glance that is busy only with the fixation of the picture in the particular position as once seen "on the level of the candlestick."

But impressionism as a rule deals only with the emotionally perceivable surface of the object, and not with its essence. The Impressionist, drowning in a sea of colors and smells, is carefully avoiding prearranged, a priori knowledge, phenomena, and ideas that are capable of disturbing the purity of the perception. In principle, impressionism is not interested in eternal values and absolute beginnings; it is completely submerged in the flow of fresh impressions radiating from *this*

and only from *this* nature. Therefore impressionism enriched
realistic art at the basic level of a concrete-emotional way of
depiction and in the transmission of visible, but not intelligible
nature.

It is interesting to note that the young Pasternak, who
clearly went beyond the limits of the impressionistic notions
concerning the nature of art, devised for himself a formula of
art that he termed "the impressionism of the eternal." * In this
formula are contained both the taste of the poet for the immediate perception of life, for a pure color touch, for *plein air*,
and his passion for a philosophical search for absolute categories. In poetical images he also tries to unite sensation and
essence, the timely and eternal, and talks about a "storm that
is momentary forever," thus giving the picture of the immediate present an immutable and unconditional meaning. The favorite "present" of the Impressionists is filled with so much
meaningful content that it registers not just the fleeting and
isolated phenomenon, but the constant and the eternal.

> The instant lasted for this second
> But it had overshadowed eternity too.

If the artist-Impressionist deliberately limits himself to the
question of how the object looks at the given moment, then
Pasternak goes further and wants to know *what* it is. He
pierces it with his vision, penetrates its depth and its very core,
and frequently builds an image as the definition of its property
and essence, giving thus not just the first impression of the object but also its idea and meaning. It is not by chance that
there are quite a few poems by Pasternak with titles like "Definition" (definition of poetry, definition of the soul, etc.); and
then there are a number of poems that reproduce as their essence the same scheme that goes back almost to the paragraphs
of some textbook or of some dictionary:

> Poetry, I shall take the oath of faith
> In you, and shall die, whispering:

* Boris Pasternak, "Chorny bokal" ("The Black Goblet"), *Vtoroy
sbornik Centrifugy*, p. 41.

You are not the carriage of the man with the sweet voice,
You are the summer with a seat in the third class
You are a suburb, and not the beginning of a song.

Pasternak is not afraid of such conclusions, which may appear at first rather dry. He is fond of dissecting the formula of the depicted object, and deals with the enumeration and the analysis of its properties and components.

> We were in Georgia. If we multiply
> The need with tenderness, heaven with hell,
> The hot house and the ice under our feet,
> Then we get the whole picture of this area.
>
> And we shall understand the delicate doses
> Needed for the mixture of heaven and earth,
> Success and work, and duty and air,
> So that man may result, as we have him here.

Pasternak, who seeks his way to the essence and penetrates frequently into the most abstract spheres, is always full of images which are whole and concrete. All his "definitions" resemble a logical construction only formally, for in reality they are reasoned pictures of life that form the basis of the whole construction.

In the poem we have quoted above, "In everything I want to get . . ." which sounds like an artistic credo, Pasternak expresses the desire to write poetry about the "properties of passion," to lay bare its "law" and "beginning." How does he imagine this cherished work that is supposed to investigate the essence of the object?

> I would divide the verses like a garden.
> With all the trembling of their sinews
> Would the lime trees blossom in it in a row
> Like a row of geese, keeping in file.
>
> I would put in the verses the breathing of the roses
> The breathing of the mint,
> Of the meadow, the sedge and the hayfield
> And the peal of thunder.
>
> Thus did Chopin once put
> The living wonder

> Of the Polish village, parks, groves and graves
> In his etudes.

Pasternak's poetry is the poetry of the concrete and the nearby. He depicts only what he himself sees. But the things depicted have an expanded meaning and some of the details constantly are transferred to a higher, general level. Everyday objects surrounding us turn into the personification of goodness, love, beauty, and other eternal categories. Uniting the concrete and the abstract, the single and the general, the temporary and the eternal, the poet creates what could be described as the ideal portrayal of the actual fact or person. Thus, for example, in the poem dedicated to the memory of Larissa Reisner, her image is expanded to an abstract concept and the person of the heroine appears as the personification of life's beauty, recalling somewhat the figures of the personified benefactors and goddesses of the art of the Renaissance:

> It could only be you, wonderfully beaten by battles,
> Who burst in like a close volley of delight.
> Not knowing life, nor the meaning of charm,
> You give life a direct answer to its face.

> You steamed like a storm of grace
> Although you've barely been in its living fire,
> Mediocrity fell immediately into disgrace
> Imperfection evoked anger.

When during the Second World War Pasternak began to speak in pathetic language and "frescoes that come to life" appeared, where the heroes "looked eternity in the eyes," and were fighting for life and death "against the naked force of evil" and were carried to the "abode of thunder-throwers and eagles," these tones were rather unexpected, although the typical Pasternakian prose still could be heard (the sinking corvette "decays like a cigarette butt") and one could hear the familiar colloquial intonations:

> The infidels fell to the ground
> With green eyes and brown eyes
> They were pulled, as if by a lasso,
> Behind the front garden, into the chancellery.

Next to the front garden the archaic "infidels" look rather abstract, despite their living faces, seen from below or from the position of a man turned on his back.

The war period, of course, put its stamp upon Pasternak's poetry and made possible, in part at least, the appearance of archaic abstractions that were then entering the literary language rather widely. However, the principles of such a combination of the pathetic-abstract with the prosaic-concrete were not really as new for the poet as they may seem at first glance. He did not change radically his system of style; rather he just strengthened and intensified for a time the qualities that were there previously anyway. The ideal contained in the actual has always emerged in his images more or less discernibly. One just has to turn to the love poetry of Pasternak during the beginning of the 1930's in order to be convinced of this. With the line: "My beauty, your figure, and your essence are pleasing to my heart," the poet addresses his beloved, and through her "figure" he discovers her "essence": the laws of beauty:

> Polycletos was praying to you
> Your laws were made public.
> Your laws of ancient times
> Have been known to me for many years.

He compares her with the future—"Measuring the quietness with your steps you enter like the future"—and sees in her the embodiment of the "beginnings" of life:

> To love others is a heavy cross,
> But you are beautiful without convolutions
> And the secret of your charm
> Is equal to life's riddles.

Life, as is characteristic for Pasternak's view of the world, has the "taste of great beginnings" in its every manifestation. And in life's presence the most ordinary objects become ideal, and are illuminated by a light which falls upon them from within. An ordinary rest in a pine forest serves as a pretext for the generalization:

And thus, immortal for a time, we
Are attracted to the faces of the pine trees
And from sicknesses, epidemics
And from death, we are freed.

Once upon a time, gods were called immortal. But here we have ordinary people, communicating with eternal nature, who thus become eternal, since immortality, according to the conviction of the poet, is to be found everywhere ("our daily immortality") and is just a synonym, another name, for life.

This intensity of the poetical idea is especially noticeable in Pasternak's art beginning with the 1930's, and the further we go the more obvious it becomes. As far as his earlier works are concerned, it is more difficult to discover this characteristic feature and the pithiness of the images have frequently been taken for pretentiousness of form. As the years pass by Pasternak becomes more and more comprehensible, and therefore, this side of his poetry is more obvious. But the greater comprehensibility of Pasternak is, to a large extent, due to the accelerated pace of his thinking, which acquires a greater structural strength and recognizes more and more its organizing and leading role in the poem.

In the early art of the poet the philosophical idea is not shown from the outside, rather it is completely obscured by the picture by means of which it is presented. We would rarely find here frank contemplations and considerations, coming from the author's ego, and the process of thought is left to nature's cognitive processes. The conception of the author is also obscured by an abundance of impressions and associations that seem to develop by chance, and also by the persistent desire of the poet to consider all the factors mutually influencing each other and to connect them with a compact metaphorical net. The young Pasternak is too consistent in his susceptibility to remain clear and although, as we have noticed before, his speech is basically natural and not artificial, what he presents is the naturalness of a chaos that dashes forward and needs to be disentangled in order to become completely understandable.

However, the profound content of Pasternak's poetry and

the naturalness of his language could not forever stay behind the locked doors of "incomprehensibility." The poet has always gravitated toward greater comprehensibility so that the "bottomless inspiration" of the images and the "unheard-of simplicity" of their linguistic expression were so closely united that they could be understood by the reader without great effort, as if by itself, like truth that does not need any additional explanations. This trend was already apparent in some of the works of the 1920's and especially in the book, *Second Birth*, from which work on, through the poetry of the 1930's and 1940's, the poet proceeds toward simplicity and clarity in his poetry.

The hero of one of Pasternak's poems, a participant in the Second World War, is daydreaming about a play which he is going to write after his release from the hospital:

> Then he shall bring
> The unique process of a
> Fantastic Life
> Into order and clarity
> Through the language of a provincial man.

"The language of a provincial man" is the everyday, living speech free from literary influences, which has been Pasternak's ideal for a long time. But here also is the concern for "order and clarity," which is something new in his understanding of the task of art, and this idea developed rather slowly. Harmonious structure and clarity are achieved by Pasternak to a great extent only because the poet ceases to play a secondary role with regard to his own perception and gives up the excessively metaphorical concentration which was characteristic of his lyric poetry in the past. He is stricter in selecting his impressions and in limiting the spontaneity of nature, and he frequently speaks up with "pure" feelings and considerations, which are not translated into the language of metaphor. If formerly the process of the description of life in Pasternak's art could have been characterized as the process of conglomeration, and one could not divide the first view of the world from the final conclusions, then we can now obviously differentiate between the process of cognition which, after understanding the objects, does not dissolve in them completely but retains its independence and brings order into the movement of the images.

The accessibility and "general comprehensibility" of poetical language were not easily achieved by the artist, who had already established an extremely individualistic view of the world and manner of portrayal. There were times when the demand for simplicity resulted in the danger of impoverishing the images and in an excessively direct and declarative solution of the problem. Sometimes during the period of these changes Pasternak wrote poems which obviously were weaker than his possibilities. Thus, for example, in the middle of the 1930's, when the poet was making a special effort to renew his method, several poems appeared of which he himself declared immediately (not without self-belittling, of course) that, for the time being, as long as he does not get used to the new style, he will have to write "badly," "write like a shoemaker." The situation was also made more complex by the fact that the new and the abstract themes were taken somewhat too abstractly and in a rather journalistic manner. As Pasternak said then, he had to "hop from position to position . . . in a space that was cut up by the methods of journalism and abstract ideas that lent themselves very little to images and concrete treatment." *

All this enables us to understand that for the later Pasternak the decisive prerequisite of artistic victory becomes the great concreteness and simultaneously the spirituality of the imagery. A picture that radiates life fills out the poem, which is free from metaphorical complexities, but still, as far as the power of the portrayal is concerned, does not lag behind his old works, and as far as their sincere and striking pithiness is concerned, is even superior to them.

It is exactly in philosophical lyric poetry that Pasternak achieves the greatest success, at a time when declarative po-

---

* "O skromosti i smelosti. Rech tov. Borisa Pasternaka" ("About Modesty and Bravery. Address of Comrade Boris Pasternak"), *Literaturnaya Gazeta*, February 16, 1936.

ems of a journalistic character, or poems on everyday life or on the landscape and not supported by a philosophical idea, are less successful. The artistic perfection is measured for the poet by the graphic and obviously meaningful quality of the idea expressed.

Having attained the desired simplicity, Pasternak also retained the most worthy features of his former achievements, for example, the perception and description of the world as a united whole. However, in the past the connections between the individual phenomena, between man and nature, between the temporal and the eternal, were achieved mainly by a metaphor which carried the objects and their properties from one place to another, and brought into the poem at the same time turmoil and a confusion of images. Now the metaphor, which still plays an important role, ceases to be the only mediator between things. Their unity is achieved by that breadth and clarity of the poet's world outlook and by that spiritual inspiration of feelings and ideas before which all barriers fall down and life is presented as a great whole, where "nothing can vanish," where man lives and dies in the embrace of the universe, and the wind

> Sways the forest and the cottage,
> Not each pine tree separately
> But all trees in sum
> With all this unlimited space . . .

In the art of the late Pasternak it is not just the connection between things but also the unification of the poet with the world that proceeds in simpler and more direct forms than before, and the "universe is simpler than some clever people may think," and the universe is built on the primacy of a few simple, uncompounded truths, comprehensible to each and every man, like earth, love, bread, sky. Sometimes the poem is built completely upon the assertion of such a cornerstone of human existence. Simultaneously, Pasternak's lyric poetry is enriched even more with the phenomena of everyday life, but without the confusing symbolism obligatory in the early poems, and in the straightforward meaning of these everyday objects, habits, and occupations. The poetry of living prose which has always inspired him now undergoes a special development.

During the half century of Pasternak's literary activity many things have changed and developed. But there are a number of ideas, principles, and preoccupations to which he remained faithful to the very end, and which were points of orientation for him in the different periods of his literary biography.

One of these profound convictions was that real art always serves higher aims than itself, since it testifies to the meaningful character of existence, the greatness of life and to the immeasurable worth of human existence. This testimony can do without declarations, without profound symbols and exalted allegories: the presence of greatness shines through the naturalness of the narration, the sharpened perception and poetical inspiration of the poet who is captivated and overwhelmed by the miracle of actual reality and who keeps "telling about this one thing," about the remarkable presence of life, about life as such, even if he is talking only about the falling snow or the sound of the wind in the forest.

Such an evaluation and appreciation of art is most applicable, of course, to the poetry of Pasternak himself. For him everyday phenomena and properties of existence told about the miraculous presence of life as such and therefore were just as important as the ancient, subconscious chaos for Tyutchev or the music of the world for Blok.

That which is most elevated, as is always the case with Pasternak, appears in the final instance in the simplest things, in life, which is all-embracing and all-exhausting. "Poetry," Pasternak said, "remains forever that celebrated height, higher than all the Alps, which is tumbling in the grass, under our feet, so that one has only to bend forward in order to see it and pick it up from the earth. . . ." *

---

* Boris Pasternak, "Vystuplenie na Mezhdunarodnom kongresse pisately v zashchitu kultury v Parizhe. Iun' 1935" ("Address to the International Congress of Writers in Defence of Culture, June, 1935"), *Mezhdunarodny kongress pisateley v zashchitu kultury v Parizhe (Stenogramma vystuplenniy)*, Moskva, 1936, p. 375.

In Defense of the Pyramid[1]

(ON YEVTUSHENKO'S POETRY)

In the April, 1965 number of *Yunost* (*Youth*) Yevgeny Yevtushenko published a long poem—at once summary and programmatic for his own art, and intended to communicate the experience of the modern age and to connect this with the experience of the past, with the history of Russia. The poem unfolds a panorama of varied human destinies and ordeals, of work and struggle. As the author states in his Foreword, the unifying principle is the dispute between two themes: "the theme of unbelief," comprised in the monologues of an Egyptian pyramid, and the "theme of faith," expressed in the monologues of a hydroelectric station and by figures, episodes, and lyrical meditations connected with its construction. Before us arise the outlines of a vast monumental scheme, and indeed in respect to its size Yevtushenko's poem clearly exceeds the customary scale of most modern poems, just as it outwardly wishes to match the structure that gave it its life and name—the Bratsk Hydroelectric Station.

To be sure Yevtushenko also explains in his Preface: "Perhaps this is not a poem, but simply my thoughts united by the dispute of the two themes." We shall not quibble. After thirty and then even forty digressions in *The Triangular Pear* by Andrei Voznesensky, we have become used to the freest composi-

167

tions and shall not look for the indispensable harmony of subject matter or for purity of genre. Digressions and monologues,
thoughts and discussions—even if they fill up the whole poem
—can be interesting and poetically justified. We shall take advantage of the appearance of such a responsible work, presented to us by Yevtushenko in the unconstrained conversation
he carries on with the reader, and we shall involve ourselves in
this and try—even if digressions are needed—not to restrict
ourselves to an evaluation of this poem, but to touch on some
general problems that his work poses for modern poetry.

The first problem is Yevtushenko himself, a man who enjoys
extraordinary success with a wide, mainly youthful audience.
Even persons who are reserved or skeptical about his verse
(among them, let us speak frankly, the author of this article)
are forced to confess that the poet's fame both at home and
abroad, perhaps the most loudly trumpeted of recent times,
has a real foundation. It cannot be reduced merely to a fleeting
fashion or to the reader's low demands or ignorance of other
more worthy objects of love and respect.

Yevtushenko owes his popularity first of all to himself—to
the very vivid and fundamental qualities of his character and
poetic talent, which permit him, for better or worse, to rule
over the minds of his time within a certain circle, and to a limited degree to fill the gap left in poetry by the departure of
Mayakovsky. After a long interval he has given back to us the
sense of a lyrical *biography*, which unfolds before our eyes in
a series of poems sustained by a single subject, namely the personality and life of the poet. Under new and different conditions and in his own personal style he has approached what
Pasternak called "the idea of a poet's biography as spectacle,"
an idea which Blok demonstrated with genius at the start of
the century, and which was later realized variously in the verse
of Mayakovsky, Yesenin, and Tsvetayeva. In spite of all the
differences of principle in the way it was interpreted individu-
ally, the essence of the "idea of spectacle" consists in the fact
that the poet does not merely compose verses, but lives in
them, so to speak, for all to see, generously and without embar-
rassment exposing to view for his contemporaries the course of

his life. The poet becomes a literary subject, a fascinating novel in verse with a vividly portrayed hero—the poet—in the center as the chief figure. The gesture of invitation to a spectacle, festive and tragic ("I do not hide from you, look at me," of Blok; "People of the future! Who are you? Here am I, all ache and bruise," of Mayakovsky); an extreme candor in telling about oneself; the striving to put oneself so fully into the verse that we almost perceive the hero physically, admire him, suffer for him, and involuntarily see him as identical with the author's own personality (although in fact they don't fully coincide) —all this Yevtushenko has adopted for himself, directly or indirectly, from his great predecessors.

Without comparing the different degrees of endowment, it is possible to distinguish features of a profound disparity in the very conception of personality and its fate, the biography. Yevtushenko, for all his proneness to self-display, lacks the stamp of an exclusive personality, the idea of a vocation or of a great and terrible fate which would impart to the poet's destiny something providential and not to be resisted, and at the same time would allow him to develop his own biography like a legend, in which personal life is raised to the level of a unique saga, half real, half invented, and created day by day before an astonished public. In comparison with the titans, masters of hyperbole and maximalists that the poets of the circle mentioned above are, Yevtushenko's hero seems like an ordinary man. His attractive features and high ideals do not prevent him from being "like everyone else," and from most often appearing in the role of "a fine fellow" or "a good guy," who is interesting, good, bold, but no means one of the elect. He is far from that myth-making about one's own personality that so attracted Yesenin and Mayakovsky, to say nothing of Blok and Tsvetayeva, and he is far from their spiritual storms and messianic pretensions. Nevertheless Yevtushenko, like them, introduces into his poetry credible details of his own life and surroundings and tells of his birth, where he lives, whom he has met, and whom he likes. He tells about his appearance and character, and thereby sustains in his verse the illusion of *acquaintance* with a living man: Yevgeni or better still Zhenya

Yevtushenko. ("Let them read on and on and say to me simply 'Zhenya' and you know that's great!") We know exactly that he is not just somebody, but Zhenya, going with his Galya to the sea on *The Moskvich*.[2]

It is here, just in the wide display of what is distinct and concrete in his personality and life that the secret of Yevtushenko lies. He has created an atmosphere of personal fascination along with other things by presenting himself to us and acquainting us with his person, and not in the capacity of some faceless "positive hero." For this confidence, friendliness, and sociability people have come to like him. If even on the street a man walks up, asks for a light and suddenly shakes hands, saying "Vasya"—that is enough for you to take him to your heart, and you walk on, recalling with a smile that there is in the world someone called Vasya who now goes on his way, and for him too life may be lonely and difficult just as at the present moment. . . . To put it briefly, Yevtushenko has entered our consciousness as a known person who furthermore embodies in his character, mimicry, and intonation substantial traits of a generation that has seen in its midst no prophets aside from this "fellow like us," about whom you say at once that he is genuine and not invented, that he is sincere and does not lie, and the proof of this is in part the perfectly authentic "mamma," and "Galya" and "The Winter Station."

All this when compared with his more demanding and self-confident predecessors ("Alexander Sergeyevich, allow me to present myself. Mayakovsky." "So says according to the Bible the prophet Yesenin, Sergei") must be described as a change, if not a diminution, of the tradition. We believe unconditionally the confused and frenzied utterances of Yesenin:

> So that for all my grievous sins,
> My lack of faith in grace,
> They should put me in a Russian shirt
> To die under the icons.

Because all this has been deeply felt and seems to have real strength, it has a majestic ring. And here is the point where one feels in Yevtushenko an affectation and a groundless pretense, even if he is seemingly like Yesenin in his disorder and negligence, for he has an incomparably more timid and easy question:

> Russian nature
> > before you
> > > in your prophetic wisdom,
> How pitiful I am
> > with my eternal haste!
> Not by scurrying
> > Nor constant fuss
> You conquer
> > by mighty slowness . . .
> When my time comes,
> > don't feel sad,
> Part with me simply,
> > without grieving.
> I shall not die!
> > You, Russian nature,
> > Take my Russian nature to yourself!

The dissolution he wants in slow Russian nature is in no way in accord with the poet's own "nature," in its perpetual hurry and fuss. On the other hand Yesenin's very sins are induced by a passionate desire for atonement and appear like grievous wounds on the body of a fallen hero who has not overcome his stormy titanic nature. (Such mutilations are significant by themselves and speak of strength or righteousness: "But if evils have nested in the soul—this means that angels lived there.")

Obviously there must be some kind of pyramid, a hierarchy of values, according to which one man's good does not suit another, and what is permissible for a Czar sounds pretentious on the lips of an ordinary mortal. Yevtushenko generally makes no pretension of playing a royal role; strictly speaking, he is less self-confident than Mayakovsky or Yesenin; but for that very reason, in his modest role of "the simple fellow," he sometimes behaves immodestly and tactlessly and seems like an upstart who has forgotten his place. The hypertrophy of his ego is paid for in the one instance by a cross, a burden, a destiny; it is motivated by the scope of the legend that has been created and the tragedy lived through; in the opposite case, when the situation is not motivated, it becomes ordinary self-love.

> On a spring night think of me
> And on a summer night think of me,
> On an autumn night think of me
> And on a winter night think of me.
> . . . .
> Be anxious for me,
> Passionately, profoundly.
> Do not stand to one side
> When I feel lonely.
>
> With empty zeal
> Don't catch me in trifles.
> For all my "later"
> Love my "now."

These lines are dedicated to the poet's beloved and to his friends, but there is a hint in them of a demanding attitude toward both love and friendship (not friends but rather admirers are treated in this way). They are all obliged to think about and remember *me*, because *I* need, *I* want it, and not because my ego is vast and universal and raised on a pedestal of unheard-of passion and torment.

Of course this the poet did not deliberately strive for, but on the level of broad literary comparisons it may be remarked that he simplifies and lowers the high tradition of Blok's love lyric when, for example, he misinterprets the "fidelity-betrayal" theme in the most ordinary, everyday terms ("Once more—to love her in heaven and betray her on earth"):

> On their knees I lay my head,
> But not to them—
>   to you I belong.

It is quite a different matter with the tradition of Mayakovsky's civic poetry, which Yevtushenko inherits and continues, since he is one of the most keenly topical poets of the new generation and eagerly assumes the role of tribune. Civic feelings largely dictated "Bratsk Hydroelectric Station" too, which has a special chapter in honor of Mayakovsky, who serves the author as an example of steadfastness, nobility, and revolutionary purity.

But the affective verse of Mayakovsky, if not supported from within by a personality of the same charge and caliber, sounds often on his lips rather bare and rarefied and declamatory, and it easily passes into a mere publicist's work (and this happens to many poets who imitate Mayakovsky). On the other hand Yevtushenko, even in the role of fighter, tribune, or agitator represents something different, a weaker variant of citizenship. Yevtushenko does not have the forcefulness of Mayakovsky, who always went straight and headlong to his goal, allowing no circumlocutions or false ideas; therefore Yevtushenko is forced to resort to maneuvers, ambushes, detours, and camouflage. ("We managed to get orders and do it all the other way around.") He has even worked out his own special "battle strategy." For him the poet "retreats in order to attack," maneuvers, lures, dodges.

> In moving artillery,
>   baggage train,
>   the flag
> A mighty hand guides him.
> Let them suppose that on the right flank
> He has concentrated his troops.
> But he,
>   he knows,
>   that on the left
> Since dawn waiting for the trumpeter
> Ready for battle
>   cavalry's behind the woods,
> Their nostrils quivering with joy.

Much, it is obvious, has changed and grown more complex since the time when the poet made no secret of the flank on which he concentrated ("Who steps to the right there? To the left, left, left!"), when he strode to the attack straight and to the front, "deploying on parade" his troops. It is hard to reproach Yevtushenko for the changes which have occurred, and still one cannot fail to notice with chagrin that his warlike temperament, boldness, and implacability toward "the scum" coexist in a startling way with compliance and adroitness, and all his complicated distribution of troops and their regrouping now on the right, now on the left flank, in short all his "battle strategy" turns out to be a very simple adjustment to the situation. He maneuvers so skillfully that you may admire his unexpected fencing sallies, but you can't feel much confidence in following him: he is capable of leading you anywhere at all, and for the sake of the next maneuver may leave you in the lurch.

Yevtushenko himself is fully aware of the compliance and halfway policy of his civic muse, and therefore the highest "strategic" considerations with which he justifies himself now and then are exchanged for other avowals: "Sometimes I am not exactly afraid, but still not very bold"; "I was as if a middle thing between wax and metal." Since he feels himself to be the poet of a time of transition, a poet still incomplete and not fully consistent, he welcomes the artist of the future who will realize his good intentions and fulfill what he has not dared to begin:

> And where I dropped the pen:
> "Not worth it"—
> He will say:
> "Worth it!"
> and take up the pen.

In his poem "Bratsk Hydroelectric Station" even Stenka Razin* repents before his death: "I resisted—half; I should have all the way." This expresses, of course, not so much the self-appraisal of Razin as it does of Yevtushenko.

At the same time these reproaches against him have a better basis than his self-praise. By not making himself into a wailing paragon of virtue, but by very often confessing his weaknesses and deficiencies, the poet strengthens our feeling of contact with a living person who for all his simplicity is not so simple and by no means naive. Most of all, these confessions tell us that he is capable of doubt and self-analysis which allow him to take a sober look at reality in all its complexity and contra-

---

* Seventeenth-century Cossack rebel.

dictions, to reflect on his own unsure position in the world and thus to step aside from his self of yesterday, and to rise above himself and reveal some other potentialities. This is the psychological basis for a number of Yevtushenko's best poems, for example his earlier "Boots," and more recently some verses under the general title of "A Trip to the North" (published in the New Year number of the journal *Znamya* [*Banner*]). In the last cycle there sounds insistently the theme of reevaluation of his own past and mistrust of himself—disputes with hope for the future:

> And really, crushed by my own icefloes,
> Cracking at the seams, fighting the ice,
> Shall I spit evil, turn about, surrender,
> Weary, and not having found myself?!
>
> . . . .
>
> That life threw me,
> I simply lied,
> There was no "All hands on deck,"
> There'll be the final bang!
>
> The sailor's coat thirsts for squalls.
> May they come more quickly
> My wind-force twelve—
> My twelve trumps.
>
> But still there's no shout "Look out!"
> And the wind has not risen . . .
> I stroll about, half cabin boy
> And half admiral.

Yevtushenko is a poet of undefined possibilities and of frequent reappraisals of his career in life and poetry. He snatches at everything and is ready to refuse everything in order to take a new chance, try himself in a new arena and finally take the road to his "real self" which is still only just getting ready to live. More than ten years ago he expressed the fear: "Shall I not really turn out to be anything, not really result?" And he still continues to worry about this theme, as though all his books were only a test of his pen, preparation, a running start, and a tuning-up. This gives his work the stamp of haste, instability, and diffuseness. He writes a lot, eagerly and often carelessly, without depth, as if he were chasing somebody he wished to overtake—most likely himself, who still has not "resulted."

But those same qualities in him which made one feel the living development of a human personality full of conflicts appealed strongly to the young. Youth too stands half-way on the road to itself, is also in a hurry to live and does not know what will result; it is full of doubt, makes choices, reappraises, seeks, finds, and does not find itself. With Yevtushenko this process has been rather extended and has assumed sharper forms, which is perhaps due to certain specific moments in his life as a writer, a life accompanied alternately by applause and reprimands and combining rare "good luck" and success with official half-recognition—and this has formed the habit in the poet of striving for something and of justifying himself in some respect or other. . . . Perhaps that is why his sincere "anxiety about himself" ("Character is knit together from one's first anxiety about oneself") at times suddenly smacks of vanity and the desire to "seem" overpowers the urge to "be"; the concern for "What am I like?" is interrupted by anxiety about "How do I look?"; the problems of the poet's fate is reduced to the trivial success of winning. Yevtushenko sometimes so insistently discusses in his verse whether his last appearance before the public has brought him victory or defeat and he so frankly seeks praise and applause (or the abuse that is their equivalent) that the central theme of his art, namely, the formation of a personality and the establishment of a character, is suddenly shifted to an entirely different plane: the author's advancement in the literary arena. In the question "Am I succeeding, or not?" one begins to hear the gambler's tone: "Will it work or won't it? Am I lucky or am I not?"

We shall not begin to reproach the poet for vanity: who does not like success? Who has not dreamed of fame? Something else is wrong too: the attitude toward oneself as a lottery ticket which may win if the occasion is right and the number turns up, but on which in reality nothing depends—a *disrespectful* attitude toward one's own personality can by this one gesture erase all the lofty monologues about faith in a humanity which has become the master of its own fate.

Fortunately there are opposed to these moods—in the light of which all life seems an endless merry-go-round, and the poet whirls just like a squirrel on a wheel, only impatiently waiting for his chance—other motifs which recently have become stronger: dissatisfaction with himself, the desire to break out of the magic circle, to rest, catch his breath, and reflect . . . These are the motifs which mark the cycle "A Trip to the North" mentioned above, the most mature and significant work, in our view, that he has written up to now. The experiences narrated here are perhaps grievous and sad and contradictory, but they can serve as a condition for a more profound view of the world; they testify to a growing exactingness in the poet and leave the impression that the constant hurry and fuss have for a while left him, yielding their place to serious thoughts about life, about himself.

> What are you, orator, what are you, prophet?
> You're confused, soaked through, shivering,
> The bullets have stopped. Your voice is hoarse.
> Rain washes out your little camp fire.
>
> But don't grieve that it's shameful enough for tears.
> About so many things one can think seriously.
> There's lots of time . . . "Long cries,"
> That's what they call the ferry.

The notes of dissatisfaction with himself and his environment and the endeavor to review the familiar, boring round of occupations and habits are to be heard clearly in "Bratsk Hydroelectric Station," which was written for the most part somewhat earlier. The appearance of the poem was motivated to a significant degree by these new needs: the poet wishes to waste no more time on trivialities, does not wish to glide over the surface, and renounces certain widespread sins of his past and that of others.

> My rivals, let's reject flattery
> And the deceptive honor of abuse.

Let us meditate on our fates.
All of us have the same
Sickness of the soul.
 Superficiality is its name.
Superficiality. You're worse than blindness.
You are able to see, but you don't want to.
Perhaps you spring from illiteracy?
Or perhaps from the fear of pulling up the roots
Of trees under which you grew,
Without putting a stake in their place?
And aren't we really hurrying,
Removing the top layer half a yard deep,
Because we've forgotten our manhood and are afraid
Of the very task: of penetrating the core of a thing?
Let's hurry . . . Giving only half an answer,
We'll carry superficiality like a treasure,
Not from cold calculation, no, no!
But from the instinct of self-preservation.
Then comes the failing of powers
And unfitness for flight and for struggle,
And with the feathers of our domestic wings
The pillows of scoundrels are already stuffed . . .

Well—it is told rather diffusely, but essentially it is quite
right. We heartily share his concern about the pressure of
superficial thoughts, of hasty decisions, half-answers, and half-
truths. This point of departure appears very serious and
topical, both with regard to contemporary life about which
Yevtushenko writes, and to his own career, so that one would
wish to take the words quoted (in their positive sense, naturally) as a rule set up by the author himself as one by which to
judge his poem. But first we must admit that we need it not
only for the sake of precision in critical analysis, which is
obliged to observe the set "rules of the game" and respect the
laws and principles which the artist subscribes to. It is also
needed as a precaution: so as not to put one's foot in it.

Yevtushenko is easy for the reader and hard for the critic.
He knows how to please, win favor, and evoke sympathy. He
is the first to criticize himself in such a way that he gives any
critic a hundred points bonus. It becomes awkward for any
other person to take up this work after him; thus it seems that
the author himself understands it all perfectly, knows every-

thing about himself, so what remains to be done? Meanwhile, though acknowledging and advancing perfectly just demands, Yevtushenko is far from consistent in applying them; his poetic thought often develops tortuously, it makes a loop, turns halfway, and leaps from subject to subject, and it evades answering the question addressed to it. And although his poems are not complex or difficult to understand, it is difficult to catch their inward essence which is inclined to change, so to speak, as the play continues. Perhaps the conditions that formed him have taught him flexibility, perhaps as a person he has not achieved final form and therefore easily loses the course he has taken, distracted by fresh ideas and impressions; or perhaps finally the historical vocation of Yevtushenko consists in removing from actuality, for the present, only the "top layer." However that may be, as you follow the logic of his art, you are often astonished at his skill in touching the acute and painful questions of our time without stating them profoundly; you are also astonished by his ability to meditate on everything in the world but not to speak to the essence of anything; and by his knack for sincerely proclaiming one thing and then just as sincerely doing something completely different. This is not always the case with him, but it can happen, and it does in "Bratsk Hydroelectric Station."

Having established our common malady—superficiality—and having expressed his firm intention of overcoming it, Yevtushenko wrote as a result his most superficial work. It is his most superficial because in design, scale, grasp of reality it aims at something immeasurably larger than, for example, a separate lyric, a cycle of lyrics, or simply a long poem, and that means that one demands more from it; his most superficial because the author has violated his own precept—one which is extremely important for him and for us all, and dear to us —almost as soon as he uttered it and, so it seems, he himself did not notice his loss. How did this happen?

Let us return to that beautiful tirade exposing superficiality which we quoted above, and let us read it attentively and observe carefully how Yevtushenko further develops the theme and what remedies he proposes for its cure.

Let each one enter life with this vow:
To help that which is supposed to flower,
And to take revenge, not forgetting this,
On everything that deserves vengeance!
Let this vengeance not be for vengeance's sake,
But a vengeance like a struggle incarnate,
In the name of justice and of honor,
In the name of affirming the good.
Through fear of vengeance we shall take no revenge.
The very possibility of vengeance decreases,
And the instinct of self-preservation
Does not preserve us but kills.
Superficiality is a murderer and not a friend,
A malady pretending to be health,
Entangling us in the nets of delusion . . .
In particular it dissipates the spirit,
Let us run away from generalizations.
The globe loses its force in the void,
Leaving generalizations for later.
But perhaps its helplessness
Is also the ungeneralizability of human fates
In the perception of the age, which is clear and simple?

Comparing this excerpt with the one before we see how the thought that was pulsing there grows thin and dries up here, how the aphorisms become trivial and the language clumsy, and the verse does not flow but marks time, since it has not the strength to overcome flabby thoughts about the need for doing what must be done and not doing what must not. "Vengeance like a struggle incarnate," "Through fear of vengeance we shall not take revenge": are *these* the revelations we expected from the poet who has gone into battle with superficiality and suddenly turned back in the middle of a phrase? What is the point of repeating these bald words ("vengeance," "honor," "justice," "vengeance," "the good," "take revenge")—or is it a game of words, twisting ideas around so that in the final result one problem is replaced by another? And the author, jumping off into generalizations about the general ungeneralizability, is already sliding along the surface of his statements which are perhaps ("But perhaps . . .") effective but have no application to what has gone before.

Yevtushenko is fond of ambiguous combinations of words

which create the appearance of dialectical contradiction, the
complexity of life, and poetical profundity: "I am making a
career for myself by not making it!"; "I am astonished—that's
why I am astonished at nothing"; "But it became easy and
simple for me, although it was not simple and not easy"; "She
did not love me, and she loved me"; "We did not understand
that it was all over because of the fact that it was all beginning." Such turns and sophistries may be successful in a
particular context, but they have long since become Yevtushenko's trademark, and for the most part they are unpleasing
because in their quite primitive way they produce an illusion
of significance.

In Yevtushenko's new poem the role of traitor is taken over
by the smart phrase about the "ungeneralizability" of the
world, and from this appears to flow the necessity for creating
artistic "generalizations" which promise to rescue us from the
hurry and fuss of superficiality (as though rhymes between
words guaranteed a connection between phenomena). Actually
the announcement made at the beginning that we shall have a
truly profound interpretation of life is not fulfilled in the continuation, since it has been crushed by the false profundity of
a "grand genre," by the grandeur of the subject, the perspective
for creating something epochal, universal, drawing some world-
historical line. "The poet, without succumbing to dismay, sums
up all that went before him," Yevtushenko affirms with unusual ease, but it so happens that this promise conflicts with
the other and excludes, even destroys it: "To penetrate to the
heart of a subject." Extending its adding up of totals over
thousands of kilometers, over decades and centuries, the poem
"Bratsk Hydroelectric Station" suffers from shapelessness and
verbosity (to read it straight through is, frankly speaking,
wearisome), it sins by its hasty attempts to speak "about everything," "taking the top layer off only half a yard deep." In
spite of being interesting in separate episodes and sketches,
the general impression it gives is that the author, not wanting
to be petty and expend himself in details, has converted it to
"generalizations" which are only outwardly full of significance,
but usually remain on the surface.

Such is in the first place the allegorical generalization which forms the basis of the poem—the dispute of Bratsk Hydroelectric Station with the Egyptian pyramid. During the whole extent of the poem the pyramid dully asserts its lack of faith in life and most boringly preaches the moral of cynicism and skepticism, whereas the power station, like a fool, objects hotly, bringing forward in defense of faith the appropriate illustrations from history and contemporary life, as a result of which the work assumes the shape it has. Ignoring for the moment what these "examples from life" amount to—each one forms a separate chapter—let us remark that Yevtushenko's symbolism appears to us strained. To be sure every poet has the right to understand in his own way images of the past, but the treatment of the pyramid jarred us: one of the great architectural wonders, based on a faith remote from our life, mysterious, but strong and deep, with an extraordinarily firm and integral conception of the world, one that down to our times serves as a symbol of immortality, creative power, monumental grandeur, for the most varied cultures—such a thing is assigned the most nihilistic program. No, whoever else may have suffered from skepticism, the pyramids did not, and they had their own thoughts evidenced in the unity of style, the harmony of detail in idea and composition, all of which creates a grandiose whole. Properly speaking we maintain in defense of their honor that Yevtushenko lacks precisely what made the fame of the pyramids, and that what is needed for any Cyclopean work in the art of yesterday and today is a firm monolithic foundation, profound thought, and artistic unity.

Having the Bratsk Hydroelectric Station before his eyes as ideal and model, Yevtushenko approached the task rather speculatively and preferred the quantitative method: his various observations, memories, and associations from the trip to Siberia are generalized and summed up by monotonously stringing them onto the central, pivotal idea of the work, the essence of which may be reduced to "you must believe" without regard to difficulties of any kind. This idea, worthy in itself, is so often insinuated and repeated that it gives rise to what is called a "bad infinity," and it imparts a single, stereotyped pattern to the vast material gathered here, and this is especially perceptible in the historical chapters which are written like paragraphs in a school textbook. The Decembrists, the Petrashevtsy, Chernyshevsky, Khalturin* appear as martyrs for this faith— all in the same form and all arranged "in order" in accordance with a schooltext program.

"Shall I be able to? I don't possess enough culture . . . A smattering promises no prophecies. . . ." Yevtushenko expresses, when beginning his poem, a serious danger, but then immediately and resolutely casts it aside: "But the spirit of Russia hovers over me and boldly bids me try." The main difficulty, however, in our view is called forth not so much from lack of culture as from excessive education which the author displays however and wherever he can, as if he were striving to put into his poem all he had ever heard, seen, read, or come across in Russian history and world art. The abundance of cultural and historical references, names, discoveries, and cryptic quotations (from Radischev to Vinokurov, from the archpriest Avvakum to Okudzhava)† is called upon to provide a broad poetical horizon. In fact it favors that superficial survey which is too often presented in "Bratsk Hydroelectric Station."

Cultural and historical references are introduced into the text of the poem so fleetingly and in phrases so ordinary and known to us all from childhood, that for all their variety they assume the character of obligatory requisites which today no man of the least education can do without: but the artist can, of course, since he possesses besides the "general baggage" his own exclusive interests and predilections. And thus when Pushkin appears among the Decembrists, then, as in a bad film, he "raises his hand, and in it holds—trembling pain" and recites "Have courage and take heed, arise, fallen slaves!" Nekrasov

---

* The Decembrists were aristocrats who revolted unsuccessfully in 1825; the Petrashevtsy were a Socialist group to which Dostoevsky belonged; Stephan Khalturin was a nineteenth-century terrorist (Translator's note).

† Radischev was a famous early opponent of serfdom. Vinokurov is a young Soviet poet. Avvakum was a seventeenth-century resistor of Church reform. Okudzhava is a popular café poet and singer of today (Translator's note).

naturally reminds us how "the Volga boatmen walk the tow-rope." Dostoevsky before his execution sees how "Rogozhin weeps and raves, Myshkin sways from side to side" and "Alyosha Karamazov roams as a quiet monk." Chernyshevsky is captured in a pose from the well-known anthology illustration recording the moment when somebody has thrown flowers to him on the scaffold, and so forth. Such associations are obvious and act automatically; in daily life one says: "Oh well, the whole works."

Wishing to show the high intellectual level of the people who built the power station, Yevtushenko, along with the popular names, introduces some rarer and more recherché ones: Skryabin, Fellini, Saint-Exupéry. . . . The builders relate:

> I see in the taiga the gardens of Gauguin,
> And Cézanne's dark blue haystacks.
> I see gleaming through the oxy-acetylene spray
> The blue girls of Degas.
>
> Forgive me the fantasy,
> But when the blizzard blows,
> All in snow, Rodin's thinker
> Sits on the edge of the dam. . . .
>
> . . . Sharing all our ordeals,
> Tolstoy walked in the furious snow,
> Dostoevsky was tormented, swayed,
> Gorki wandered with a baby in his arms.

Thus, between the commas in each verse, sometimes with a line for each person, the whole "kit" is presented, the kit necessary for the contemporary young man who wants to be associated with art. About the variety of aesthetic tastes and cultural interests, which he has grasped as a sign of the times, there is no need to argue. The unfortunate thing is that in Yevtushenko's rapid speech this variety has no foundation, and merely to say that it is the heroes of the poem, not the author, who think and speak like this, does not alter the prevailing stylistic confusion which fully accords with the author's taste. "I see gleaming through the oxy-acetylene spray the blue girls of Degas. . . .": Often Yevtushenko's images are constructed according to this formula and his words and themes are connected by the same principle. Outwardly pretty and fashionable, with pretensions of precision and measure, it is, so to speak, a proletarian production formula—but it cries out to heaven about the poetic eclecticism to which Yevtushenko pays tribute in his new poem.

In this respect he is not alone. We encounter now and then attempts to join together what may not be joined and, speaking crudely, to marry Andrei Rublyov* with radar, in the work of A. Voznesensky, who, more sharply than Yevtushenko, has aimed for formal innovation. In the visual arts the same tendency may be found in the works of Ilya Glazunov, who recently caused a sensation among young lovers of painting who did not sense the tastelessness of his showy imitations of the old Russian icon which was crossed with the method of Käthe Kollwitz, Ioganson, and the Kukryniksy. †

It is not impossible that this eclecticism stems from too fervent adoption and superficial appropriation of two different kinds of ideas, which in principle are completely legitimate and fruitful. First we all know well (even too well) that art develops by basing itself on a classical tradition. On the other hand, in modern art and especially with the work of the young school of artists, there is a legitimate striving to enlarge and renew the traditional range of art. But in hasty practice ("And that is why we hurry. . . .") the combination of these tendencies can give rise to inconceivable hybrids, like the cross between a dachshund and a collie. If the poet has been so far content, for example, with the tradition of Demyan Bedny,‡ but now has had enough of this, he "enriches" Bedny with Bryusov§ without giving up his old orientation. Each of the authors mentioned is worthy of having followers, but the mixing of styles leads to something monstrous.

* Famous Russian icon painter of the late fourteenth and early fifteenth century.
† Ioganson is a Soviet realist painter; the Kukryniksy are well-known cartoonists.
‡ Proletarian poet of the Stalin era.
§ Symbolist poet, later accepted by Soviets (Translator's note).

In the introduction to "Bratsk Hydroelectric Station," in accordance with the rules of the devout masters of the Middle Ages, Yevtushenko pronounces a "prayer before the poem." In it he turns for help simultaneously to seven Russian poets: Pushkin, Lermontov, Nekrasov, Blok, Pasternak, Yesenin, and Mayakovsky, and in passing he gives them each a rapid characterization, paraphrasing in his own fashion their winged utterances—which appears for the most part as cheap cliché or in places as parody. In trying to disclose in two words each one's specific quality, Yevtushenko for instance paraphrases the well-known line from Yesenin's poem "To Kachalov's Dog": "Give, Jim, for luck your paw to me. . . ." as "Yesenin, give for luck your tenderness to me. . . ." The worst part is that the respectful pupil, in his desire to imitate all that is most valuable in his great teachers, does not consider how all this will fit into his poem. Although "Bratsk Hydroelectric Station" is, as the saying goes, large enough for everyone, it is hard to suppose that in the new poetic amalgam Pushkin's "melodiousness" (all these definitions are Yevtushenko's and appear as "gifts" he asks of the classic authors) would harmonize with the "inelegance" of Nekrasov, the "mistiness" of Blok, and the "venom" of Lermontov. If one imagines that the poets mentioned really did give the author of "Bratsk Hydroelectric Station" these mutually exclusive qualities, it would turn out to be a disaster and his structure would immediately collapse. There remains another road which Yevtushenko takes in practice: to take a little from each classic author—a little "mistiness," a little "roughhewnness," a little "melodiousness," etc. Then there would result a neutral stylistic mixture, unexplosive, and devoid of the brilliant features which the donors possessed, eclectic to a degree and often peculiar. But is it worth praying for so earnestly?

Obviously we should not confuse the artistic heritage in a broad sense with the tasks of an individual work of art. If we all, society, literature, and readers, strive to take the best in world culture and seek a variety of tastes and styles, this by no means signifies that a specific author in a specific work is obliged to appropriate all these traditions directly and to display them clearly. The large scale of his proposed work may have confused Yevtushenko and impelled him to turn to such numerous supporters, but it makes no difference. Dante's one guide was Virgil. Who was Pushkin's in *Eugene Onegin,* Tolstoy's in *War and Peace*? The whole of culture, presumably, and no single person.

We have dwelt thus on the "prayer before the poem" because unfortunately it is typical of widespread notions today as to how masterpieces are created; one would like to oppose to it a prayer of another kind made by an exacting artist before his work. It was written by Kipling—a judge who may not be very authoritative for us, but in questions of the psychology of art and the creation of unique aesthetic values he was an expert. Kipling's poem "Evarra and His Gods" tells about a certain Evarra, "maker of Gods in lands beyond the sea," who personifies any artist, to whatever country he may belong, and thus every time, in each new life of his, he solves his problem differently. Depending on the place and time in which he lives, Evarra now makes his God out of gold and pearl, now hews it from the rude stone, now carves himself an idol from wood with hair of moss and a straw crown, and finally moulds it from mud and horns. Each time he sets on his work the proud inscription: "Thus Gods are made, / And whoso makes them otherwise shall die." But then in his next incarnation, forgetting the past, he will trace ever new the same immutable law which serves him for the creation of a different image.

> Yet at the last he came to Paradise,
> And found his own four Gods, and that he wrote;
> And marvelled, being very near to God,
> What oaf on earth had made his toil God's law,
> Till God said mocking: "Mock not. These be thine."
> Then cried Evarra: "I have sinned!" "Not so.
> If thou hadst written otherwise, thy Gods
> Had rested in the mountain and the mine,
> And I were poorer by four wondrous Gods,
> And thy more wondrous laws, Evarra. Thine,
> Servant of shouting crowds and lowing kine!"

The moral of this tale is that the artist in the process of creation should not be omnivorous, but rather impatient with anyone else's performance, and convinced of the absolute rightness of his own unique course. It is not that in general and in principle he is not able to value other people's works or show breadth of view and taste. Like any man he may have access to a very wide variety of things. But with regard to himself he knows for sure that he is able to work only in one way and no other, and that his proposed version is unshakable, his stylistic system, tradition, and aesthetic true and unique: "Thus Gods are made." We know many instances of one genius being unjust to another: Tolstoy abused Shakespeare, Gorky at one time had no special liking for Mayakovsky, and Mayakovsky attacked the Arts Theater. To us they are all dear and we often feel bewildered by the unexpected narrowness and partisan prejudice of such judgments; we forget that the splendid variety of the works we love came about only because each one of them wanted to be unlike the next one and therefore in its obstinate singularity at times it was deaf to a foreign method of artistic perception. It is not necessary, of course, to create artificially such conflicts, but they indirectly bear witness once again to the fact that in the field of art the one-sided fanatics of their own idea and their own style usually win.

In the poem "Bratsk Hydroelectric Station" there is much talk about faith and steadfastness. But there is too little that is steadfast in style and taste, and at times the text wavers, attuning itself to the theme of a well-known song or to a familiar quotation; heavy didactic bits fall out of the living tissue of the verse which is linked to pictures of the real world. Yevtushenko has long since formed his direct and immediate connection with actuality, and has a keen eye for details of daily life, and an ear not spoilt by lack of faith in familiar daily speech; therefore, when he forgets to make grand literary summations and simply writes about the life about him, everything becomes normal, so to speak.

> And again I absorbed, falling on the steering wheel,
> Into my insatiable eyes

Palaces of culture.
　　　Tearooms.
　　　　　Barracks.
Regional committees
　　　Churches.
　　　　　And car-inspection posts.
Factories.
　　Peasant huts.
　　Slogans.
　　　Birches.
Roar of jets in the sky.
　　Vibration of sledges.
Silences.
　　　Overgrown statuettes
Of dairymaids, pioneers, miners.
Old woman's eyes, looking like icons.
Broad bottoms of peasant women.
　　　Children's jumble.
Artificial limbs.
　　Oil derricks.
　　　Slag heaps
Like the breasts of recumbent giantesses.
Men drove tractors.
　　Sawed.
Went to check in, then hurried to the bench.
Went down the mine shafts.
　　　Drank beer,
Sprinkling salt at the brim.
And the women did the cooking.
　　　Laundered.
Darned, crowding the work into a moment.
They painted houses.
　　　And stood in queues.
Founded the earth.
　　　Hauled cement.

In this section there is no pretense of special philosophical conclusions, but a list of features of the country and the times, and it has more love and wisdom than the following strained efforts that try to "interpret" and "generalize" what he has seen ("And looking into the many-starred night, ahead, I thought that great illuminations were fastened into saving links"); here everything is appropriate and natural, unless perhaps the old woman's eyes "looking like icons": a familiar cliché. But in the "many-starred night" full of meditation, beside the "broad-bottomed peasant women" (and just how did he contrive to put such words side by side?) one feels a forced assortment: just as sometimes the customer may be loaded up with unsalable goods and to the box of oatmeal he wanted may be gratuitously added some quite superfluous canned fish in tomato sauce.

The best parts and chapters of the poem (for example "Nyushka," "Bolshevik," "The Controller of the World," "The Night of Poetry") are written like scenes taken from nature and the characters are captured directly from reality. Here the poet appears not in his usual position of the main actor, but is himself a spectator and listener who has realized the intention expressed earlier in the lines "to overhear everyone at once, to spy on everything at once." From the art of lyrical biography he passes over to metamorphoses; of this too he wrote in a recent poem ("I must be, in accord with duty and love, trees, tramways, people") and this is often achieved in the poem.

At the same time the wide range and Yevtushenko's eagerness to render "everything at once" creates the effect in places of having read the best parts before or having seen them in a movie theater. Thus it happens that in a recent film *The Chairman* we have already met Yevtushenko's chairman (in the chapter "Nyushka"), and the dramatic experiences that fall to his lot.

> "Give us the plan" they drummed from the center.
> The telephone went crazy with ringing,
> Well, the hands vainly pressed
> The dried-up udders of the cows . . .
>
> He took an old photo of Lenin
> And for hours looked and smoked,
> And seemed to be asking something,
> And talking to him about something.

We have already encountered on the screen something like the wish expressed by Yevtushenko at the grave of the rank-and-file worker (in the chapter "Don't die, Ivan Stepanovich!"):

> Among the broad-pawed pines
> Let the whole nation follow the coffin,
> And removing their hats in silence
> Let the government follow it.

In giving these quotations we are not trying to establish the source of Yevtushenko's images. It is merely a question of showing that in spite of their concreteness, their liveliness and credibility, his images somehow live at times in a secondary, reflected light. It is not necessarily so that a particular film or book served as the intermediary link, but readers of the poem may involuntarily recall a Polish film *The Passenger*, when for instance the poem (in the chapter "The Controller of the World") tells the tragic story of love in a German concentration camp and there follows such a soul-rending scene:

> And she runs, runs in a circle in Riva,
> Stumbling among the stones,
> And the soldiers' shiny snouts
> Smirk at her from the towers.
>
> My God, I asked her to die, remember?
> Why is she still alive?
> I scream, rush to her aid,
> And my comrades stuff my mouth.
>
> And she runs, runs in a circle,
> Fall, gets up, her face is bloody.
> My God, stretch out your hand to her,
> And forever abandon her!

Another tacked-on element, permitted entrance by the poet in his truthful stories about life, is evident when he exploits pathetic tones and touching gestures which are calculated to produce an impression and to soften up the reader. Hence the abundance of tears shed in the poem, hence the theatrical parting words of the old woman (in the chapter "Zharki"):

> And that lean, gnarled
> Peasant hand
> Makes the sign of the cross over the excavators
> And over us—for all time . . .

Presumably the author needed this gesture to bring together loose ends and to create logical bridges to another chapter near the beginning ("A Fair in Simbirsk"), where the youth Lenin is depicted in similar company. But such little bridges (there are several in the poem) are entirely contrived and invented, without mentioning the fact that the episode with the drunken peasant woman whom Lenin symbolically lifts out of the mud marks the future rebirth of Russia, which sounds here extremely sentimental and false:

> He carefully leads her by the elbow,
> And he does not even think how it looks.
> "May God keep you,
>   clear-browed man,
> And somehow I'll make it alone . . .
> And he goes away
>   goes along the barges
> On the banks of the Volga,
>   and, sad in the sequel,
> The old woman quietly makes the sign of the cross for him,
> As if making the sign over her child.

There is no doubt that in the poem "Bratsk Hydroelectric Station" Yevtushenko has set about the solving of very serious problems of the past and present; in such a field of activity, naturally, he was not able to solve everything at the required level. It is also sometimes said that a writer has in general no obligation to "solve" anything, and that he need only "pose" the questions of his times while leaving the answers to his generation, to society and history. This opinion, however, needs just one qualification: to pose questions means more than to name them, hint at something serious and then pass quietly on as if merely to mention it were the last word on the given subject. Perhaps it would be better if a writer in general did not touch at all those aspects of life about which for whatever reasons he cannot say more than others have already said. Is not meditative "narrowness" better than a superficial "breadth"? Is not a conscious limitation of theme and material at times capable of helping create a more concentrated approach to reality and of achieving more than a light, all-embracing glance at things?

These unhappy thoughts come to mind when Yevtushenko in his poem touches on what is perhaps the sorest and most "accursed" question of our recent past, and tries to deal with the theme of the concentration camps. It would have been better if he had left it alone. Without trying to provide the answer to *how* he should have written on this theme, one may confidently assert that he should not have done it as it appears in the text published in *Yunost* (*Youth*). Probably, in trying to exalt the unyielding faith of those who suffered innocently under Stalin, he proceeded along the well-tried and easy path of celebrating their workers' enthusiasm, just as there were scarcely any materials which indicated where, why, and under what conditions this enthusiasm had to be shown. As a result, against his own wishes, the concentration camps become a stronghold of our military and industrial might, almost a pledge of victory, and the people who perished there a kind of Communist labor brigade—which sounds altogether blasphemous.

> Roundabout, watching, stood the escort,
> And you did not understand, Comrade Stalin,
> That, far from your prison convoy,
> We, the politicals you had numbered,
> Went through seas and through rivers
> And reached Berlin with the army.
>
> Still remaining an "enemy of the people,"
> I built the hydroelectric station on the Volga, not giving up.
> They hid us from foreign eyes.
> And we broke records. We spat on the fact
> That they never photographed or drew us
> And wrote no sketches about us.

Too facile and illusory too is the solution of the problem connected with the above, namely that of "fathers" and "children," although it may seem seductive at first glance. The "children" do not dare to betray the honorable "fathers" who had faith and toiled heroically even in the labor camps.

But remember the other fathers—who knocked,
Who locked us up or were basely silent,
Don't forget such fathers either.
Spit on their threats or caresses!
Go, my boy, clean as a commissar,
With the truth of your fathers against the scoundrels!

This is told sharply and boldly, but it is a shallow thought. If the question is put a shade more profoundly, the proposed separation of the "fathers" into honorable believers and base unbelievers will appear a fiction: were there not among the "other fathers," who "knocked and locked us up," people of the most sincere faith? Does this aspect of things exhaust the tragedy that was lived through?

The idea of "faith," around which turn the majority of episodes in the poem, might well in conclusion be equipped and supplemented with another idea expressed by Yevtushenko himself, and sounding in his verses like a kind of invitation from the new poetry to the young generation: "Let us think."

Let us think. We are all guilty
Of the annoyance of big details—
Of empty verses, countless quotations,
Of stereotyped conclusions to speeches . . .

We do not wish to live the way the wind blows.
We shall gain an understanding of our becauses.
Greatness calls. Let us think.
Let us be equal to it.

Together with other attractive qualities in our author, this invitation, expressing the spirit of the time and becoming practically the motto for a good deal of thought in contemporary literature, has enabled Yevtushenko in recent years to play the role more than once of sharpshooter or choir-leader. It has not happened in this poem. Here, if it may be said that way, he falls short of his own demands, and is concerned with developing his theme in breadth when he ought to have done it in depth and thought it out to the end and penetrated to the essence. "Yes, into the heights and the depths—and both at once!"—he proclaims in the poem, as always understanding what should be done, but not coping with the task he recognized and turning away from it. For us there is nothing left but to support the poet in his challenge: "Yes, into the heights and the depths! . . ." Yes, this is the way, the only way.

Notes

Notes

✣

Introduction

1. It was mentioned at the trial that the pseudonym Abram Tertz is taken from an obscene, and possibly anti-Soviet, "bandit" song from Odessa of the 1920's and that it had Jewish connotations. (We could not identify the song—Editors.) Because they had found alleged anti-Semitism in Sinyavsky's works, the prosecution wanted to utilize the pseudonym as a proof of Sinyavsky's anti-Semitism and hypocrisy, to demonstrate his "amoral" character. Sinyavsky denied the charges, but did not explain where the pseudonym is from. See: *On Trial* (translated and edited by Max Hayward, Harper & Row, New York, 1966), pp. 82, 87.

2. See the testimony of D. V. Duvakin in *Grani* (Frankfurt am Main), No. 62, 1966, p. 95.

3. *Literaturnaya Gazeta*, February 16, 1966. "There is no Moral Justification"—unsigned.

4. The periods of the 1920's and the first years of the war, 1941–1943, were the most liberal periods in the history of Soviet literature. Sinyavsky's interest in these periods is a clear indication that he, like other disillusioned former Communists of his generation, felt the need to find some positive tradition in the history of Soviet Russia, and found these two above-mentioned periods the most encouraging.

5. *On Trial*, p. 4.

6. Sinyavsky described himself at the trial as a "non-Marxist" and an "unorthodox Soviet writer," i.e., implying that he was not anti-Soviet, like Valery Tarsis. *On Trial*, p. 128.

7. At the trial, Sinyavsky reports the shock he had in 1951 when his father was arrested by the NKVD. His diaries were also confiscated, and since then, he developed a habit of hiding his manuscripts. This is why some of his manuscripts were at a friend's house (Dokukina) when Sinyavsky was arrested in 1965. *Grani*, No. 62, 1966, p. 82. Also, *On Trial*, p. 125.

8. Reference to the so-called "doctors' plot," in which nine doctors, six of them Jewish, were accused of having conspired in the interests of Western powers and international Jewish organizations to poison Stalin and other Soviet leaders. Only Stalin's death on March 5, 1953, saved the lives of the accused. The "doctors' plot" was used by Soviet authorities to launch a malignant anti-Semitic campaign in the Soviet Union. *The Trial Begins* by Tertz has the "doctors' plot" atmosphere as background.

9. *On Trial*, p. 5.

10. *On Socialist Realism* and *The Trial Begins* were ready in 1956, and Sinyavsky gave them to Zamoyska in December, 1956. The last two pages of the manuscript *On Socialist Realism* Sinyavsky wrote later (1959) and had them sent abroad by Andrei Remezov, a staff member of the Library of Foreign Literature in Moscow. *On Trial*, p. 45, and *Grani*, No. 62, 1966, pp. 89–90.

11. Zamoyska writes that Sinyavsky warned her not to have his manuscript published by so-called "anti-Soviet" publishers. Thus, Tertz's first work, *On Socialist Realism*, was, oddly enough, published by a French left-wing Catholic magazine, *Esprit* (February, 1959), in an abbreviated French translation. In the United States, Pantheon Books, New York, published the book in 1960. The works of Tertz are now available in a Russian edition, *Fantastichesky Mir Abrama Tertsa*, Inter Language Literary Associates, 1967, 454 pp. (*Thoughts Unaware* not included.)

12. *Istoriya Russko-Sovyetskoi Literatury*, Vol. I, Moscow, Izd. Akad. Nauk, 1955, pp. 99–167 and 397–420.

13. *Novy Mir*, 1959, No. 2, pp. 211–222; *Novy Mir*, 1959, No. 8, pp. 248–254.

14. *Novy Mir*, 1960, No. 5, pp. 225–236.

15. *Voprosy Literatury*, 1960, No. 1, pp. 45–59; *Literaturnaya Gazeta*, 1960, May, No. 1; "Realism Fantastiki."

16. A. D. Sinyavsky, I. N. Golomshtok: *Picasso*, "Znanie" Publishing House, Moscow, 1960, 63 pp.

17. Abram Tertz: *Fantastic Stories*, Random House, 1963, pp. 213. In 1961 the *Fantastic Stories* were published in Polish by the Institut Litteraire, S.A.R.L. in Paris. They are now included in the Russian edition *Fantastichesky Mir* . . . , as is the short story "Pkhentz."

18. *Novy Mir*, 1961, No. 1, pp. 224–244.

19. *Novy Mir*, 1961, No. 8, pp. 248–252.

20. *Istoriya Russko-Sovyetskoi Literatury*, Vol. III. Moscow, Izd. Akad. Nauk, 1961. Sinyavsky's article opens the volume—"Literatura perioda Velikoi Otechestvennoi voiny," pp. 5–54.

21. *Novy Mir*, 1962, No. 3, pp. 261–263.

22. *The Makepeace Experiment*, New York, Pantheon Books, 1965. The Russian version, *Lyubimov*, was published in 1964 by Boris Filippov in Washington, 66 pp.

23. *Novy Mir*, 1964, No. 1, pp. 260–263.

24. A. Menshutin, A. Sinyavsky, *Poeziya Pervykh Let Revolyutsii, 1917–1920*, Moscow, Izd. Akad. Nauk, 1964, p. 440.

25. *Novy Mir*, 1964, No. 6, pp. 174–176.

26. *Novy Mir*, 1964, No. 12, pp. 228–233.

27. *Novy Mir*, 1965, No. 3, pp. 244–248.

28. Boris Pasternak: *Stikhotvoreniya i Poemy*, Moscow-Leningrad, 1965, Sovyetsky Pisatel. With an introduction by A. Sinyavsky, pp. 5–62.

29. "Pkhentz," *Encounter* (London), March, 1966. In Russian, in *Fantastichesky Mir*.

30. *Thoughts Unaware*, first English text in *New Leader*, New York, July 19, 1965. Published in Russian by Boris Filippov in Washington, 1966, 157 pp.

31. In *Encounter* (London), April, 1967. In Russian, *Grani*, No. 63, 1967, pp. 114–140.

32. *On Trial*, pp. 107, 134.

33. *Grani*, No. 62, 1966, pp. 86–87.

34. A. Tertz: *On Socialist Realism*, New York, Pantheon Books, 1960, pp. 94–95.

35. *On Trial*, p. 106.

36. *On Trial*, p. 123.

37. *Sinyavsky i Daniel na skame podsudimykh*, Inter-Language Literary Associates, New York, 1966, p. 10.

38. Alexey Alexandrovich Surkov (1899–   ), Stalinist poet, functionary of the Writers' Union, "peace and friendship" delegate. Recently he has tried to expiate his former behavior by helping to rehabilitate formerly oppressed writers.

39. A popular magazine, similar to the U.S. *Life*.

40. *Grani*, No. 62, 1966, p. 22.

41. *On Trial*, p. 22.

42. *Izvestiya*, January 13, 1966. "The Turncoats" by D. Yeremin.

43. *Literaturnaya Gazeta*, January 22, 1966.

44. *Pravda*, February 15, 1966. "Slanderers Sentenced" by T. Petrov.

45. Paragraph 70 of the Civil Law is a deliberately vaguely formulated article punishing "agitation and propaganda . . . subverting the Soviet state." *Ugolovny Kodeks*, R.S.F.S.R., Moscow, 1962, pp. 47–48.

46. In the meantime it has been reported that the editor of the *White Book* is A. Ginzburg (editor of the underground literary periodical *Sintaksis*), who also contributed a letter to the *White Book*, *Grani*, 1966, No. 62, pp. 33–38. Allegedly he has been arrested by the Soviet authorities for sending a copy of the "White Book" to Soviet Premier Kosygin.

47. The number of organizations and individuals protesting against the trial is too numerous to be listed here. We list here just a sample of newspaper articles reporting the protests: *The New York Times*, April 24, 1966 ("Set the Writers Free—U.S. Colleges and Universities Protest"); Washington *Post*, April 19, 1966 ("Pleas for Jailed Soviet Writers"); New York *Herald Tribune*, February 24, 1966 ("N.J. Academics' Plea"); *Christian Science Monitor*, February 18, 1966 ("Western Reds Protest"). A world-wide list of articles protesting the trial compiled by Radio Liberty stretches to almost ten pages.

48. For the protest of the West European Communist parties see: Washington *Post*, February, 1966 ("French Reds Protest"); Baltimore *Sun*, February 17, 1966 ("Italian Reds Protest"); *Christian Science Monitor*, February 17, 1966; ("Nyekul'turno"); *L'Unità* (Italian Communist daily); *L'Humanité*, February 16, 1966 (Louis Aragon's article).

49. *Pravda*, April 2, 1966.

50. Our selection includes all magazine articles Sinyavsky published in the Soviet Union. We have omitted two articles; one, published in the *Literaturnaya Gazeta* (1960, May, No. 1), because it deals with the same topic as Sinyavsky's other article, "On Science Fiction," translated here, and the other, a review article on Pasternak's poetry (*Novy Mir*, 1962, No. 3, pp. 261–263, English, *Encounter*, March, 1966), because of the more complete article included here. We did not want to include the critical longer studies by Sinyavsky—for reasons of space and magnitude, for example, we did not include the essay Sinyavsky wrote for the *Istoriya Russko-Sovyetskoi Literatury*, or the whole book on *Poeziya Pervykh Let Revolyutsii, 1917–1920*, which alone would require an individual volume. The interesting analysis of Picasso's paintings, which Sinyavsky wrote together with I. N. Golomshtok, is not included here either. If, however, as we assume, Sinyavsky is going to have a lasting influence on the history of Russian literature and literary criticism, we are confident that his other works will also find their way to the English-speaking public.

On a Collection of Verses by Anatoly Sofronov

(A. Sinyavsky, "O novom sbornike stikhov Anatoliya Sofronova," *Novy Mir*, 1959, No. 8, pp. 248–254.)

1. Anatoly Vladimirovich Sofronov (1911–   ), Socialist-realist poet, playwright, Stalin prize-winner, 1959. Sofronov, together with Vitaly Kochetov, another Socialist-realist writer, serves as constant target also for A. Tertz. See, for example, the conversation between the two policemen Vitya (from Vitaly) and Tolya (from Anatoly) arresting Karlinsky in *The Trial Begins*. Kochetov appears in the *Makepeace Experiment* as the "universal secret agent" who sends his intelligence reports to Sofronov.

During the "re-Stalinization" campaign connected with the 25th anniversary of German defeat in World War II, Anatoly Sofronov also joined the campaign with a super-patriotic poem attacking Stalin's critics. Charlotte Saikowski, correspondent of the *Christian Science Monitor* (May 4, 1970) wrote from Moscow: ". . . the Kremlin's current theme is that the Soviet people have a glorious past of which they need not be ashamed. The theme is vividly reflected in a poem by an archconservative literary figure, Anatoly Sofronov, in a chapter of the poem entitled 'The Burden of Courage,' which is a paean to Soviet soldiers who fought in the war; the author angrily assails the 'penpushers' who try "to cross out the past." This is a 'theft of the soul,' he says, and goes on with burning nationalistic pride:

> They would like
> to convince me,
> That I lived
> for thirty years,
> suffocating in a dark cell
>
> That I walked,
> with clanking shackles.
> No, I will not allow them
> to take from me
> those years!"

2. Nikolay Semyonovich Tikhonov (1896–   ), Stalin prize-winner (1942, 1949, 1952). Socialist-realist poet, author of super-patriotic and "peace and friendship'" poems.

3. Sergei Alexandrovich Yesenin (1895–1925); one of the leading poets of the early twentieth century; Mikhail Vasilyevich Isakovsky (1900–   ); Socialist-realist poet, Stalin prize winner 1943 and 1949.

4. Edvard Grieg (1843–1907), Norwegian composer.

5. Alexander Alexandrovich Blok (1880–1921), leading symbolist writer. The reference is to Blok's famous poem "The Scythians" (1918).

6. Reference is to Mayakovsky's poem "The Brooklyn Bridge."

7. "Laponka" (Russian)—affectionate colloquial usage, approximately in the meaning of the U.S. "honey."

No Discount (ON SCIENCE FICTION)

(A. Sinyavsky, "Bez Skidok" [O sovremennom nauchnofantasticheskom romane] *Voprosy Literatury*, 1960, No. 1, pp. 45–59.)

1. Veiled, vague reference to the destructive effect of Socialist-realism on the development of Soviet literature.

2. Sinyavsky's sarcasm is directed again at the perpetrators of the "thaw-freeze," "freeze-thaw" game.

3. "To decipher the Mystery of Mars" is the task of science, just as to decipher the mystery of life is the aim of art, Sinyavsky says in his collection of philosophical aphorisms: *Thoughts Unaware.*

4. This statement is identical to Sinyavsky's artistic credo at the end of *On Socialist Realism.*

5. The last three paragraphs describing clearly Sinyavsky's theory of "fantastic realism" are very useful, indeed, for a better understanding of Sinyavsky's fantastic tales, especially the latest ones: *The Makepeace Experiment* and "Pkhentz."

6. The assertion about the unlimited nature of history applied to a future ideal society has dangerous implications in the Soviet Union, where according to the Marxist scheme Communism is the "logically" final stage of historical development.

7. Sinyavsky ridicules a similar phenomenon in his *Makepeace Experiment,* where the backward Russian provincial town Lyubimov pretends to be the model of a "future" Socialist community.

8. Stanislaw Lem (1921–   ), Polish science-fiction writer, author of the *Man from Mars* (1946) and other science-fiction stories.

9. Konstantin Eduardovich Tsiolkovsky (1857–1935), aeronautical inventor, made major discoveries in aerodynamics, rocketry, and the theory of interplanetary flights. Father of Russian space research.

10. Sir Arthur Conan Doyle (1859–1930), English novelist and historian, creator of the modern detective story, and of the character Sherlock Holmes.

11. Soviet popular scientific and technological periodicals.

12. *Detgiz*: Children's Books Publishing House; *Trudrezervizdat*: Publishing House of Vocational Training; *Molodaya Gvardiya*: Publishing House of the Young Communist League; *Yunost*: Literary monthly, published by the Writers' Union; *Pionerskaya Pravda*: Daily of the Pioneer Organization.

13. Faddey Venediktovich Bulgarin (1789–1859), Minor writer of the Pushkin period, publisher of the periodical "Northern Bee."
14. Alexander Romanovich Belyaev (1894–1941), Russian-Soviet writer of science-fiction stories. The novel *The Amphibious Man* (1928) referred to by Sinyavsky is attacked in the *Bolshaya Sovyetskaya Entsiklopediya*, Vol. 4, p. 581, as ". . . [bearing] the clichés of bourgeois science-fiction stories, which [sometimes] forced the author to abandon realism" (*sic!*).

The Poetry and Prose of Olga Berggolts

(A. Sinyavsky, "Poeziya i proza Olga Berggolts," *Novy Mir*, 1960, No. 5, pp. 225–236.)
1. Olga Fyodorovna Berggolts (1910–   ), Soviet poetess, her early poetry was influenced by Anna Akhmatova. Her late husband, the poet Boris Kornilov, was arrested in 1937 and he died some time later in a labor camp.
2. Blockade of Leningrad, in early September, 1941. German troops blockaded Leningrad, and the siege lasted for some 900 days. The suffering of the Leningrad population, but also their heroism and human readiness to help each other, is Berggolts' important topic.
3. Mamison Height: mountain pass over the central Caucasus.
4. Alexander Ivanovich Herzen (1820–1870), leading Russian revolutionary thinker and philosopher, publisher of the émigré magazine *The Bell* (London). *My Past and Thoughts* (1858) is his autobiography and a brilliant picture of the Russian intellectual life in the 1840's.
5. Reference to the German blockade of Leningrad.
6. Obukhovskaya: industrial district in Leningrad.
7. "There will be no more time"—reference to Revelation 10:5–7.
8. Uglich: city, pop. 28,000 (1959) in the Yaroslav region.
9. Lenin monument at the Finland station commemorates Lenin's return from exile in Switzerland in April, 1917. Sculptures of Petergoff: Petergoff, built in 1709–1710 under Peter I as his summer residence; it has beautiful parks and palaces with many sculptures and fountains. Since 1944, the place is called Petrodvorets, in order to eliminate the German sounding ending (-goff: Hof).
10. Ulitsa Zodchego: street in Leningrad commemorating the great architect of the city, Peter the Great.
11. Altai: mountain system in S. W. Siberia and Mongolia.
12. Reference to the Bartholomew Night (August 24, 1572) when the Huguenots were massacred by the Catholics in Paris. The "cross"—the form of the paper stripes used to black out the

windows against air attacks, must have reminded Berggolts of the crosses made on the Bartholomew Night on the windows of the Huguenots marked for extinction.

13. Samson rending the lion, Judges 14:6.

14. Fatherland War, or the Great Patriotic War—Soviet terms for World War II. They are sometimes the "second" because the Napoleonic War (1812–1815) counts as the first.

15. Leather Jackets: Members of the first Soviet political police, the Cheka, wore leather jackets.

16. Reference to the post World War I and Civil War (1917–1920) inflation in Russia. By 1920 the ruble-dollar exchange rate climbed to 1:1200 (from the 1918 rate of 1:9). Vernadsky, *A History of Russia*, New Haven, Yale University Press, 1954, p. 316.

17. Tsokane: northern Russian dialect, palatalized "t" is pronounced "ts."

18. February, 1942: the hardest winter of the German blockade of Leningrad.

"Come Walk with Us" (ON ROBERT FROST'S POEMS)

(A. Sinyavsky, "Poidyom so mnoi. . . ." [Robert Frost, Iz devyati knig. Perevod s angliiskogo pod redaktsiyei i s predisloviyem M. A. Zenkevicha. Izd. Inostrannoi Literatury. Moscow, 1963] *Novy Mir*, 1964, No. 3, pp. 261–263.)

1. Robert Frost visited the Soviet Union in 1963. The volume under review was probably prepared for this occasion. This article is based on a translation by L. Tikos and F. C. Ellert, which appeared in *The Massachusetts Review*, Vol. VII No. 3, 1966, pp. 431–441.

2. In Sinyavsky's understanding Frost and Pasternak are related in spirit exactly for this reason—insistence upon the ethical and aesthetic unity of the world.

The Unfettered Voice (ON ANNA AKHMATOVA)

(A. Sinyavsky, Raskovanny Golos [K 75-letiyu A. Akhmatovoy] *Novy Mir*, 1964, No. 6, pp. 174–176.)

1. The title of this essay is taken from a Pasternak poem from *Above the Barriers* (1917). See *Stikhotvoreniya*, 1965 (with an introduction by A. Sinyavsky), p. 84.

2. Anna Andreyevna (Gorenko) Akhmatova (1888–1965), poetess, associated with the Acmeists. Her husband, the poet N. Gumilyov,

was executed in 1921 for participation in a supposed anti-Bolshevik conspiracy. In 1937 their son was arrested and spent 15 years in Stalin's labor camps. *Requiem,* a beautiful cycle of poems written between 1935 and 1957, commemorated Akhmatova's feelings about the fate of her beloved. (A. Akhmatova: *Sochineniya,* New York, Inter Language Literary Associates, 1965, p. 464.)

3. "Yezhovshchina"—the years of the "Great Purges" (1936–1938), derived from the name of the NKVD chief of the times, N. I. Yezhov (1894–1939) who in 1938 was released from his post and executed.

The stanza is taken from the *Requiem* still unpublished in the Soviet Union. This is one of Sinyavsky's devices, intended to broaden the limits of the permissible by quoting from works as yet unpublished in the Soviet Union, but known by heart by people of the literary profession. He used the same method to introduce Pasternak's poetry from *Doktor Zhivago.* (*Novy Mir,* No. 3, 1962, pp. 261–263.)

4. Tsarskoye Selo: settlement near Leningrad, made famous by A. S. Pushkin, who graduated in 1817 from the Lycée at Tsarskoye Selo established by Alexander I for children of the nobility. Sinyavsky's reference is to Akhmatova's poems devoted to Tsarskoye Selo. Simultaneously, this also indicates that those poems were non-political, poems turned toward the past of Russia.

5 & 6. Untranslatable puns—*rugatsa kak popadya*—to swear using obscene words. *Zhrali kak pop*—derogatory reference to the greediness of the uneducated lower clergy in prerevolutionary Russia.

7. Yevgeny Abramovich Baratynsky (1800–1844), outstanding poet of the Pushkin group.

8. Osip Emilevich Mandelshtam (1892–1940), Acmeist poet, arrested in 1934 for writing an epigram against Stalin, died in a concentration camp.

9. Korney Ivanovich Chukovsky (1882–   ), literary critic and writer for children. The reference is made to Chukovsky's reminiscences on A. Blok in *Literaturnaya Moskva,* Moscow, 1956.

Pamphlet or Lampoon (ON A NOVEL BY IVAN SHEVTSOV)

(A. Sinyavsky, "Pamflet ili paskvil?" [Ivan Shevtsov: *Tlya.* Roman-pamflet. Sovetskaya Rossiya, Moscow, 1964], *Novy Mir,* 1964, No. 12, pp. 228–233.)

1. Alexander Ivanovich Laktionov (1910–   ), well-known Socialist-realist painter, member of the Academy of Arts of the Soviet Union.

2. Ivan Shevtsov, minor Socialist-realist writer.

3. Realist: Socialist-realist.

4. Modernists, cosmopolites, etc.—pejorative adjectives used with particular vehemence during the "Zhdanovshchina" denote non-Socialist–realist artists.

5. The implication is that he was on the "White" side; i.e., anti-Bolshevik. By this Shevtsov uses the good old Stalinist method of denigrating the enemy. A person opposing any form of the party's rule (here aesthetic) must also be a morally inferior character. The same method, known also as "demonology," was applied against Sinyavsky and Daniel at their trial.

6. S.R.: Marxist political party (Social Revolutionaries) opposed to the Bolsheviks, and suppressed by them in 1920. "S.R." was used as a derogatory adjective under Stalin. (The S.R.'s are still not rehabilitated.)

7. Trotsky is still not "rehabilitated," and being or having been a "Trotskyite" is still used as a pejorative term.

8. Obvious derogatory reference to Ilya Ehrenburg's novel *The Thaw* (1954) which started the de-Stalinization process in literature and gave the name to the entire post-Stalin period. *The Thaw* describes the life of a painter and his friends—therefore Shevtsov's novel, which is meant as a refutation of the entire *Thaw*-trend, also deals with the life of painters.

9. Sinyavsky's double sarcasm is directed against those "old traditions," i.e., Stalinism.

10. Sinyavsky's obvious desire is to show the harm done to the prestige of the Soviet Union by primitive Communist warriors of the Shevtsov type, and to plead for "normalcy" in artistic life.

11. Abbreviation for *Moskovsky Khudozhnik* (*Moscow Artist*), an art periodical.

12. Ilya Yefimovich Repin (1844–1930), painter of the naturalist school.

13. Possibly a reference to Sinyavsky's book on Picasso (written in cooperation with I. N. Golomshtok, Moscow, "Znanie" Publishing House, 1960).

14. The entire passage is a heavy and almost undisguised attack upon Stalinism—as exemplified by Khrushchev and his art critics. Khrushchev is caricatured also in Sinyavsky's *Makepeace Experiment*.

15. Reference to the modern art exhibition in December 1962 in Moscow, visited also by Khrushchev, where he reacted furiously to the exhibited paintings and looked ridiculous in his clumsy boorish way. *Izvestiya*, December 23, 1962. See also: *Khrushchev and the Arts, The Politics of Soviet Culture, 1962–64*, text by Priscilla Johnson, Cambridge, Mass., The M.I.T. Press, 1965, pp. 101–105.

16. D. J. Shchukin, pre-revolutionary art collector. His collection is now part of the A. S. Pushkin Moscow Museum of Fine Arts.

17. Tretyakov Gallery—the world-renowned art museum in Moscow. Named after Paul Mikhaylovich Tretyakov (1832–1898), Moscow merchant, founder of the gallery (1892).

18. Moskovsky Khudozhestvenny Teatr—or abbreviated MKHAT —is one of the leading theaters of the Soviet Union.

19. Now part of the Museum for Western and Eastern Art in Kiev and in Odessa.

20. Karl Pavlovich Bryullov (1799–1852), Russian painter. His paintings are in the Tretyakov Gallery.

21. Sinyansky's footnote has absolutely deadly implications—not only as far as Laktionov is concerned, but furthermore because it shows that the conditions described in the *Plant-Louse* indeed do exist in Soviet literature, but contrary to Shevtsov's picture they are created by the party and its supporters, not by the "modernists."

22. Vladimir Ivanovich Dal (1801–1872), writer, ethnographer, linguist; Nikolay Nikolayevich Karamzin (1766–1820), Russian historian and novelist.

23. The March 30, 1970 issue of *The New York Times* and the April 21, 1970 issue of the *Christian Science Monitor* have reported on a new Stalinist potboiler of Ivan Shevtsov: *In the Name of the Father and Son.* The correspondent of the *Christian Science Monitor,* Charlotte Saikowski writes: "The Shevtsov book brims with shining heroes and black villains. Among the latter are corrupted young people who talk in a crude jargon, fawn on Western culture, show pornographic films, drop out from universities and factories, and deceive their parents—the 'transistor, twist, vodka' crowd. Also under attack are the liberal artists of Soviet society. . . . Counterposed to the assorted scoundrels and opportunists is a party committee secretary in a Moscow factory, a staunch Communist whose aim is to be builder of the new world" and who seeks solace at Lenin's tomb after he has been victimized by a provocation. Another positive character is an old-time sculptor who lashes out at modernism and innovation in the arts. (p. 2)

Apparently Shevtsov's now novel represents the same type of Socialist-realist novel which Sinyavsky demolished several years ago in the review article translated here into English.

There Are Such Verses (ON YEVGENY DOLMATOVSKY'S POETRY)

(A. Sinyavsky, Yest takiye stikhi [Yevgeny Dolmatovsky: *Stikhi o nac s.* Russky Pisatel Moscow, 1964] *Novy Mir,* 1965, No. 3, pp. 244–248.)

1. Yevgeny Avronovich Dolmatovsky (1915–   ), Socialist-realist poet, Stalin prize-winner, 1950.

2. The list of "virtues" follows the order of the Russian alphabet: A, B, V, G, D, etc.

3. Reference to Mayakovsky, who described himself this way in his unfinished narrative poem: "At the Top of My Voice" (1930). Sinyavsky points out, as early as his *On Socialist Realism* (1956) that the Socialist-realist poets plagiarize Mayakovsky's poetry, but they do not understand the essence of Mayakovsky's art: rebellion against pretensions and the established order of things.

4. Ilya Lvovich Selvinsky (1899–   ), Soviet poet, follower of Mayakovsky and Pasternak.

The Poetry of Pasternak

(Boris Pasternak, *Verses and Poems* with an introductory article by A. D. Sinyavsky, Moscow-Leningrad, 1965.)

1. Boris Pasternak, *Stikhotvoreniya i poemy*. Biblioteka Poeta, Sovyetsky Pisatel. Moscow-Leningrad, 1965. Introduction by Andrei Sinyavsky, edited by L. A. Ozerov. Sinyavsky's Introduction: pp. 5–62.

2. Valery Yakovlevich Bryusov (1873–1924), leading symbolist poet, scholar, translator, editor of the collected works of Pushkin.

3. Alexander Nikolayevich Skryabin (1871–1915), composer, considered forerunner of modern music.

4. Reinhold Moritsevich Gliere (1875–1956), composer, conductor, teacher, winner of three Glinka and three Stalin prizes.

5. Nikolay Nikolayevich Aseyev (1889–   ), poet, member of the Cubo-Futurist group. Sergey Pavlovich Bobrov (1889–   ), poet, translator, writer of Socialist-realist science fiction; in the 1920's one of the leaders of the Futurist literary group called "Tsentrifuga."

6. "LEF": Levy Front Isskustva ("The Left Front of Art"), literary group in Moscow in 1923. Mayakovsky played a leading role in it.

Sergei Tretyakov (1892– ?), left-wing Futurist, theoretician of the "LEF," poet and playwright. Arrested in 1938 and most likely died in a labor camp.

Osip Maximovich Brik (1888–1945), writer, literary critic and dramatist, close friend of Mayakovsky, editor of the periodical *LEF*.

7. Innokenty Annensky (1856–1909), poet, translator, loosely connected with the symbolist movement. Andrei Bely (1880–1934), pen name of Boris Bugayev, poet, novelist of the symbolist generation. Alexander Blok (1880–1921), the greatest poet of the Russian symbolist movement.

8. Vera Fyodorovna Komissarzhevskaya (1864–1910), famous Russian actress.

9. Velemir Khlebnikov (1885–1922), poet, founder of Russian futurism.

10. Yuri Nikolayevich Tynyanov (1894–1943), critic of the "formalist" school; also creative writer.

11. Kazbek: mountain in Soviet Georgia.

12. Veche: the name of town meetings in medieval Russia. Ceased to exist in 1510, after Moscow established its autocratic rule.

13. *Potyomkin*: Russian battleship on the Black Sea. Her sailors rebelled in 1905. Presnya: district in Moscow, one of the leading areas of the December, 1905 armed uprising.

14. Trial of Beiliss: anti-Semitic trial (1911–1913) in which a certain Beiliss was charged with having committed a "Jewish ritual murder" of a Russian child. Beiliss was finally acquitted.

15. Stolypin's assassination: Pyotr Arkadyevich Stolypin (1862–1911), minister of interior and later prime minister, originator of agrarian reforms. Assassinated by the social revolutionist, D. Bogrov.

16. Vladislav Khodasevich (1886–1939), classicist poet, adversary of Futurism.

In Defense of the Pyramid (ON YEVTUSHENKO'S POETRY)

(A. Sinyavsky, *Grani* No. 63, 1967, pp. 114–139. Parts of this appeared translated by Henry Gifford in *Encounter*, April, 1967, pp. 33–34.)

1. *Grani*, 1967, No. 63, p. 114. Notes on the works of Yevgeny Yevtushenko and his poem "The Bratsk Hydroelectric Station."

The editors of the journal *Phoenix 1966* prefaced this article with the following commentary:

The present article by the important Russian critic and artist A. D. Sinyavsky was written for the journal *Novy Mir* shortly before his arrest. At the time the article was rejected by the editors of *Novy Mir*, probably because of censorship considerations.

When we take into account the topical value of the questions treated in the article and the great mastery of the author and his capacity for profound socio-economical and psychological analysis, we publish this article with the intention of acquainting a broader section of society with it. We consider it our duty to note the fact that the present article convincingly refutes the charge, put forward at the trial of Sinyavsky and Daniel by the official press, that they were "two-faced."

By comparing this article by A. Sinyavsky, for example, with his article "What is Socialist Realism," published abroad earlier under the pseudonym of Abram Tertz, the reader may easily convince himself of the identity of the author's view of the world.

We think that this article once again will convince the reader that the reason which inspired A. Sinyavsky with Yu. Daniel to publish their works abroad is not that they are two-faced or immoral, but simply that there was a complete absence of freedom of work and freedom of the press in present-day Russia.

2. "The Moscovite" (*Moskvich*), small Russian-made car.